Intercultural Communication and Language Education

Series Editors

Stephanie Ann Houghton, Saga University, Saga, Japan

Melina Porto, Universidad Nacional de La Plata, La Plata, Argentina

This book series publishes top quality monographs and edited volumes containing empirical research that prioritises the development of intercultural communicative competence in foreign language education as part of intercultural citizenship. It explores the development of critical cultural awareness broadly aimed at triggering and managing personal and social transformation through intercultural dialogue. Citizenship education and interculturally-oriented language education share an interest in fostering learner exploration, critical analysis and evaluation of other cultures within dynamic socio-political environments.

To complement existing research on the development of intercultural communicative competence, this book series explores the techniques, processes and outcomes of intercultural language pedagogy and intercultural citizenship inside and outside the classroom. It also explores the nature, dynamics and impact of intercultural dialogue outside the classroom in real-world settings where various language codes are in use, including World Englishes and English as a Lingua Franca.

Further, this book series recognizes and explicitly attempts to overcome wide-ranging real-world barriers to intercultural dialogue and intercultural citizenship. This is especially important in the field of English language education considering the status of English as a global language and associated problems connected to linguistic imperialism, ideology and native-speakerism among others. To promote the development of deeper understandings of how such social problems connect to the use of foreign languages in general, contributions are also sought from disciplines outside foreign language education such as citizenship education, social justice, moral education, language policy and social psychology that shed light upon influential external social factors and internal psychological factors that need to be taken into account.

Textbooks containing teaching materials relevant to this series are also welcome at all levels. Textbooks containing teaching materials used in the classroom research projects reported in academic monographs and edited books published in this series are especially welcome.

Please contact Melody Zhang (email: melodymiao.zhang@springer.com) for submitting book proposals for this series.

More information about this series at https://link.springer.com/bookseries/13631

Martin East · Constanza Tolosa · Jocelyn Howard · Christine Biebricher · Adèle Scott

Journeys Towards Intercultural Capability in Language Classrooms

Voices from Students, Teachers and Researchers

Martin East
School of Cultures, Languages
and Linguistics
University of Auckland
Auckland, New Zealand

Jocelyn Howard
School of Teacher Education
University of Canterbury
Christchurch, New Zealand

Adèle Scott
Post-Primary Teachers' Association
Wellington, New Zealand

Constanza Tolosa
School of Curriculum and Pedagogy
University of Auckland
Auckland, New Zealand

Christine Biebricher
School of Curriculum and Pedagogy
University of Auckland
Auckland, New Zealand

ISSN 2520-1735   ISSN 2520-1743 (electronic)
Intercultural Communication and Language Education
ISBN 978-981-19-0990-0   ISBN 978-981-19-0991-7 (eBook)
https://doi.org/10.1007/978-981-19-0991-7

© The Editor(s) (if applicable) and The Author(s) 2022. This book is an open access publication.
Open Access This book is licensed under the terms of the Creative Commons Attribution 4.0 International License (http://creativecommons.org/licenses/by/4.0/), which permits use, sharing, adaptation, distribution and reproduction in any medium or format, as long as you give appropriate credit to the original author(s) and the source, provide a link to the Creative Commons license and indicate if changes were made.
The images or other third party material in this book are included in the book's Creative Commons license, unless indicated otherwise in a credit line to the material. If material is not included in the book's Creative Commons license and your intended use is not permitted by statutory regulation or exceeds the permitted use, you will need to obtain permission directly from the copyright holder.
The use of general descriptive names, registered names, trademarks, service marks, etc. in this publication does not imply, even in the absence of a specific statement, that such names are exempt from the relevant protective laws and regulations and therefore free for general use.
The publisher, the authors and the editors are safe to assume that the advice and information in this book are believed to be true and accurate at the date of publication. Neither the publisher nor the authors or the editors give a warranty, expressed or implied, with respect to the material contained herein or for any errors or omissions that may have been made. The publisher remains neutral with regard to jurisdictional claims in published maps and institutional affiliations.

This Springer imprint is published by the registered company Springer Nature Singapore Pte Ltd.
The registered company address is: 152 Beach Road, #21-01/04 Gateway East, Singapore 189721, Singapore

Introduction and Acknowledgements

The importance of enhancing young learners' intercultural capability as an essential component of preparation for our increasingly diverse and globalised world has underpinned recent curricular developments in many countries. Learning an additional language or L2 (i.e., a language other than one's first language) is often considered as an important vehicle through which intercultural capability may be developed. As L2 learners engage with a new language, they are automatically confronted with difference and "otherness." Intercultural capability represents the ability to recognise, appreciate and deal with these differences in interaction with others.

In line with international trends, the current national curriculum for English-medium schools in New Zealand—the *New Zealand Curriculum* or NZC (Ministry of Education, 2007)—is both forward-focused in its aspirations and clear in acknowledging that L2 learning is now a key component of education in and for the twenty-first century. Intercultural capability is seen as a new and transformative goal, both more broadly across the curriculum and specifically within the curriculum area known as *Learning Languages*. Integral to this is the expectation that narrow conceptualisations of culture should be replaced in L2 programmes with interwoven, exploratory and reflective approaches through which learners can gain deeper understandings of *themselves*, as well as linguistic and cultural *"others,"* as they develop their capability to become effective intercultural communicators.

The purpose of this book is to present the findings of a project funded by New Zealand's Ministry of Education. Our project sought to investigate how five teachers working in four primary/intermediate schools in New Zealand supported young beginner language learners to develop their intercultural capability through learning an L2. Over two years, we worked with the teachers to introduce them to the intercultural principles underpinning the *Learning Languages* learning area, scaffold them as they attempted to enact these principles through two cycles of implementation (one in each year), and finally worked with them to present their stories as vignettes to encourage and support other teachers. Our work with the teachers revealed to us that developing young learners' intercultural capability through L2 learning can be an exciting and meaningful endeavour. It is also highly challenging and raises questions about exactly what is and what is not possible in L2 classrooms.

This book presents the journeys of three groups of stakeholders during this two-year endeavour—students, teachers and researchers/teacher educators. We use the voices of each of these groups to present what happened and consider the implications for language education. The book builds on a range of publications that we wrote at different points on the journeys. Several academic articles have reported on aspects of the first of the two interventions undertaken by the teachers (i.e., in Year 1 of the project), alongside some of the lessons that began to emerge for us as researchers (Biebricher et al., 2019; East, Howard et al., 2018; Howard et al., 2019; Tolosa et al., 2018). At the end of the project, one short locally published and teacher-oriented booklet, co-constructed with the teachers, was designed to give examples to other New Zealand-based teachers about what might be possible in their own classrooms (East, Tolosa et al., 2018a). A final report submitted to our funder summarised the key findings and their implications (East, Tolosa et al., 2018b). This book adds substantially to our previous work in several important ways.

First, the book has provided us with the opportunity to present findings from both years of the project, including both of the interventions the teachers undertook, thereby documenting growth and development as the teachers progressed through the project. Second, the book has enabled us to present the perspectives of each of the stakeholder groups in one place, drawing connections and synergies across different sources of data. Third, the book has allowed us, as researchers and teacher educators, to take a step back from the student and teacher data and thereby to consider in some depth the implications of our findings for language education. Finally, and perhaps most importantly, the book has created the opportunity to present a multi-faceted and in-depth account of the journeys of three intersecting stakeholder groups, and to draw out in a coherent way the lessons learned from these intersecting voices—something that simply is not possible in a range of short and focused articles.

The end result is a book that tells a comprehensive story of different journeys towards intercultural capability in language classrooms that took place across two academic years, with a focus on young language learners. While rooted in a particular national context, its findings have implications for those working in a range of contexts across the globe who have a stake in young learners' intercultural capability as it might be developed through learning an L2. The book will be invaluable reading for all those who are interested in the interface between intercultural communication and language education, whether as teachers, policy makers, curriculum developers, teacher educators or researchers.

We would like to take this opportunity to acknowledge our primary funder, New Zealand's Ministry of Education through the Teaching and Learning Research Initiative (TLRI). Established in 2003, the TLRI seeks to enhance the links between educational research and teaching practices to improve outcomes for learners (http://www.tlri.org.nz/). Without the funding we secured, which enabled us to support the teacher partners in this endeavour, this study could not have taken place. We are also grateful to Tui Tuia (https://www.learningcircle.co.nz/), funded by the Ministry of Education to support the professional learning and development of teachers of languages in schools, for the generous funding that enabled this book to be published Gold Open Access. We would also like to thank our teacher partners (Lillian, Kelly,

Kathryn, Mike and Tamara) who committed to the project enthusiastically, but also no doubt with some trepidation, and who were willing to try out with their classes ideas that were new to them and therefore involving some risk. We also thank one of our colleagues for her willingness to read and comment on an earlier draft of this manuscript—Nicola Daly (The University of Waikato, New Zealand, and researcher-partner in earlier discussions about this project).

We commend the different journeys to you, and we trust that, by reading them, you will gain new insights into what it means to travel on roads towards interculturality in the context of language learning, and the benefits and challenges that emerge along the way.

Auckland, June 2022

Martin East
Constanza Tolosa
Jocelyn Howard
Christine Biebricher
Adèle Scott

References

Biebricher, C., East, M., Howard, J., & Tolosa, C. (2019). Navigating intercultural language teaching in New Zealand classrooms. *Cambridge Journal of Education, 49*(5), 605–621.

East, M., Howard, J., Tolosa, C., Biebricher, C., & Scott, A. (2018). Isolated or integrated? Should the development of students' intercultural understanding be separated from, or embedded into, communicative language use? *Babel, 52*(2/3), 20–25.

East, M., Tolosa, C., Biebricher, C., Howard, J., & Scott, A. (2018a). *Enhancing language learners' intercultural capability: A study in New Zealand's schools*. Languages Research NZ.

East, M., Tolosa, C., Biebricher, C., Howard, J., & Scott, A. (2018b). *Enhancing the intercultural capability of students of additional languages in New Zealand's intermediate schools*. Teaching and Learning Research Initiative Final Report.

Howard, J., Tolosa, C., Biebricher, C., & East, M. (2019). Shifting conceptualisations of foreign language teaching in New Zealand: Students' journeys towards developing intercultural capability. *Language and Intercultural Communication, 19*(6), 555–569.

Ministry of Education. (2007). *The New Zealand curriculum*. Learning Media.

Tolosa, C., Biebricher, C., East, M., & Howard, J. (2018). Intercultural language teaching as a catalyst for teacher inquiry. *Teaching and Teacher Education, 70*, 227–235.

Contents

1	**Beginning the Journeys Towards Intercultural Capability**	1
	1.1 Introduction	1
	1.2 The Significance of Our Study	2
	1.3 The Language–Culture Relationship	3
	1.4 Communicative Competence	4
	1.5 Communicative Language Teaching	4
	1.5.1 Weak CLT	5
	1.5.2 Presentation-Practice-Production	6
	1.5.3 Strong CLT	6
	1.5.4 Task-Based Language Teaching	7
	1.6 What Has Been Lacking in CLT Approaches	8
	1.7 Intercultural Communicative Competence	9
	1.8 Intercultural Communicative Language Teaching	10
	1.9 Challenges in Practice	11
	1.10 Introducing the Present Study	13
	1.10.1 The New Zealand Context for Language Teaching	13
	1.10.2 Our Project	15
	1.11 Presenting the Journeys	18
	1.12 Conclusion	18
	References	20
2	**Studies on the Intercultural Dimension Across the Globe**	25
	2.1 Introduction	25
	2.2 The Intercultural Dimension	25
	2.3 Intercultural Competence	26
	2.4 Critiquing the Models of Intercultural Competence	28
	2.5 Third Place Positioning	29
	2.6 Interculturality in Curricula	30
	2.6.1 Interculturality in Language Classrooms	32
	2.6.2 Challenges for L2 Teachers	33
	2.7 Studies into the Intercultural in L2 Teaching	35

		2.7.1	Studies into the Intercultural with Young Learners	36
		2.7.2	Embedding Intercultural Explorations in School Contexts	37
		2.7.3	Collaborations Between Teachers and Teacher Educators/Researchers	40
		2.7.4	Promoting Explicit Teaching and Scaffolding for Intercultural Learning	41
	2.8	Conclusion		42
	References			43
3	**The Intercultural Dimension in the New Zealand Language Teaching Context**			49
	3.1	Introduction		49
	3.2	A History of Language Policy Development in New Zealand		49
	3.3	New Zealand's 2007 School Curriculum		52
	3.4	Te reo Māori		55
	3.5	Supporting Enactment of the *Learning Languages* Learning Area		56
		3.5.1	The Ellis (2005) Report	56
		3.5.2	The Newton et al. (2010) Report	58
	3.6	Supporting Teachers with Enacting the Strands		59
	3.7	Studies into the Intercultural in the New Zealand Context		62
	3.8	Conclusion		66
	References			67
4	**Introducing the Two-Year Study**			71
	4.1	Introduction		71
	4.2	Background		72
	4.3	Research Framework		73
		4.3.1	Inquiry-Based Approaches	73
		4.3.2	Inquiry Learning	74
		4.3.3	Teaching as Inquiry	75
		4.3.4	Collaborative Inquiry	76
	4.4	Data Collection Methods		77
		4.4.1	Student Data	77
		4.4.2	Teacher Data	78
		4.4.3	Researcher Data	80
	4.5	Ethical Considerations		80
	4.6	Teacher Participants		80
		4.6.1	Lillian	81
		4.6.2	Kelly	82
		4.6.3	Kathryn	83
		4.6.4	Mike	83
		4.6.5	Tamara	84
	4.7	Researchers		85
	4.8	Research Procedures		86

		4.8.1 Phase I (February 2016–June 2016)	86
		4.8.2 Phase II (July 2016–December 2016)	87
		4.8.3 Phase III (February 2017–September 2017)	88
		4.8.4 Phase IV (September 2017–December 2017)	88
	4.9	Data Analysis and Reporting	89
		4.9.1 Data Source Identifiers	91
	References		92
5	**Journeys Towards Intercultural Capability: The Students' Voices**		95
	5.1	Introduction	95
	5.2	Contextual Background	96
	5.3	Lillian	97
		5.3.1 Phase II Inquiry: Discovering Different Perspectives of School Sports	97
		5.3.2 Phase III Inquiry: Using Senses and Feelings to Compare Schooling	98
	5.4	Kelly	99
		5.4.1 Phase II Inquiry: Exploring Concepts of Family Through Language and Culture	99
		5.4.2 Phase III Inquiry: Comparing Values and Beliefs Reflected in Colours and Clothing	100
	5.5	Kathryn	101
		5.5.1 Phase II Inquiry: Noticing Similarities and Differences in the Use of Time	101
		5.5.2 Phase III Inquiry: Using Student Inquiries About Food for Intercultural Exploration	102
	5.6	Mike	103
		5.6.1 Phase II Inquiry: Challenging Notions of "Normal" Through Food and Drink	103
		5.6.2 Phase III Inquiry: Reflecting on School Systems	104
	5.7	Tamara	105
		5.7.1 Phase II Inquiry: Making Connections Through Movement	105
	5.8	The Students' Journeys: Emergent Intercultural Growth	106
		5.8.1 Facts About the Target Cultures	106
		5.8.2 Noticing Differences	107
		5.8.3 Openness to Difference	108
		5.8.4 Comfortableness with Difference	109
		5.8.5 "Third Place" Positioning	110
	5.9	Teachers' Perceptions of Students' Intercultural Learning Gains	110
	5.10	Unanticipated Outcomes	111
		5.10.1 Increased Engagement	111
		5.10.2 Greater Use of the Target Language	112

		5.10.3	Heightened Motivation for Future Language Use and Language Learning	113
	5.11	Reflections on the Outcomes		113
		5.11.1	The Issue of Age	114
		5.11.2	Affective Impacts	115
	5.12	Conclusion		116
	References			117

6 Journeys Towards Intercultural Capability: The Teachers' Voices ... 119

6.1	Introduction		119
6.2	Contextual Background		120
6.3	The Participating Teachers		121
6.4	Preparing Teachers for Their Inquiry Cycles		121
6.5	Initial Reflections		122
6.6	Challenges Encountered in Practice		123
6.7	Pedagogical Approaches		123
6.8	Addressing Stereotypes		125
6.9	The Language–Culture Interface		127
6.10	Time Constraints		129
6.11	Teachers' Reflections and Learnings from the Project		131
6.12	Realisations About the Teaching Approach		131
6.13	Self-Reflection and Critical Thinking		133
6.14	Benefits of the Project		135
	6.14.1	Motivation and Student Engagement	135
	6.14.2	Increased Critical Reflection	136
	6.14.3	Additional Realisations	136
	6.14.4	The Broader Context	137
6.15	Conclusion		138
References			138

7 Journeys Towards Intercultural Capability: The Researchers' Voices ... 141

7.1	Introduction		141
7.2	Contextual Background		142
7.3	Beginning the Journey		143
7.4	Phase I		144
7.5	Phase II		145
	7.5.1	Critical Friend Conversations	146
	7.5.2	Promoting Reflective Practices	148
7.6	Phase III		150
	7.6.1	Challenges Emerging from the Inquiry Cycles	154
7.7	Phase IV		156
7.8	Conclusion		157
References			158

8 Journeys Towards Intercultural Capability: Retrospective Reflections 161
- 8.1 Introduction 161
- 8.2 What We Found 161
  - 8.2.1 Students' Journeys: Developing Intercultural Capability 162
  - 8.2.2 Teachers' Journeys: Developing Intercultural Teaching and Learning 164
  - 8.2.3 Researchers' Journeys: Uncovering What Is Feasible 165
- 8.3 Language Teaching and Learning: Theoretical Considerations 167
  - 8.3.1 Target Language or First Language Use? 167
  - 8.3.2 Isolated or Integrated? 169
- 8.4 Implications for Language Education 171
  - 8.4.1 Planning 171
  - 8.4.2 Teaching 172
  - 8.4.3 Reflecting 173
- 8.5 Further Implications for Language Education 173
  - 8.5.1 Implications for the L2 Classroom—Integrating Culture and Language 174
  - 8.5.2 Implications Beyond the L2 Classroom—Isolating Culture from Language 175
  - 8.5.3 Reconciling the Language–Culture Interface in the New Zealand Context 176
- 8.6 Limitations and Directions for Further Research 177
- 8.7 Conclusion 179
- References 180

Chapter 1
Beginning the Journeys Towards Intercultural Capability

1.1 Introduction

The intercultural dimension of the language learning experience is one that has taken on increasing significance over the past decades. As Byram (2018) reminded us, "intercultural competence" (IC) as a term of relevance to language pedagogy arose in the 1980s as a development to "communicative competence." The construct of communicative competence was, by that time, beginning to become embedded as informing the principal aim of language teaching and learning programmes. That is, for many years students have been learning languages in a variety of ways and in a range of different contexts, but with a primary goal of learning how to *communicate* in the target language (TL). However, as TL users in real-world contexts initiate communication with TL speakers, they are necessarily confronted with situations that move communication beyond the pure use of language and require them to negotiate with, as Byram (e.g., 2021) put it, beliefs, meanings, values and behaviours that may be very different from their own. This has implications for effective communication. Indeed, all TL interactions are encounters with "otherness" that require navigation beyond just choosing the appropriate words for the context; hence the emergence of IC as a construct of interest in language education.

The study we present in this book is rooted in the diverse multilingual and multicultural context of New Zealand. Ours was a two-year project, funded by New Zealand's Ministry of Education, that sought to investigate the ways in which five teachers working at the intermediate school level[1] could be supported to embrace an intercultural dimension in the context of students learning an additional language (L2). We began from the premise that the increasing diversity of backgrounds of learners and their families in New Zealand creates an imperative to utilise L2 programmes as vehicles to increase L2 learners' capacity to understand and relate effectively to diversity, not only the diversity represented in the TL, but also the diversity that makes up

---

[1] See Table 1.2 for an overview of the New Zealand school sector.

the classroom environment. Through data collected in a range of ways—classroom observations, reflective interviews with the teachers, focus groups with students, meetings, email correspondence and our own reflections—this book presents the journeys and voices of three groups of stakeholders in the intercultural educational endeavour—students, teachers and researchers/teacher educators.

The purpose of this introductory chapter is to set the scene for the journeys we will present later in this book. The chapter begins by outlining what we see as the significance of the study we undertook. We go on to provide a brief historical overview of how, and to what extent, a cultural/intercultural dimension has been included in the communicative L2 classroom over the years. We raise some of the challenges that have been encountered in more contemporary understandings of the "intercultural" in the context of the construct of communicative competence. We then briefly describe the site of the present study—New Zealand. We conclude by providing an overview of how the journeys of the different stakeholders in our study will unfold in the remainder of the book.

1.2 The Significance of Our Study

To date, very little research has been conducted into the intercultural dimension in L2 learning among young language learners (i.e., those who are beginning to learn a new language at the school level), particularly in what might be termed acquisition-poor contexts where these young learners are exposed to very minimal teaching time for the L2 and might not even encounter TL speakers with whom they can interact authentically. The paucity of research at this level means that we know little as yet about young language learners' capacity for intercultural development. Byram (1997) argued, however, that research was needed to "provide a more systematic base for formulating the cultural learning aims of language teaching in the early years" (p. 46). More recently, Perry and Southwell (2011) highlighted the need for more research into how the intercultural dimension can be developed among school-aged students. Our study sought to add to current knowledge and understanding of how young language learners might develop intercultural skills in time-limited language learning contexts.

Our study is also significant in its focus on three groups of stakeholders—students, teachers and researchers/teacher educators. We present and reflect on what happened as *students* in different language classes experienced a range of ways of engaging with otherness and difference as they were learning an L2. We look at what happened when the *teachers* with whom we worked as researchers enacted "teaching as inquiry" cycles[2] to explore the intercultural dimension with their students. We also take a step back from the project and the data and consider what we, as *researchers and teacher educators*, learned as we reflected on the extent to which the intercultural dimension can be developed in young students who are at the beginning stages of learning a

---

[2] See later in this chapter for a definition of this action research approach.

new language and as we reflected on how teachers could be supported to reframe their language teaching in intercultural terms.

Looking back on what we experienced during the two years of our project, we drew a conclusion that needs to be stated at the outset of presenting the journeys of the different stakeholders: for many reasons, the development of the intercultural dimension through L2 learning (particularly with younger students) is fraught with challenges. Dervin et al. (2020), for example, asserted that the notion of IC "has been with us for decades" (p. 4) and that "[t]oday it feels like everything has been said and written about IC" (p. 5). If that is the case, its enactment and development in the context of L2 learning should be a straightforward process. Nevertheless, Dervin and colleagues went on to present a collection of studies that illustrated not only "the diverse and uneven pathways which educators have taken" towards understanding IC, whereby they have confronted "personal and pedagogical risk, growth, and, in a number of cases, struggle and frustration" (p. 9), but also problematised the very construct of IC in the face of real-world experiences. Furthermore, as Brunsmeier (2017) suggested in the European context, the development of L2 learners' IC is hugely challenging because the construct is yet to be adequately defined, both more broadly and, in particular, with regard to young learners. The knowledge and understanding emerging from our study therefore includes careful consideration of the complexities involved in developing young language learners' intercultural skills in time-limited contexts. Hence, we frame what we present as "journeys towards." We cannot claim to have arrived.

1.3 The Language–Culture Relationship

A relationship between language and culture has long been acknowledged in the field of language teaching and learning. As Brown (1994) put it, "[a] language is a part of a culture and a culture is a part of a language; the two are intricately interwoven so that one cannot separate the two without losing the significance of either language or culture" (p. 165). Brown (2014) subsequently expanded on this notion when he argued that language and culture are components of "a 'package' that the L2 learner must grapple with in the journey to successful [L2] acquisition" (p. 197). At the time of first writing this chapter, we googled the phrase "language and culture" and came up with over 100 million results. Many of these results either indicated an inextricable link between the two concepts or posed questions about what the inter-relationship is or should be. It is one thing to recognise the potential interface; it is quite another to pinpoint exactly what that interface means and how it might be realised. Indeed, the interface finds different expressions depending on the pedagogical paradigm in question. In what follows, we consider that interface with reference to the construct of communicative competence and its outworking through pedagogical approaches that may broadly be labelled as Communicative Language Teaching (CLT). We follow this with an exploration of intercultural communicative competence (ICC), and Intercultural Communicative Language Teaching (ICLT).

Table 1.1 The four components of communicative competence (Canale, 1983)

Competence	Students of an L2 need to …
Grammatical or formal	Develop knowledge and understanding of the rules of language (grammar, lexis and phonology) so that communication is accurate
Sociolinguistic	Know what kinds of language are appropriate for different social contexts and relationships
Discourse	Move beyond knowledge and understanding of isolated words and phrases, and be able to use language in extended contexts (e.g., listen to a lecture, give a speech, read a report)
Strategic	Develop skills to enable communication to be maintained when knowledge is lacking (e.g., guess the meaning, ask for clarification, use gestures)

1.4 Communicative Competence

The construct of communicative competence finds its genesis in the arguments of Hymes (e.g., 1972), described by Sherzer et al. (2010) as a leading figure in linguistic anthropology and sociolinguistics whose pioneering work included "the study of relations between and among language, culture, and society" (p. 301). Walker et al.'s (2018) introductory chapter provides a useful overview of the development of the construct, using Hymes' work as a starting point, and outlining advances that have occurred over time.

One significant model of communicative competence which continues to influence thinking in the field of language education was presented by Canale and Swain (1980). Canale (1983) concisely presented its four components (Table 1.1).

Embedded within the concept of sociolinguistic competence was the understanding that the *social context* needed to play a role in determining the *language* that was suitable to initiate and maintain an interaction. The social context may be referred to as "the culture-specific context embedding the norms, values, beliefs, and behaviour patterns of a culture," such that "[a]ppropiate use of the language requires attention to such constructs" (Alptekin, 2002, p. 58). The model thereby began to raise consciousness that an interface needed to exist between language and culture in L2 education.

1.5 Communicative Language Teaching

CLT emerged in the latter half of the last century as a response to calls for greater emphasis on genuine communication in L2 classrooms. Aligned with theoretical constructs of communicative competence as articulated, for example, by Canale and Swain (1980) and Canale (1983), the ability to communicate effectively with others in the TL increasingly became fundamental to the aims and goals of many L2 programmes across the globe (Richards, 2001; Richards & Rodgers, 2014). L2

1.5 Communicative Language Teaching

programmes began to emphasise the comprehension and production of meaningful language in authentic contexts (Hedge, 2000).

In parallel with CLT was the emergence of what Kramsch (1986, 1987) referred to as the proficiency movement in the United States which similarly encouraged, as a primary goal, the ability to communicate in authentic settings (Higgs, 1984). For Kramsch (1986), this meant that "the final justification for developing students' proficiency in a foreign language" was "to make them interactionally competent on the international scene" (p. 367).

The 1970s and 1980s represented the beginnings of what Richards (2006) referred to as the "classic" CLT phase. In light of different understandings about what makes L2 teaching and learning effective (see, e.g., Mitchell et al., 2019), several polarisations to CLT became apparent during this phase. These polarisations were fundamentally informed by theoretical arguments about where, and how, attention to grammar should be situated. That is, Canale and Swain (1980) had identified grammatical competence as an important component of communicative competence. At the level of the classroom, teachers' understanding of how to attend to this component essentially led CLT in two contrasting directions—a teacher-led behaviourist-influenced approach that placed strong emphasis on teaching and practising the rules (so-called weak CLT), and, by contrast, a learner-centred constructivist-informed approach that gave learners room to discover the rules for themselves (so-called strong CLT).

1.5.1 Weak CLT

The established approach that had dominated L2 pedagogy since the eighteenth century had come to be known as grammar-translation. As the name suggests, this pedagogical approach placed strong emphasis on studying, practising and mastering the rules of the TL, often through the direct translation of sentences and texts. The medium of instruction was the students' first language (L1), and L1 explanations became the gateways into L2 acquisition. Thus, knowing a language under the grammar-translation method meant knowing its grammar and vocabulary, with the benchmark of competence being a "native-like" (i.e., L1) level.

A strong component of the grammar-translation approach, particularly as students advanced in their studies, was exposure to authentic texts in the TL. In turn, original (authentic) texts became the windows through which another culture might be viewed, and the primary means to develop "cultural knowledge." Thus, a language–culture interface was attempted within the grammar-translation paradigm, but the cultural dimension could be interpreted as "high culture" or "culture as artefact" (Crozet et al., 1999; Sehlaoui, 2001). Culture was perceived to focus both on and in a canon of literature (Peiser & Jones, 2013), and cultural knowledge was built on "the conviction that language and culture are two separate domains of language learning, with language competence being given priority over cultural" (Piątkowska, 2015, p. 398).

As the communicative agenda began to take hold, the "traditional anglocentric assumptions" underpinning grammar-translation that "the main purpose of learning foreign languages was to broaden the mind" began to give way to a recognition that students were "learning languages because they needed to *use* them in an ever-shrinking world" (Benson & Voller, 1997, p. 11). The essential criticism of grammar-translation was that it failed to help learners to develop the ability to communicate. However, for the most part, teachers who were emerging from approaches such as grammar-translation still tended to place grammar teaching at the forefront of their classroom practices, even when there was tacit recognition that effective communication in the TL was now the goal. Thus, grammatical competence continued to take a central place in weak CLT.

1.5.2 Presentation-Practice-Production

One expression of the weak CLT paradigm came to be known as the "classic lesson structure" of Presentation-Practice-Production or PPP (Klapper, 2003). In this teacher-led approach, teachers would begin their lessons by teaching a particular grammatical principle to the class. Students would then practise the grammatical rule through various focused practice activities. Only after the rule had been practised would students be asked to utilise the rule in a pseudo-authentic context that aimed to replicate the domains in which the L2 might be used authentically in real-world contexts—for example, buying food and drink in a restaurant, purchasing a train ticket at a station, booking into a hotel. This was often done through structured role-play scenarios. Intercultural notions were implicit in how the TL user was supposed to interact appropriately, for example with the waiter, the ticket clerk or the hotel receptionist (i.e., sociolinguistic competence). However, the main focus of practice for these encounters was on (grammatically correct) *language*, not on the dynamics of real-world interaction.

Where culture was attended to in the PPP-based classroom, it was frequently enacted in ways that Byram described over twenty years ago as "something to talk over if there are a few minutes free from the *real* business of language learning" (1991, pp. 17–18, our emphasis)—for example, "on Friday afternoon we will learn about the Eiffel Tower." The language–culture interface was effectively minimised. When it came to the intercultural dimension, a PPP-oriented approach to CLT was found wanting.

1.5.3 Strong CLT

Some communicatively oriented teachers perceived significant limitations in grammar-translation, and focused primarily on meaning and fluency, alongside dominant or exclusive use of the TL. The principle here was that students should be "immersed" in the TL, that is, exposed to wide-ranging authentic TL input, and being given extensive opportunities to use language creatively. It was left up to the students to work out and assimilate the grammar rules for themselves, by noticing in the input patterns and structures, and how they were used.

At its strongest, CLT was proposed as a wholly learner-centred and experiential approach to the extent that the teacher had little, if any, role to play. Although this extreme reaction to teacher-dominant pedagogy did not prove to be as popular as PPP, Richards (2006) spoke of a *developmental* phase to the CLT model (from the 1990s onwards) which, according to Brown (2014), continued to de-emphasise the structural and cognitive aspects of communication, with its focus on accuracy as a necessary component of successful communication, in favour of exploring its social, cultural and pragmatic dimensions. This, Brown argued, has focused teachers' and learners' attention on "language as *interactive communication* among individuals, *each with a sociocultural identity*" (p. 206, our emphases). This has arguably created greater space for attention to the sociolinguistic and intercultural due to the wide range of authentic input to which learners would be exposed, and the centrality of "learning by doing."

1.5.4 Task-Based Language Teaching

A more strongly constructivist-oriented approach, where the role of the teacher shifts from instructor to facilitator, emerged in the 1980s as the phenomenon of task-based language teaching or TBLT—an approach that sees "important roles for holism, experiential learning, and learner-centered pedagogy" alongside "the interactive roles of the social and linguistic environment in providing learning opportunities, and scaffolding learners into them" (Norris et al., 2009, p. 15). In contrast to PPP, TBLT starts with language in use and subsequently focuses on the forms of the language on the basis of the errors that students make with language and/or the language structures that they notice as they attempt to use language for themselves—a kind of PPP in reverse. In TBLT, language learners have a crucial level of responsibility to work out how language functions through engagement in communicative "tasks"—that is, "the hundred and one things that people do in everyday life at work, at play, and in between" (Long, 1985, p. 89) or "the real-world activities people think of when planning, conducting, or recalling their day" (Long, 2015, p. 6). The teacher's role is nonetheless crucial in helping learners to notice (and then correct) errors through such mechanisms as corrective feedback.

TBLT offers some potential for a stronger focus on the intercultural dimension in line with Brown's (2014) acknowledgement of a pedagogical shift in emphasis. As learners engage in a series of tasks, they are able to focus on authentic samples of language as used in genuine real-world contexts. In TBLT, the broader cultural contexts for language use take on added relevance and significance. Indeed, the interface between TBLT and the intercultural dimension is something that is beginning to emerge in the task-based literature as potentially important (see, e.g., East, 2012a; Gonzáles-Lloret, 2020; Müller-Hartmann & Schocker, 2018). Nevertheless, it must be acknowledged that TBLT is built on particular understandings and theories of second language acquisition, and that exploration of the TBLT-intercultural interface is in its infancy.

1.6 What Has Been Lacking in CLT Approaches

The isolationist approach to culture that was apparent in the early days of CLT might have been seen as a valuable starting point for language learners who may have enjoyed learning about "a series of selected facts, customs and traditions learners need to understand and appreciate in order to become 'culturally competent'" (Flinders Humanities Research Centre, 2005, p. 3). Nevertheless, when cultural knowledge is viewed as "the marginalized sister of language" (Hennebry, 2014, p. 135), separated from learning the L2, it effectively becomes an "optional extra," not regarded as an important component of the development of learners' communicative competence. The problem, however, is that this approach does not help learners of an L2 to appreciate and navigate the challenges that might emerge in encounters with TL speakers.

Kramsch (1986) gave an early illustration of what appeared to be absent from a CLT model in which language and culture were essentially separate. She took as her example "[t]he difficulty in ordering the legendary cup of coffee in a French restaurant after three years of French" (p. 368). That is, in the traditional communicative classroom students might learn the basics of how to order a cup of coffee through being taught appropriate language and grammar, effectively practised through some kind of role-play. In Kramsch's view, if, in a subsequent real-world scenario, the customer could not secure the wanted cup of coffee, this could hardly be put down to not knowing, or not being able to put to use, the right vocabulary or grammar. Something was amiss that went *beyond* language. Kramsch continued that the lack of intended outcome was:

> ... more likely due to a lack of awareness of the different social relationships existing in France between waiters and customers, of the different affective, social, and cultural values attached to cups of coffee, of the different perception French waiters might have of [for example] American citizens. (p. 368)

Kramsch (1986) concluded, "[i]n short, the difficulty lies in the differences in expectations, assumptions, and general representations of the world between two speakers" (p. 368). Kramsch thus viewed an approach that stresses grammar and lexis (even in specific communicative contexts) as overlooking what she referred to as the "*dynamic* process of communication" (p. 368, our emphasis). Effective communication, as Kramsch later asserted, is "*more than* just learning to get one's message across," even if that message is delivered "clearly, accurately, and appropriately" (Kramsch, 2005, p. 551, our emphasis).

Kramsch's (2005) "more than" element has become the focus of debates around the integration of the intercultural into language learning and language use. This developed understanding of what it means to communicate effectively has given rise to a rich and varied literature spanning several decades which we will explore in subsequent chapters (e.g., Byram, 1997, 2009; Byram et al., 2002; Liddicoat, 2005b, 2008; Liddicoat & Crozet, 2000; Lo Bianco et al., 1999). Furthermore, this developed understanding has influenced the refinement of pedagogical practices aligned to CLT approaches.

1.7 Intercultural Communicative Competence

More recent thinking about the communicative competence construct has recognised that the intercultural dimension must be made more explicit. Martinez-Flor et al. (2006), for example, made the implicit elements of the Canale and Swain model more visible when they suggested that the development of communicative competence needed to include intercultural competence. They went on to define this competence initially in *linguistic* terms, that is, as knowledge of appropriate language use within a specific sociocultural context (i.e., sociolinguistic competence). However, from this perspective the intercultural dimension included, in *addition* to appropriate language choice, an awareness of "the rules of behavior that exist in a particular community in order to avoid possible miscommunication" as well as "non-verbal means of communication (i.e., body language, facial expressions, eye contact, etc.)" (p. 150).

East (2016) put it like this: if interactions between two interlocutors are to be effective, what the interlocutors arguably need is "some level of understanding of, and competence in, appropriate interactional *behaviour* (when, for example, it is appropriate, in France, to shake someone's hand or kiss them on the cheek – *faire la bise*)" (p. 29). In other words, "[i]nappropriate behaviour may lead to a breakdown in communication that is not related to *linguistic* proficiency but is nonetheless related to *intercultural* proficiency (or lack thereof)" (p. 29). Thus, a view emerges that intercultural competence entails not only a "culture-in-language" element, made apparent in helping learners to acquire proficiency in handling *language* appropriately in a range of contexts, but also a behavioural element, made apparent in helping learners to understand what is and what is not appropriate *behaviour* in a given context.

A further dimension of intercultural competence which embraces *attitudinal* or *positioning* elements becomes apparent, for example, in Byram's five-facet *savoirs* (knowledge or skills) model of Intercultural Communicative Competence or ICC (e.g., Byram, 1997, 2021), a model we present in more depth in Chaps. 2 and 4. Essentially, Byram's *savoirs* took us beyond linguistic and behavioural appropriacy to the *attitudes* that intercultural speakers hold towards their interlocutors. Although for Byram et al. (2002) a crucial element of ICC is knowledge, this is not primarily knowledge *about* the target culture (or even about appropriate language and behaviours)—even though such knowledge is important; rather, it is knowledge *of* how individuals and societies function and what that means for interaction with others. The *savoirs* enable language learners and language users to step back from their own views of the world (to "de-centre," as Byram et al. put it), and to consider and take into account the views of their interlocutors in comparative terms.

Byram et al. (2002) concluded, "it is not the purpose of teaching to try to change learners' values, but to make them explicit and conscious in any evaluative response to others" (p. 8). Ultimately this would lead to "knowing how to negotiate several potentially conflicting codes of acting and thinking, and how to handle the feelings that those negotiations evoke, which may at times be uncomfortable" (East, 2012b, p. 140). As we explain in more detail in Chap. 2, this place of negotiation or "intercultural positioning" has been variously labelled as a "third place" (Lo Bianco et al., 1999), "third space" (Bhabha, 1994), "third culture," "third stance," or "thirdness" (Kramsch, 2009). MacDonald (2019) acknowledged ongoing tensions and contradictions in the ways in which these terms are used and interpreted, but found the "third place" emerging as a term to represent "a pedagogic site where the 'hybrid' identity of the language learner/intercultural subject can be worked out" (p. 106).

1.8 Intercultural Communicative Language Teaching

All that we have presented so far suggests that intercultural competence must be a component of communicative competence, that there can arguably be no communicative competence without the intercultural, and that L2 learning must involve elements that enable learners to focus on the intercultural in comparative terms. Liddicoat (2008) put it like this: "[a] language learner who has learnt only the grammar and vocabulary of a language is … not well equipped to communicate in that language." In his view, "learners require *cultural* knowledge *as much as* they require grammar and vocabulary" (p. 278, our emphases). However, this cultural knowledge moves beyond facts about the target culture (which may have been how this knowledge was interpreted in the early days of CLT); it also moves beyond knowledge of linguistic and behavioural appropriacy (elements that were implicit in the foundations of CLT, even if not fully realised); it includes attitudes and positioning in relation to the "other." As Liddicoat (2005a) argued, cultural knowledge is "not [just] a case of knowing *information* about the culture," as might have been the emphasis in grammar-translation or earlier realisations of CLT; rather it is "about knowing *how to engage* with it" (p. 31, our emphases).

Discourses around the language–culture interface, and the development of theoretical frameworks such as ICC, have given rise to the concept of Intercultural Communicative Language Teaching (ICTL). Piątkowska (2015) provided a useful summation of the aims of ICLT. She argued that, central to the ICC construct as operationalised in an ICLT model, culture is viewed as a dynamic concept where language and culture are interdependent and where focus is put on both awareness of inseparability of language and culture and the need to prepare learners to communicate across cultures.

As part of this preparation for interaction, intercultural teaching focuses learners' attention on both the TL culture and their own culture in an exploratory, comparative way. The goal of teaching is not to introduce the TL culture or L1 speakers in a static and exclusively facts-based way, thereby "neglecting the skills of analysis, evaluation and interpretation of cultural meanings, beliefs and values" (p. 400). It is, rather, to reach a range of cultural outcomes. Such teaching, Piątkowska asserted, is "in line with constructivist approaches in that it is a learner-centred approach that promotes student autonomy, meaning construction and transfer of abilities to other contexts not previously met by a learner," where the learning outcomes are no longer seen in terms of a uniform view of culture, but rather of culture as dynamic and heterogeneous. The focus therefore is "on *attitudes and skills* in the first place and *knowledge* in the second" (p. 403, our emphases). ICLT as conceptualised in this way shares much in common with TBLT.

1.9 Challenges in Practice

The above presentation of developments to our understanding about the intercultural dimension, and the interface between language and culture, leads, in both theory and practice, to several significant challenges. Indeed, even though Piątkowska (2015) appeared to conclude that ICC provides the most comprehensive, meaningful and integrative theoretical framework by which to understand what IC is, what it entails, and how it might be developed, she accepted nonetheless that culture is "a complex phenomenon" (p. 397). Likewise, although Kramsch (2005) acknowledged the shortcomings of the traditional linguistic foci of language learning, she also highlighted a lack of consensus about what intercultural competence in the context of L2 learning actually was and entailed. Furthermore, the proliferation of a range of acronyms, including those we have so far included in this chapter (IC, ICC, CLT, PPP, TBLT, ICLT) can lead to confusion about exactly which label most adequately applies and which stances to pedagogy should be taken as teachers seek to enact and enhance the language–culture interface. A fundamental challenge is the very nomenclature that should apply to the intercultural dimension in L2 learning and L2 use, and the meanings that nomenclature carries.

Dervin et al. (2020), for example, viewed the construct of IC as sufficiently problematic that they decided not to define the construct in their opening chapter, but, rather, to allow their readers to uncover and reflect on how each individual chapter author in their collection understood the concept. In this regard, they argued:

> We each have our own (incomplete) understandings of IC, of course. We agree on some aspects while disagreeing on others … and would not want to give the impression that ours is THE right understanding of IC. That is why we have decided not to share our definitions. (pp. 4–5)

In the same volume, Dervin (2020) argued, "[t]here is a clear lack of agreement about the notion of interculturality in research, practice and decision-making today," leading to a "multiplicity of approaches and meanings" (p. 59). Dervin et al. asserted on this basis, "[w]ho has the power to decide what the intercultural is, how IC is defined?" (p. 8).

Certainly, the notion of IC is very established and frequently used in the literature (see, e.g., Bennett, 2014; Byram, 2018; Deardorff, 2009). Interestingly, Rehbein (2013) also drew on the IC acronym, but reframed this as *intercultural communication*, which he described as "the mediation of cultural differences between social groups through verbal or nonverbal interaction" (p. 1). Arguably the differentiation here is between the underlying competence and the realisation of that competence in practice, but use of the same acronym is potentially confusing. *Intercultural awareness* is another proposed construct (Baker, 2011; Hennebry, 2014). Yet another construct, *intercultural understanding*, features prominently in documents emanating from Australia, where explorations of the intercultural in language teaching and learning have been going on for many years (Australian Curriculum, n.d.). In one Australian state (Victoria State Government, 2018), however, *intercultural capability* is a chosen label (and, indeed, the one chosen by us for our study, for reasons we explain later in this chapter). How, if at all, do these constructs differ? If they do differ, where and why do they differ? Which construct best represents the knowledge, skills and understanding for interaction that we would wish learners of an L2 to acquire in the context of that learning?

The above arguments indicate that defining constructs such as IC and ICC, and enacting them through CLT and ICLT, leads to significant challenges. Furthermore, in practice the apparently simultaneous goals of exploring culture-in-language and critical comparison and contrast across cultures—within the broader overarching goal that, at the end of the day, students will learn how to communicate in the TL (with all that continues to imply about grammar and vocabulary)—lead to a confusing scenario for L2 programme planning. That is, and as we have already acknowledged, the (inter)cultural in language teaching and learning has often been approached in isolation from what Byram (1991) labelled the perceived "real business" of language learning. An integrated approach, especially an approach which is required to build in opportunities for critical reflection, comparison and contrast, is likely to place significant demands on L2 teachers who, with limited time available to them as it is, might view the language itself as their more pressing priority. Additionally, if standard practice in the L2 classroom is principally or exclusively to focus on language, adopting an intercultural stance in the classroom "implies a radical rethinking of one's goals for teaching a language" (Crozet, 2017, p. 157). When it comes to the practices of actual teachers, it is apparent that there is a strong and persistent mismatch between the ideal goal of language–culture integration and the implementation of an integrated approach in real classrooms.

Furthermore, prior studies have emphasised teachers' uncertainty about how to implement intercultural language teaching (see, e.g., Castro et al., 2004; Driscoll et al., 2013; Kohler, 2015). The early language learning years arguably present a particularly challenging (and therefore particularly intriguing) environment for the integration of the intercultural into L2 learning. Despite Byram's (1991) early assertion that separating out culture from language was "fundamentally flawed," carrying with it the implication that the L2 could be "treated in the early learning stages as if it were self-contained and independent of other sociocultural phenomena" (p. 18), studies to date (which we explore in Chaps. 2 and 3) indicate that many teachers still persist in separatist practices that demonstrate limited (or perhaps non-existent) understanding of intercultural integration, even when they may demonstrate a level of openness to the concept.

1.10 Introducing the Present Study

The study we present in this book is grounded in global debates about, and developments to, the CLT paradigm and, in particular, how the intercultural within this paradigm might be operationalised. It is also situated within the challenges facing the integration of language and culture in the L2 school classroom, particularly at the primary school level. In what follows we introduce the study, beginning with the New Zealand context in which it is situated.

1.10.1 The New Zealand Context for Language Teaching

In Chap. 3, we explore in some detail the New Zealand context for language teaching, and endeavours that have been made to enhance the intercultural dimension in that context. In what follows here, we provide a brief introduction to language education within the New Zealand school system in order to contextualise the study we report in this book.

In common with other western Anglophone contexts, New Zealand's approach to L2 learning in the school sector over the last few decades has focused on learning a language for purposes of genuine communication, realised through approaches aligned to the CLT paradigm. In the New Zealand school system, students can receive instruction for thirteen years (Years 1–13; ages 5+ to 18+). In the English-medium state or public school system, schools operate in a primarily two- or three-division model, as illustrated in Table 1.2.

Since 2010, teaching and learning in the state school system has been governed by a document known as the *New Zealand Curriculum* or NZC (Ministry of Education, 2007). The curriculum encourages learner-centred and experiential pedagogical approaches. Within the NZC, the learning area that focuses on L2 teaching and learning is appropriately called *Learning Languages*. It comprises three components. These are described as "strands," suggesting that the components are to be interwoven:

Table 1.2 New Zealand's state school system

School year	Age	Sector	
1	5+	Primary	Full primary
2	6+		
3	7+		
4	8+		
5	9+		
6	10+		
7	11+	Intermediate	
8	12+		
9	13+	Secondary	Junior
10	14+		
11	15+		Senior
12	16+		
13	17+		

1. The core *communication* strand
2. The supporting *language knowledge* strand
3. The supporting *cultural knowledge* strand.

Communication in the target language is seen as the overarching goal of L2 programmes. Language knowledge (a focus on grammar) and cultural knowledge (a focus on culture) are seen as equal components that are there to support the communicative agenda. Theoretical constructs of communicative competence inform the three-strand model.

The *cultural knowledge* strand sets out the primary learning expectations with regard to culture (Ministry of Education, 2007): students will not only "learn about culture"—an assumption here about learning facts about the target culture—but also about "the interrelationship between culture and language"—an assumption here about the interface between how language is used and the cultural meanings that language carries. Students will also be expected to "compare and contrast different beliefs and cultural practices, including their own" so that they "understand more about themselves and become more understanding of others" (p. 24)—an assumption here about the importance of "third place positioning."

Separately published achievement objectives (Ministry of Education, 2009) are designed to help teachers to understand how the elements of the three strands might be evaluated. With regard to cultural knowledge, it is made clear that beginners with learning a language might be expected to recognise that the target culture is organised in particular ways, and, as they progress, to be able to describe, compare and contrast cultural practices.

To support New Zealand-based teachers with understanding and implementing the *cultural knowledge* strand in the context of communication, a set of principles was published that explored so-called intercultural CLT (Newton et al., 2010).[3] The published principles are that an intercultural approach to CLT:

1. integrates language and culture from the beginning
2. engages learners in genuine social interaction
3. encourages and develops an exploratory and reflective approach to culture and culture-in-language
4. fosters explicit comparisons and connections between languages and cultures
5. acknowledges and responds appropriately to diverse learners and learning contexts
6. emphasises intercultural communicative competence rather than native-speaker competence (p. 63).

In essence, the principles encourage L2 learners to explore and reflect on how cultural practices may be similar and different across both the learners' own cultures and the target cultures. This reflects both the expectations of the *cultural knowledge* strand (Ministry of Education, 2007) and the curriculum achievement objectives (Ministry of Education, 2009).

In summary, the *Learning Languages* area of the NZC places a definite expectation on teachers to develop their students' intercultural skills in the context of a communicative approach to L2 learning. In practice, however, the expectation is not being realised because, in many cases, teachers are either not aware that they need to do this, or do not know how to do this. The challenge is arguably greater in New Zealand's primary/intermediate school sector because the vast majority of language teachers working in this sector have not received any dedicated teacher education in language acquisition theories and language pedagogy, are inexperienced in teaching languages, and may often be learning the language they are teaching alongside their own students (Scott & Butler, 2007). Students in the primary/intermediate sector are also beginners and, in many cases, receive only minimal instructional time in the L2. The addition of an intercultural element to teachers' practices and students' experiences is therefore a significant step and a huge challenge.

1.10.2 Our Project

As we noted at the start of this chapter, and explain in more detail in Chap. 4, our two-year project sought to investigate how five teachers working in four primary/intermediate schools in New Zealand could be supported to develop the intercultural dimension of L2 learning for their students.

---

[3] Newton et al. (2010) chose the acronym iCLT (rather than ICLT) as a context-specific means of reflecting the NZC emphasis on communication as the *core* strand and "the concept of intercultural language learning as an effective means of approaching the *supporting* strand of cultural knowledge in the curriculum for learning languages" (p. 4, our emphasis).

The study was framed as a collaborative partnership between the researchers and the teachers. Our teacher partners were Lillian[4] (L1 speaker of Mandarin and teacher of Mandarin); Kelly (L2 speaker of Mandarin and teacher of Mandarin); Kathryn (L2 speaker of Japanese and teacher of Japanese); Mike (L2 speaker of French and teacher of French); and Tamara (L2 speaker of Māori and teacher of Māori). Across all subject areas, the NZC encourages reflective approaches to teaching and learning, that is, approaches that involve some kind of inquiry, whether on the part of the learners (inquiry learning) or on the part of the teachers (teaching as inquiry). This inquiry emphasis became the means through which we aimed to create spaces with and for the teachers and their students for the kinds of intercultural reflections and explorations that we wished to encourage.

On the part of students, the NZC promotes inquiry learning as a means to facilitate students' self-reflective inquiries into specific phenomena, and the development of so-called key competencies such as thinking, managing self, relating to others, and participating and contributing (Ministry of Education, 2007, pp. 12–13). Inquiry learning may be defined as "an investigation into a topic, idea, problem, or issue with a focus on students constructing their own learning and meanings." Inquiry thus "enables students to learn through curiosity, discovery, and collaboration rather than being presented with facts through direct instruction" (National Library of New Zealand, n.d., para. 3).

In turn, teachers are encouraged to approach their own teaching through a teaching as inquiry approach (see Chap. 4 for further details). Teaching as inquiry is carefully articulated in the NZC as a cyclical process through which teachers investigate how a particular teaching strategy plays out in the classroom (Ministry of Education, 2007, p. 35). This is essentially an action research model which facilitates what Burns (1999) described as "a process for enhancing reflective practice and professional growth and development" (p. 24), because it "addresses questions of real practical and theoretical interest to many educational practitioners" (p. 25).

The overarching research question that we posed at the outset of the project was as follows: can a teaching as inquiry process in the context of learning an L2 enhance intermediate school learners' intercultural capability? Unlike Dervin et al. (2020) who explicitly stated that they would not define the intercultural dimension in their opening chapter on the basis that the concept might be interpreted in a multiplicity of ways, we chose, at the beginning of the project, to state our stance. In terms of the operationalisation of the construct of interest for the purposes of our study, we chose the label *intercultural capability* and defined the intercultural dimension as follows:

> [W]e use the term 'intercultural capability' … as the ability to relate comfortably with people from diverse linguistic and cultural backgrounds, appreciating and valuing the learners' own cultures and uniqueness alongside the cultures and uniqueness of others. Moreover, we use 'capabilities' rather than the most commonly used 'competence' to acknowledge the highly personal individual trajectories that the development of interculturality seems to take. (Biebricher et al., 2019, p. 606)

---

[4] In line with the expectation of the funder of this project that the study would represent genuine teacher-researcher partnerships, these are the teachers' actual names, and not pseudonyms.

1.10 Introducing the Present Study

We argued that our choice and interpretation were context-bound. That is, where teachers are guided by published achievement objectives (Ministry of Education, 2009), it was important for us to stake a claim to a definition of the intercultural dimension in line with, and not in opposition to, those objectives. The choice of an operational definition also enabled us to support the teachers in thinking through what they wished to investigate, and how they might frame their classroom activities for purposes of inquiry.

One of our aims during the two-year project was to co-construct with the teachers two teaching as inquiry cycles, both lasting up to six months, with an intercultural focus embedded within their L2 programmes. This was essentially a bottom-up process whereby we encouraged teachers to come up with their own context-suitable inquiries. That is, working within the above operational definition of the intercultural, we encouraged the teachers to think through how they might best achieve the outcome—enhanced intercultural capability in the context of L2 learning—in ways that were meaningful and realistic to their own contexts. We did not therefore prescribe which intercultural outcomes the teachers should aim to promote, or how the teachers should enact and then investigate them.

In essence, our project, framed as research with and by teachers, was intended to document how teachers moved forward in planning effective intercultural learning opportunities in line with the learner-centred stance of the NZC, the *cultural knowledge* outcomes anticipated in the *Learning Languages* learning area, and the intercultural achievement objectives teachers were presented with (Ministry of Education, 2007, 2009).

As we indicated at the start of this chapter, the project, as it unfolded, presented several challenges, and what we found in practice was actually quite different to what we had initially anticipated. That is, we began our project with high expectations and optimistic assumptions about what it means to develop young learners' intercultural capability in the context of learning a new language. As we engaged with the process, our thinking about what was possible was developed and refined. Two research questions (RQs) therefore underpin the journeys we will present in this book:

1. How do stakeholders' understandings about enhancing language learners' intercultural capability change and develop over time?
2. What are the implications for language education going forward?

To answer these questions, we take a retrospective look at the whole project and the findings that emerged (RQ1). We then consider the lessons we learned as we reflected on what the findings revealed (RQ2). This book therefore looks back on our journeys, from a range of perspectives, and the stops and redirections we made on the way, as we attempted to address what it means to enhance intercultural capability in the context of L2 learning. It presents and discusses the tensions, challenges and classroom realities, and the ways in which our journeys were shaped by those as our own understandings of what was possibly developed.

1.11 Presenting the Journeys

In this chapter, we have introduced the project in the broader context of discussing the intercultural dimension of L2 teaching and learning. In Chap. 2, we review the international literature on the intercultural dimension alongside a range of empirical studies that have investigated the development of this dimension in L2 learning, with a particular focus on younger learners. Chapter 3 builds on what has been outlined in this introductory chapter: we revisit and describe in more detail the context of the study—New Zealand—and present prior studies into the intercultural dimension in the New Zealand context. Chapter 4 presents the methodology for our two-year project in more detail, including the teaching as inquiry model as one means for teachers to investigate their own practices.

Chapters 5–7 present the findings of our study. In Chap. 5, we describe the inquiries the teachers undertook by presenting accounts of aspects of their lessons, based on observations of teachers in their classrooms. The chapter also presents findings pertaining to the students, gleaned principally from a series of summative focus groups. Our attention is on the evidence of intercultural learning that students reported had taken place, alongside the problems these revealed. Chapter 6 presents findings pertaining to the teachers, gleaned from discussions they had with the researchers, both individually and collectively, and follow-up reflective interviews. We present the teachers' reflections on the effectiveness of the inquiries they instigated, alongside the problems they encountered. In Chap. 7, we take a step back from the classroom and teacher data and present an account of how we worked with the teachers, alongside how we aimed to enhance reflection on practice through the "critical friend" conversations we undertook at different stages in the project. We reflect on the evidence we collected from the teachers and students, once more alongside the problems we came up against, and what these might mean for an effective focus on the intercultural in L2 classrooms.

Chapter 8, the concluding chapter, draws each of the strands from Chaps. 5–7 together. Bearing in mind challenges with defining the intercultural, and all this means for research and teaching, the concluding chapter revisits some of the problems raised in this introductory chapter and in Chaps. 2 and 3 and discusses the implications of these in light of the findings we report in Chaps. 5, 6 and 7. In particular we focus on the lessons we learned and the recommendations we would make, as both researchers and teacher educators, to move the debates forward about developing the intercultural dimension in the context of classroom-based L2 learning.

1.12 Conclusion

We have argued in this chapter that L2 pedagogy needs to prepare students for intercultural encounters, and that a pure focus on language, without any attention paid to difference and otherness, will be insufficient. Furthermore, the classrooms

1.12 Conclusion

and contexts in which students are learning the L2 are often multicultural, with students brought together from diverse backgrounds who collaborate with each other in the language learning endeavour. Attention needs to be paid to the intercultural dimension of communicative interactions, both in and beyond the TL. In Byram's (2018) words, the intercultural dimension serves to enhance the development of communicative competence by focusing on "skills, knowledge, and attitudes for interaction" (p. 1).

As we stated at the start of this chapter, the intercultural as a dimension of communicative L2 teaching and learning began to become apparent in the 1980s and was debated as necessary as a *development* to the construct of communicative competence (e.g., Byram, 2018). As Spada (2018) put it, "twenty-first century CLT" has developed and broadened considerably since its early beginnings, and now reflects "a greater balance, scope and depth" (p. 12). For Spada, this has meant that, in *addition* to an emphasis on language used appropriately for communicative purposes—the central element of "traditional" or PPP-oriented CLT—there needed to be the inclusion of "functional and intercultural competence" (p. 12). Moreover, learner-centred and experiential pedagogical approaches may hold out greater possibilities for intercultural exploration than more teacher-dominant approaches.

Two key problems emerge. First, L2 pedagogy often remains largely teacher-led and language-focused in many contexts, and separated from culture, even though Byram (2021) noted that addressing culture as "decontextualised factual information with minimal relationship to the language being learnt" (p. 92) represents a worst-case scenario. It must be acknowledged that, quite early on, the PPP approach quickly became embedded as "more or less standard practice" (Howatt, 1984, p. 279). Furthermore, it persists as a model in many L2 classrooms across the world. Indeed, in the context of reporting a recent interesting study that compared the effectiveness of PPP and TBLT with very young, beginner learners of English as L2 in Japan, Shintani (2016) underscored the ongoing dominance of PPP, both in and beyond her immediate setting.

Second, Byram (2018) problematised the notion of IC, speaking of several different models and interpretations of the concept, and noting that the interface between language and culture can often be obscure. The construct of IC was further problematised by Dervin et al. (2020), who asserted that, despite apparent clarity around IC as the underpinning theoretical construct they had selected, IC is in reality "a mish-mash of a concept" (p. 6), and the "roads of IC in education" are "muddy" (p. 5).

The journeys we present in the remainder of this book illustrate the pedagogical realities highlighted, for example, by Shintani (2016), Byram (2018, 2021) and Dervin et al. (2020). They demonstrate just how the stakeholders got their boots dirty as they made their journeys towards L2 learners' enhanced intercultural capability. In this book, our aim is that, through presenting the journeys of three distinct but intersecting groups of stakeholders—students, teachers and researchers/teacher educators—and by including, as Dervin et al. had expressed it, emerging stories that illustrate risk, growth, struggle and frustration, we will add to the ongoing debates about how to promote and develop the intercultural dimension in L2 classrooms.

References

Alptekin, C. (2002). Towards intercultural communicative competence in ELT. *ELT Journal, 56*(1), 57–64.

Australian Curriculum. (n.d.). *Intercultural understanding.* https://www.australiancurriculum.edu.au/f-10-curriculum/general-capabilities/intercultural-understanding/

Baker, W. (2011). Intercultural awareness: Modelling an understanding of cultures in intercultural communication through English as a lingua franca. *Language and Intercultural Communication, 11*(3), 197–214.

Bennett, J. (Ed.). (2014). *Sage encyclopedia of intercultural competence.* Sage.

Benson, P., & Voller, P. (Eds.). (1997). *Autonomy and independence in language learning.* Longman.

Bhabha, H. K. (1994). *The location of culture.* Routledge.

Biebricher, C., East, M., Howard, J., & Tolosa, C. (2019). Navigating intercultural language teaching in New Zealand classrooms. *Cambridge Journal of Education, 49*(5), 605–621.

Brown, H. D. (1994). *Principles of language learning and teaching* (3rd ed.). Prentice Hall Regents.

Brown, H. D. (2014). *Principles of language learning and teaching* (6th ed.). Pearson.

Brunsmeier, S. (2017). Primary teachers' knowledge when initiating intercultural communicative competence. *TESOL Quarterly, 51*(1), 143–155.

Burns, A. (1999). *Collaborative action research for English language teachers.* Cambridge University Press.

Byram, M. (1991). Teaching culture and language: Towards an integrated model. In D. Buttjes & M. Byram (Eds.), *Mediating languages and cultures: Towards an intercultural theory of foreign language education* (pp. 17–30). Multilingual Matters.

Byram, M. (1997). *Teaching and assessing intercultural communicative competence.* Multilingual Matters.

Byram, M. (2009). Intercultural competence in foreign languages: The intercultural speaker and the pedagogy of foreign language education. In D. K. Deardorff (Ed.), *The Sage handbook of intercultural competence* (pp. 321–332). Sage.

Byram, M. (2018). Intercultural competence. In C. Chapelle (Ed.), *The encyclopedia of applied linguistics.* Wiley.

Byram, M. (2021). *Teaching and assessing intercultural communicative competence: Revisited* (2nd ed.). Multilingual Matters.

Byram, M., Gribkova, B., & Starkey, H. (2002). *Developing the intercultural dimension in language teaching: A practical introduction for teachers.* Council of Europe.

Canale, M. (1983). On some dimensions of language proficiency. In J. W. J. Oller (Ed.), *Issues in language testing research* (pp. 333–342). Newbury House.

Canale, M., & Swain, M. (1980). Theoretical bases of communicative approaches to second language teaching and testing. *Applied Linguistics, 1*(1), 1–47.

Castro, P., Sercu, L., & Méndez-García, M. C. (2004). Integrating language-and-culture teaching: An investigation of Spanish teachers' perceptions of the objectives of foreign language education. *Intercultural Education, 15*, 91–104.

Crozet, C. (2017). The intercultural foreign language teacher: Challenges and choices. In M. Dasli & A. Díaz (Eds.), *The critical turn in language and intercultural communication pedagogy* (pp. 143–161). Routledge.

Crozet, C., Liddicoat, A. J., & Lo Bianco, J. (1999). Intercultural competence: From language policy to language education. In J. Lo Bianco, A. J. Liddicoat, & C. Crozet (Eds.), *Striving for the third place: Intercultural competence through language education* (pp. 1–20). Language Australia.

Deardorff, D. (Ed.). (2009). *The Sage handbook of intercultural competence.* Sage.

Dervin, F. (2020). Creating and combining models of Intercultural Competence for teacher education/training—On the need to rethink IC frequently. In F. Dervin, R. Moloney, & A. Simpson (Eds.), *Intercultural competence in the work of teachers: Confronting ideologies and practices* (pp. 57–72). Routledge.

References

Dervin, F., Moloney, R., & Simpson, A. (2020). Going forward with Intercultural Competence (IC) in teacher education and training: Beyond the 'walls built by ghosts'? In F. Dervin, R. Moloney, & A. Simpson (Eds.), *Intercultural competence in the work of teachers: Confronting ideologies and practices* (pp. 3–16). Routledge.

Driscoll, P., Earl, J., & Cable, C. (2013). The role and nature of the cultural dimension in primary modern languages. *Language, Culture and Curriculum, 26*(2), 146–160.

East, M. (2012a). Addressing the intercultural via task-based language teaching: Possibility or problem? *Language and Intercultural Communication, 12*(1), 56–73.

East, M. (2012b). *Task-based language teaching from the teachers' perspective: Insights from New Zealand*. John Benjamins.

East, M. (2016). *Assessing foreign language students' spoken proficiency: Stakeholder perspectives on assessment innovation*. Springer.

Flinders Humanities Research Centre. (2005, March 24). *Language and intercultural communication (LInC) group—Discussion paper*.

Gonzáles-Lloret, M. (2020). Using technology-mediated tasks in second language instruction to connect speakers internationally. In C. Lambert & R. Oliver (Eds.), *Using tasks in second language teaching: Practice in diverse contexts* (pp. 65–81). Multilingual Matters.

Hedge, T. (2000). *Teaching and learning in the language classroom*. Oxford University Press.

Hennebry, M. (2014). Cultural awareness: Should it be taught? Can it be taught? In P. Driscoll, E. Macaro, & A. Swerbrick (Eds.), *Debates in modern languages education* (pp. 135–150). Routledge.

Higgs, T. V. (Ed.) (1984). *Teaching for proficiency: The organizing principle*. National Textbook Company.

Howatt, A. P. R. (1984). *A history of English language teaching*. Oxford University Press.

Hymes, D. (1972). On communicative competence. In J. B. Pride & J. Holmes (Eds.), *Sociolinguistics* (pp. 269–293). Penguin.

Klapper, J. (2003). Taking communication to task? A critical review of recent trends in language teaching. *Language Learning Journal, 27*, 33–42.

Kohler, M. (2015). *Teachers as mediators in the foreign language classroom*. Multilingual Matters.

Kramsch, C. (1986). From language proficiency to interactional competence. *The Modern Language Journal, 70*(4), 366–372.

Kramsch, C. (1987). The proficiency movement: Second language acquisition perspectives. *Studies in Second Language Acquisition, 9*(3), 355–362.

Kramsch, C. (2005). Post 9/11: Foreign languages between knowledge and power. *Applied Linguistics, 26*(4), 545–567.

Kramsch, C. (2009). Third culture and language education. In V. Cook & L. Wei (Eds.), *Contemporary applied linguistics Vol. 1: Language teaching and learning* (pp. 233–254). Continuum.

Liddicoat, A. (2005a). Culture for language learning in Australian language-in-education policy. *Australian Review of Applied Linguistics, 28*(2), 28–43.

Liddicoat, A. (2005b). Teaching languages for intercultural communication. In D. Cunningham & A. Hatoss (Eds.), *An international perspective on language policies, practices and proficiencies* (pp. 201–214). Fédération Internationale des Professeurs de Langues Vivantes (FIPLV).

Liddicoat, A. (2008). Pedagogical practice for integrating the intercultural in language teaching and learning. *Japanese Studies, 28*(3), 277–290.

Liddicoat, A., & Crozet, C. (Eds.). (2000). *Teaching languages, teaching cultures*. Language Australia.

Lo Bianco, J., Liddicoat, A., & Crozet, C. (Eds.). (1999). *Striving for the third place: Intercultural competence through language education*. Language Australia.

Long, M. (1985). A role for instruction in second language acquisition: Task-based language teaching. In K. Hylstenstam & M. Pienemann (Eds.), *Modelling and assessing second language acquisition* (pp. 77–99). Multilingual Matters.

Long, M. (2015). *Second language acquisition and task-based language teaching*. Wiley-Blackwell.

MacDonald, M. (2019). The discourse of 'thirdness' in intercultural studies. *Language and Intercultural Communication, 19*(1), 93–109.

Martinez-Flor, A., Usó-Juan, E., & Alcón, E. (2006). Towards acquiring communicative competence through speaking. In E. Usó-Juan & A. Martínez-Flor (Eds.), *Studies on language acquisition: Current trends in the development and teaching of the four language skills* (pp. 139–157). Walter de Gruyter.

Ministry of Education. (2007). *The New Zealand curriculum.* Learning Media.

Ministry of Education. (2009). *Curriculum achievement objectives by learning area.* http://nzcurriculum.tki.org.nz/The-New-Zealand-Curriculum

Mitchell, R., Myles, F., & Marsden, E. (2019). *Second language learning theories* (4th ed.). Routledge.

Müller-Hartmann, A., & Schocker, M. (2018). The challenge of thinking task-based teaching from the learners' perspectives: Developing teaching competences through an action research approach to teacher education. In M. Ahmadian & M. Garcia Mayo (Eds.), *Recent perspectives on task-based language learning and teaching* (pp. 233–257). De Gruyter.

National Library of New Zealand. (n.d.). *Understanding inquiry learning.* https://natlib.govt.nz/schools/school-libraries/library-services-for-teaching-and-learning/supporting-inquiry-learning/understanding-inquiry-learning

Newton, J., Yates, E., Shearn, S., & Nowitzki, W. (2010). *Intercultural communicative language teaching: Implications for effective teaching and learning—A literature review and an evidence-based framework for effective teaching.* Ministry of Education.

Norris, J., Bygate, M., & Van den Branden, K. (2009). Introducing task-based language teaching. In K. Van den Branden, M. Bygate, & J. Norris (Eds.), *Task-based language teaching: A reader* (pp. 15–19). John Benjamins.

Peiser, G., & Jones, M. (2013). The influence of teachers' interests, personalities and life experiences in intercultural languages teaching. *Teachers and Teaching: Theory and Practice, 20*(3), 375–390.

Perry, L., & Southwell, L. (2011). Developing intercultural understanding and skills: Models and approaches. *Intercultural Education, 22*(6), 453–466.

Piątkowska, K. (2015). From cultural knowledge to intercultural communicative competence: Changing perspectives on the role of culture in foreign language teaching. *Intercultural Education, 26*(5), 397–408.

Rehbein, J. (2013). Intercultural communication. In C. Chapelle (Ed.), *The encyclopedia of applied linguistics.* Wiley Blackwell.

Richards, J. C. (2001). *Curriculum development in language teaching.* Cambridge University Press.

Richards, J. C. (2006). *Communicative language teaching today.* Cambridge University Press.

Richards, J. C., & Rodgers, T. S. (2014). *Approaches and methods in language teaching* (3rd ed.). Cambridge University Press.

Scott, A. J., & Butler, P. J. (2007). My teacher is learning like us: Teachers and students as language learners. *The New Zealand Language Teacher, 33,* 11–16.

Sehlaoui, A. S. (2001). Developing cross-cultural communicative competence in pre-service ESL/EFL teachers: A critical perspective. *Language, Culture and Curriculum, 14*(1), 42–57.

Sherzer, J., Johnstone, B., & Marcellino, W. (2010). Dell H. Hymes: An intellectual sketch. *Language in Society, 39*(3), 301–305.

Shintani, N. (2016). *Input-based tasks in foreign language instruction for young learners.* John Benjamins.

Spada, N. (2018). Isolating or integrating attention to form in communicative instruction: A dilemma? *Babel, 53*(1), 7–12.

Victoria State Government. (2018). *Intercultural capability.* https://www.education.vic.gov.au/school/teachers/teachingresources/discipline/capabilities/Pages/intercultural.aspx

Walker, I., Chan, D., Nagami, M., & Bourguignon, C. (Eds.). (2018). *New perspectives on the development of communicative and related competence in foreign language education.* De Gruyter.

Open Access This chapter is licensed under the terms of the Creative Commons Attribution 4.0 International License (http://creativecommons.org/licenses/by/4.0/), which permits use, sharing, adaptation, distribution and reproduction in any medium or format, as long as you give appropriate credit to the original author(s) and the source, provide a link to the Creative Commons license and indicate if changes were made.

The images or other third party material in this chapter are included in the chapter's Creative Commons license, unless indicated otherwise in a credit line to the material. If material is not included in the chapter's Creative Commons license and your intended use is not permitted by statutory regulation or exceeds the permitted use, you will need to obtain permission directly from the copyright holder.

Chapter 2
Studies on the Intercultural Dimension Across the Globe

2.1 Introduction

In Chap. 1, we introduced the study that is the focus of this book alongside the New Zealand language teaching and learning context in which the study is situated. In this chapter, we present arguments from the international literature on the intercultural dimension, starting with an attempt to synthesise key debates around defining this crucial dimension. In the first part of this chapter, we locate the concept of interculturality in education, in particular in curricular reforms in different jurisdictions and in the teaching/learning of additional languages (L2s). In the second part, we present a range of empirical studies that have investigated the intercultural dimension as it relates to pedagogy, teachers and learners, with a particular focus on younger (school-aged) language learners.

2.2 The Intercultural Dimension

Interest in understanding the skills required to engage with cultures and learning about cultures is not new, and certainly not exclusive to language education. Several academic fields have contributed to the knowledge base regarding what today is known as "interculturality." Contributions from anthropology, communication studies, education, linguistics and psychology, to name a few, have resulted in a rich and complex interdisciplinary field with numerous definitions, theorisations and applications. Authors like Holmes and MacDonald (2020) consider that the concept of interculturality is present in all aspects of contemporary life and characterise the development of interculturality "through the different forms of ethical practice which we carry out, moment by moment, in the unfolding of our daily lives" (p. 1).

Although scholars agree that culture shapes how individuals communicate, behave and interact with others, defining precisely what *culture* is has been less straightforward. As Byram (2021) put it, "[d]efinitions of 'culture' are many" (p. 50), and it is important to be mindful of the risks of presenting a given culture "as if it were unchanging over time or as if there were only one set of beliefs, meanings and behaviours in any given country" (p. 51). Broadly speaking, the conceptualisation has changed from viewing culture as a relatively static entity made up of "facts" to be learned, to seeing culture as dynamic and constantly changing through interaction and communication. According to Paige et al. (2000), a change in perspective from static to dynamic has been characterised by "conceptual shifts from culture-specific to culture-general models of intercultural competence, cultural stereotypes to cultural generalizations, cultural absolutes to cultural variations (within and across cultures), and culture as distinct from language to culture as integral to language" (p. 5).

The interest in researching the intercultural dimension of human interaction can be traced to the 1950s, with documentation of cross-cultural communication problems encountered by Westerners working overseas followed by three decades of expanded interest in contexts as varied as study abroad or immigrant acculturation (Sinicrope et al., 2007). However, just as there are many meanings to the word "culture," determining exactly what the intercultural dimension is and entails is also complex. Indeed, we pointed out two problems in the opening chapter. First, a range of labels is used in the literature with regard to the intercultural dimension. These include: intercultural *competence*; intercultural *communication*; intercultural *awareness*; intercultural *understanding*; and intercultural *capability* (the label we have chosen for this book). Fantini and Tirmizi (2006) offered a comprehensive list of 19 terms that they noted were often used interchangeably. Intercultural competence (IC) has emerged as a predominant label. However, this label has been used and variously defined by different scholars over the last 30 years, and no single definition has been agreed upon (Deardorff, 2006), making the construct itself messy and difficult to pin down (Dervin et al., 2020).

2.3 Intercultural Competence

Sercu et al. (2005) provided a multi-faceted description of what intercultural competence might entail:

> the willingness to engage with foreign culture, self-awareness and the ability to look upon oneself from the outside, the ability to see the world through the others' eyes, the ability to cope with uncertainty, the ability to act as a cultural mediator, the ability to evaluate others' point of view, the ability to consciously use culture learning skills and to read the cultural context, and the understanding that individuals cannot be reduced to their collective identities. (p. 2)

Taking the above description as a starting point, it can be argued that, despite differences that have emerged, all definitions and conceptualisations acknowledge that IC involves the ability to interact effectively and appropriately with people from other cultures. Such interaction includes both what people do and what people say, and typically encompasses four dimensions: knowledge, attitudes, skills and behaviours (Perry & Southwell, 2011). These four dimensions can be seen in many definitions and models of intercultural competence (see reviews by Dervin, 2016; Perry & Southwell, 2011; Sinicrope et al., 2007; Spitzberg & Changnon, 2009). These models generally agree that intercultural competence refers to "the appropriate and effective management of interaction between people who, to some degree or another, represent different or divergent affective, cognitive, and behavioral orientations to the world" (Spitzberg & Changnon, 2009, p. 7).

In what follows, we briefly describe three models considered influential to current operationalisations of the intercultural dimension in education, each including cognitive, affective and behavioural components operating within an ongoing process of individual and interactional development.

Cited as one of the earlier models of intercultural competence, Bennett's (1986) *Developmental Model of Intercultural Sensitivity* was created as a framework to explain the reactions of people to cultural difference. Drawing on concepts from cognitive psychology, the model charts stages of the individual's evolution from "ethnocentrism" (believing that one's culture is the best) to "ethnorelativism" (realising that all cultures contain elements that are both "good" and "bad"). According to Bennett (2004), in order to navigate intercultural situations successfully, a person's worldview must shift from *avoiding* cultural difference to *seeking* (i.e., consciously not avoiding) cultural difference. The model has been used in both academic and business contexts to inform educational programmes to facilitate individuals' development across stages.

In the context of efforts to develop interculturally competent students at tertiary level who can engage in international education, Deardorff (2006) developed the *Process Model of Intercultural Competence*. Using both a questionnaire completed by administrators of international offices in US universities and a Delphi process (see, e.g., Rowe & Wright, 1999), developing consensus among a panel of intercultural scholars, the resulting framework contains five essential components of intercultural competence: knowledge, attitudes, skills, desired internal outcome and desired external outcome. Deardorff argued that one of the advantages of this model is that it lends itself to the possibility of *assessing* the development of intercultural competence.

Perhaps the most widely known framework used as a standard for intercultural education and development programmes in the European Union is Byram's (1997) *Intercultural Communicative Competence* (ICC). This model, arguably one that has the most direct relevance to language teaching and learning in a range of contexts, traces its origins to work on communication, and the concept of *communicative competence*, proposed initially by Hymes (1972) and subsequently extended by others (e.g., Canale, 1983; Canale & Swain, 1980).

Acknowledging the importance of communicative competence in language education, the ICC model has shown considerable endurance, with its ongoing relevance being recently reaffirmed in a revised edition of the original 1997 work (Byram, 2021). Indeed, in the Foreword to the revision Byram argued that his model has not been substantially changed, but that, on the contrary, "the central message … remains" (p. xiii). Byram (1997, 2021) argued that the primary intent of L2 education must be to develop a level of competence whereby individuals of different cultures and experiences can understand and relate to one another—or ICC. He based his framework around three essential characteristics that he argued an intercultural speaker should possess: attitudes, knowledge and skills. Furthermore, Byram framed his perception of what was required for intercultural capability in terms of the development of several *savoirs* (knowledges). These represent different dimensions of knowledge, not only about the general processes involved in societal and individual interaction, but also about social groups and how they might behave both in the target language country and in the learner's own country (we present the *savoirs* in more detail in Chap. 4 where we discuss their relevance for the project we undertook).

Diversity with representing what IC might be provides educators with a variety of approaches to understanding and researching the intercultural dimension. Additionally, a consistent element of the intercultural across different conceptualisations is the development of the kind of capability that compares, contrasts and evaluates across cultures. For example, underpinning and informing the development of the *savoirs* is the suggestion that, to attain the goal of becoming *intercultural* speakers, students of an L2 need to abandon their typical role of "tourist" (with the implication of being an outsider and temporary visitor). Instead, they will assume the more active role of "sojourner"—someone who goes beyond "visiting" a target culture to experiencing several aspects of it, exhibiting willingness to engage in new encounters and suspend judgement of others, with openness to question the values and practices of their own culture (Byram, 1997; Sercu, 2010).

2.4 Critiquing the Models of Intercultural Competence

The above three models of intercultural competence—Bennett (1986), Deardorff (2006), and Byram (1997, 2021)—have not been without comment or criticism. Piątkowska (2015), for example, provided an important caution with regard to the notion of comparison and contrast across cultures. She argued that a contrastive approach to cultural knowledge whereby learners are encouraged to "look for connections and find a bridging gap" between their own culture and the target culture can lead to the danger of creating "a very monolithic and static picture of cultures" (p. 400) which does not sufficiently take into account heterogeneous societies, minority groups and other non-mainstream members of a given society.

While the encouragement of comparison may be to develop in learners "the distinction between 'us' and 'them', that is, between our own and another culture" (Piątkowska, 2015, p. 400), this, Piątkowska warned, may well lead to stereotypical conclusions and does not help to foster attitudes of respect towards difference and variations within cultures. As Byram (2021) put it, it is important to "be aware of the dangers of presenting 'a culture' as if it were unchanging over time or as if there were only one set of beliefs, meanings and behaviours in any given country." Rather, "it is *individuals* who meet and not *cultures*" (p. 51, our emphases). Individuals are unique and bring their own unique understandings to different interactions.

Dervin (2016) has also criticised the three models because of what he perceived as their emphasis on the individual and that individual's positioning, disregarding the relationships in which these individuals are involved or the interactions in which they engage. He went on to warn that models of intercultural competence that are focused on the blurring of difference may run the risk of dissolving the shared values, beliefs and behaviours of specific cultural groups. In fact, he warned that concepts developed in the contexts of Europe and North America may serve the needs of their more heterogeneous and developed societies, but may be problematic for less heterogeneous, less developed societies. Further criticisms point to the fact that such a wide range of theoretical frameworks and models "complexifies the task of communicating about related ideas in a systematic and consistently interpretable way" (Sinicrope et al., 2007, p. 2).

2.5 Third Place Positioning

Despite critiques, comparison, contrast and evaluation appear to be consistent elements of the intercultural across different conceptualisations. In the process of developing a comparative and reflective intercultural stance, learners need to consider how their capability develops by drawing on their own language and culture as part of the process of coming to understand those from other cultures (Papademetre, 2000). This means that learners need to "decentre" from their own culture and see their own positioning from the perspective of another (Kramsch, 1993). Learning languages has the potential to expose learners to other ways of viewing the world and thereby develop flexibility, independence and separation from a single linguistic and conceptual system (Kramsch, 1993; Liddicoat, 2005).

Underlying the complexity of encounters across cultures is what we introduced in Chap. 1 as the metaphors of "third space" (e.g., Bhabha, 1994) or "third place" (e.g., Lo Bianco et al., 1999). Other labels that have been used include "third culture," "third stance," or simply "thirdness" (Kramsch, 2009). Each label seeks to capture the dynamic nature and multi-faceted relationality of communications that are intercultural. As we acknowledged in the opening chapter, MacDonald (2019) labelled developing understandings of the concept as constituting a "discourse of thirdness," and acknowledged tensions and contradictions in the ways in which the terms are used and interpreted in contemporary studies. He argued nonetheless that "third place" has emerged as a term to represent the space where "the 'hybrid' identity of the language learner/intercultural subject" can be worked out in a pedagogical context (p. 106). However labelled, the concept "draws our central focus *beyond* the entities that interlocutors are conceivably 'locked into' towards a *new site* opened up *between* interlocutors" (Zhou & Pilcher, 2019, p. 1, our emphases). Kramsch (1993) described these interlocutors as "brokers" who will use language in its double role of medium and shaper of culture (Paige et al., 2000).

Preparing students to be brokers and culture learners requires putting culture at the core of language education. The move to language learning as a social practice of meaning-making and interpretation is a much more expanded view than having a pure language focus, and is claimed to provide a more engaging educational experience for students (Scarino & Liddicoat, 2009). Liddicoat (2011) argued that this expanded view "implies a transformational engagement of the learner in the act of learning." This kind of learning "involves the student in oppositional practice that seeks to decentre learners from their existing linguistic and cultural positioning and to develop intercultural identity as a result of an engagement with another culture" (p. 838). To become effective intercultural learners, students must develop a variety of learning strategies, ranging from reflective observation to active experimentation, or what Kolb (1984) referred to as an "experiential" learning style.

2.6 Interculturality in Curricula

At a conceptual level, there may be challenges in identifying exactly what the intercultural dimension entails. Nonetheless, this dimension has recently been incorporated into national curricular documents in a range of contexts, highlighting the perceived importance of helping learners to develop "complex abilities needed to perform effectively and appropriately when interacting with others who are linguistically and culturally different" (Fantini, 2006, p. 12). An intercultural approach has gained relevance in different contexts because of its potential to contribute to overarching educational objectives (Chan et al., 2015; Hill & Cowie, 2012), in particular to prepare learners for global citizenship, an aim also considered one of the key competencies of the twenty-first century (Byram, 2018; Noddings, 2005; OECD, 2016).

As Byram et al. (2013) argued, the appearance in curriculum documents of references to *culture, intercultural competence, intercultural understanding* and other such phrases, suggests that the "theorists" have persuaded curriculum designers that these concepts are significant and worthy of attention through educational initiatives. These efforts have been widely documented in Europe where countries belonging to the European Union have been at the forefront of reforms to educational policies that reflect the changing demographics of their populations, developing an approach to interculturalism that targets education on three fundamental levels: societal, institutional and pedagogical (Neuner, 2012). Addressing the challenges associated with building multicultural societies, the Council of Europe (2003), for example, has recognised education as an invaluable medium through which to develop intercultural capabilities and support the ideal of "learning to live together" (p. 4).

In Australia, the wider national curriculum has recently included *intercultural understanding* as a general capability articulated as: (1) recognising culture and developing respect; (2) interacting and empathising with others; and (3) reflecting on intercultural experiences and taking responsibility (Australian Curriculum Assessment and Reporting Authority [ACARA], 2011).

2.6 Interculturality in Curricula

Within a more broadly articulated intercultural interest that has permeated curriculum documents around the world, language education is arguably in a privileged position to advance the intercultural dimension. For example, in the early 1990s, policymakers in Australia put forward a progressive language and literacy policy (Department of Employment, Education and Training, 1991) which motivated a number of initiatives, spearheaded by the Australian Federation of Modern Language Teachers Associations (AFMLTA). These initiatives included the publication of the *Principles for Intercultural Language Learning* (Dellit, 2005) and the *Professional Standards for Accomplished Teaching of Languages and Cultures* (AFMLTA, 2005), which were included in a countrywide professional learning and development programme for L2 teachers. In this context, the growth of an intercultural approach to language teaching and learning has been labelled "the most significant development in Australian language pedagogy in the last 20 years" (Harbon & Moloney, 2013, p. 8).

In the United States, a report demonstrating the influence of language learning on economic growth, cultural diplomacy and productivity has advocated for a twenty-first-century education that fosters *international competencies* and "nurtures deep expertise in world languages and cultures" (American Academy of Arts & Sciences, 2017, p. 19). The American Council on the Teaching of Foreign Languages (ACTFL) published the *Standards for Foreign Language Learning* in 1996 to guide language teaching and learning. These standards were later arranged into five areas that were designed to guide the teaching of a range of L2s: communication, culture, connections, comparisons and communities. A revised version (ACTFL, 2014) included *global competence*, defined as the ability to communicate with respect and cultural understanding in different languages inside and outside the classroom.

A milestone for L2 teaching in the European context was the development of the *Common European Framework of Reference for Languages* or CEFR (Council of Europe, 2001), a document adopted throughout Europe and used as a benchmark around the world (including New Zealand, as we note in the next chapter). The CEFR provides guidelines for defining common descriptors for language proficiency levels and language qualifications. Pedagogically relevant points are the recognition that competence is relative and not absolute, and the formulation of *levels of competence* alongside a general orientation of L2 teaching towards output and outcomes (e.g., interaction with others to achieve specific goals) instead of input and content (e.g., reading and processing texts in the target language [TL]), as was previously the case (Hu, 2013). The framework also highlights the importance of developing intercultural awareness and intercultural skills, to enhance intercultural communication and prevent intercultural misunderstandings.

To support the implementation of the CEFR framework in curricula across the European Union, a group of scholars developed a guide (Beacco et al., 2010) using the concept of plurilingualism as a special feature of multicultural and multilingual member states. It was argued that since plurilingualism is linked to the maintenance of democratic values across Europe, it should be paired with interculturalism. From those initial guidelines, Beacco and colleagues developed an intercultural L2 curriculum addressing both macro issues (e.g., syllabus, professional development standards) and micro issues (e.g., course content, textbooks, resources) to be adapted by the various school systems in Europe. The aim was to provide stakeholders with the necessary resources to implement an approach to the development of intercultural competencies in an effective way, drawing on the theoretical work developed in the Anglophone context by Byram and others (e.g., Byram, 1997). More widely, UNESCO (2013) outlined a vision for the development of intercultural competence within L2 education that insisted that ministries of education, policy makers, teacher education programmes, materials developers and teacher educators, as well as administrators and schools, must all provide classroom practitioners with the knowledge, skills, experiences, resources and support they require. The pivotal role of teachers in the intercultural endeavour was therefore clearly recognised.

In summary, the goal of developing intercultural competence has become significant at both curricular and policy levels, both within and beyond the L2 context. It must be noted, however, that these efforts at the level of vision and even policy have not resulted in the effective implementation initially envisioned (Byram, 2014). This, it seems, is a consequence of the complexity of defining and then operationalising the construct of intercultural competence in the L2 classroom. This complexity in practice is an issue we take up in what follows.

2.6.1 Interculturality in Language Classrooms

Both scholars and policymakers have agreed that developing intercultural competence needs to be addressed explicitly in learning and teaching; more specifically, from this perspective language teaching needs to enable L2 students to develop into multilingually and multiculturally aware world citizens, something that might be labelled a "cultural turn" (Byram et al., 2013). As we discussed in the previous chapter, this growing emphasis can be traced in L2 pedagogy back to the emergence of Communicative Language Teaching in the 1970s, to perceived gaps in what CLT was aiming to achieve, and to the theorisation of intercultural communicative competence or ICC.

Byram's ICC model (1997, 2021), which we referred to earlier, provides one means of articulating for teachers the skills that might be developed in the L2 teaching and learning context. Taking into account sets of principles for language learning and teaching that have been developed in different contexts, Liddicoat (2011) proposed a complementary means of articulating the intercultural dimension for teachers. He clarified that intercultural language teaching does not constitute a language teaching "method." Nor is it a set of prescribed pedagogical practices. Rather, it should be viewed as a "stance" which Cochran-Smith and Lytle (1999) described as "positions teachers and others ... take toward knowledge and its relationship to practice" (p. 289). This means that intercultural language teaching and learning "is best considered as a set of shared assumptions about the nature of language, culture and learning that shapes an overall understanding of what it means to teach language and to do this in an intercultural way" (Liddicoat, 2011, p. 840). Liddicoat's review identified a number of themes:

- an active engagement with the culture of the target language community as a form of lived experience;
- positioning the learners as mediators across a multiplicity of cultures;
- an engagement in processes of reflection about language and culture and their relationship as a component of language learning.

In essence, language learning from an intercultural perspective requires "an understanding of culture as facts, artifacts, information and social practices, as well as an understanding of culture as the lens through which people mutually interpret and communicate meaning" (Liddicoat & Scarino, 2013, p. 46). Byram and Wagner (2018) concluded that if language educators move from teaching "knowledge about" cultures to developing in their students the skills and attitudes to "know how to" develop intercultural competence, students will "value language education as an education for developing their identity rather than as the learning of a code that can only be used in some restricted environments" (p. 147).

In the last decade, Byram has further broadened the treatment of intercultural competence to include, in addition to the competencies of intercultural communication, the competencies of intercultural citizenship (e.g., Byram, 2012). The concept of education for intercultural citizenship brings together L2 education and citizenship education (Byram & Wagner, 2018). This is an attempt to integrate the notion of ICC from L2 education with an emphasis on civic action in the community as addressed in citizenship education (e.g., Porto, 2016). This further illustrates the interest in the intercultural that moves *beyond* language education and the L2 classroom.

2.6.2 Challenges for L2 Teachers

The development of the intercultural dimension in the context of language learning has posed several challenges for many L2 teachers, who must often assume this responsibility without adequate supporting mechanisms. As Peiser (2015) asserted, the re-conceptualisation of language teaching as encompassing *both* linguistic *and* intercultural elements has not been easy to realise in practice. When it comes to the implementation of an intercultural dimension into language pedagogy, Rauschert and Byram (2018) acknowledged the multiple challenges experienced by teachers in the form of expertise, logistics, curriculum design and methodology.

First, a significant problem for the implementation of an intercultural dimension in L2 teaching and learning, which we have noted both in Chap. 1 and earlier in this chapter, is that there is, as yet, no agreement on a definition of what the intercultural dimension is and what it entails. Teachers are therefore being asked to implement a dimension of learning for which there currently exists no definitive or universally accepted characterisation.

Second, Byram's use of the term "interculturally competent" highlights a significant shift in thinking with regard to the goals of L2 learning. Byram differentiates between the cultural competence of the "native" (L1) speaker, who identifies with one language, and the "intercultural" (L2) speaker, who is able to "see the relationships between the learner's and the native-speaker's languages and cultures, to perceive and cope with difference" (Byram & Risager, 1999, p. 2).

The notion of *"the"* native speaker, where the definite article suggests uniformity among users of a language, is now much challenged and discussed (May, 2014), and has given way to the notion of the *interculturally competent* speaker as someone who is able to mediate between several languages and cultures (Byram, 2012). That is, Byram's model of intercultural competence recognises the illusory nature of the Chomskyan concept of the "ideal speaker-listener" (Chomsky, 1965) and challenges the consequent notion that the goal of L2 learning should be to help learners to reach native-speaker-like (or perfect) competence in the L2. It also recognises that perfect or error-free command of the TL is no longer the goal of the communicatively oriented classroom (a positioning that is tangibly realised, for example, in the different levels of competence articulated in the CEFR). In terms of language acquisition, Fantini and Tirmizi (2006) argued that the shift from a monolingual speaker possessing (perfect) communicative competence and a single worldview in their own language to a second language speaker possessing a multicultural worldview with communicative competence in an L2 requires an intercultural pedagogy that develops *both* communicative competence *and* intercultural competence, and that recognises that neither of these competences is absolute, but, rather, relative. This, in turn, requires a significant pedagogical shift in thinking with regard to linguistic accuracy.

Third, if teachers are to be the key brokers between theoretical understandings of interculturality and their application to the L2 within language classrooms (Young & Sachdev, 2011), they have to be equipped with the necessary knowledge, skills and attitudes required to accomplish this wider task appropriately (Sercu, 2006). Developing intercultural stances is a process that is both cognitive and affective and it impacts teachers' personal theories of teaching as well as their professional identities (Byram, 2015). A key conceptual barrier is that interculturality, in addition to being theoretically abstract, is usually "presented in universalist terms, i.e. independent of context and age of the learners" (Hu & Byram, 2009, p. xii). What is more, teachers themselves may not have confronted their own conceptualisations and understandings of interculturality and often do not fully understand their role in the development of intercultural stances in their students (Moloney, 2008).

Fourth, the focus on the intercultural in L2 classrooms requires teachers to move from the role of "instructor" to that of "facilitator" who supports learners in developing their own interpretations of language and culture (see, e.g., Moeller & Nugent, 2014; Moloney et al., 2015; Peiser, 2015). This constructivist-informed pedagogical approach places the learner into a central position, and emphasises learners' *active construction* of their own knowledge, in contrast to taking a passive role and developing their knowledge via input from teachers or textbooks. From this standpoint, learners require opportunities to construct their own meanings as they collaborate with others and "raise their own questions, generate their own hypotheses and models as possibilities and test them for validity" (Fosnet, 1996, p. 29). This approach acknowledges the support and facilitation that teachers need to offer, but emphasises what the learners themselves are required to bring to their own learning.

The shift away from a central (and often teacher-led) focus on *the language* and towards a wider, more learner-centred and reflective stance also demands the development of "interculturally sensitive language teachers" (Siqueira, 2017, p. 398) who are willing to take a step back from their current practices and reflect on what might need to change. In Siqueira's view, teachers need to be supported to deal with "issues like identity, power, racial conflicts, social change, global mobility, just to cite a few" (p. 400). Siqueira encouraged the development of *critical* intercultural teachers who develop a critical consciousness and "put reflection into action" (p. 402).

The importance of reflection is also highlighted by Jokikokko (2016) who saw reflective teachers as those who evaluate and develop themselves. With regard to intercultural learning, this implies an ability to reflect critically on situations, to consider the context and to accept that IC is continuously developing. Jokikokko identified a need for teachers to learn to "examine their assumptions, values and beliefs towards different learners" (p. 220), and to realise how those influence their practices. Teachers need to question their own beliefs and confront potentially discomforting emotions attached to those beliefs.

Critical reflection and awareness are also emphasised by Díaz (2016) as essential skills needed by teachers so that they become aware of their own assumptions but can also reflect critically and interpret information with which they are presented. According to Díaz, critical awareness can be triggered by moments of "cognitive dissonance" (p. 123), that is, the mental conflict people experience when they are presented with evidence that their beliefs are limited. This can be achieved by being confronted with beliefs that contradict existing beliefs. The mind is then compelled to modify beliefs or develop new understandings. In doing so, we become more consciously aware of our own and others' beliefs and have the opportunity to transform our perspective, a crucial part in developing intercultural understanding. Thus, Díaz argued that uncritically acquired assumptions are called into critical consciousness and have the potential to transform a person's perspective.

2.7 Studies into the Intercultural in L2 Teaching

Having highlighted a gap between policies, academic literature and perceived values of intercultural capabilities and their implementation in practice, as well as the range of additional (and often new) responsibilities and expectations of teachers relating to intercultural education, there remains the question of whether and how educators have used approaches to help their L2 learners enhance their intercultural capability. It must be acknowledged that, as interculturality grows in attention from academics and practitioners, empirical studies have investigated—with relative degrees of success— the development of intercultural capabilities in learners of widely different ages and in vastly different contexts. Our particular focus here is on those studies that relate to learners of an L2 in school contexts. These studies highlight different dimensions of practice and the different complexities of the inclusion of an intercultural dimension in classrooms. We start by reporting promising findings of several studies related to younger L2 learners. We go on to present studies that can be organised into those that (1) illustrate the challenges that teachers of languages face when implementing an intercultural dimension; (2) advocate a collaboration between teachers and teacher educators or researchers; and (3) promote the explicit teaching and scaffolding of intercultural learning to aid critical reflection.

2.7.1 Studies into the Intercultural with Young Learners

In a report on primary-level learners in England, Barton et al. (2009) discussed a six-term language awareness initiative, designed to address a government-initiated new emphasis on L2 teaching in the primary school sector, in which generalist teachers in seven primary schools learned the basics of five languages alongside their Year 5 and 6 (9–11-year-old) students. Several objectives for the "Discovering Language" programme were set, including increasing learners' motivation to learn languages; highlighting similarities and differences between learners' L1 and a range of European and non-European languages; and enhancing students' intercultural awareness and understanding. The researchers used a summative student questionnaire to investigate students' perspectives on the programme. Additionally, the perceptions of teachers and head teachers, and a subset of students, were collected by interviews.

One of the intercultural aims of the programme was "to make pupils aware of the cultural context of each of the languages they studied." This included "exploring the various differences and similarities between, for instance, traditions and schooling in their home country and overseas" (Barton et al., 2009, p. 154). The researchers reported "generally positive intercultural awareness" (p. 159) among the students, but also mixed findings in relation to the programmes' motivational objectives. Barton et al. were also uncertain of the extent to which the students' more positive attitudes could be attributed to the programme itself or to the students' overseas travel experiences outside of the teaching and learning context.

In the Australian setting, Morgan (2010) described a lesson with a group of eight primary 6–7-year-old students learning Indonesian. Her focus was on linguistic interactions designed to enhance these young L2 learners' intercultural understandings regarding ways of talking about self, and about and to others, in both Indonesian and Australian contexts. Interactions were planned so that there could be scaffolded comparative exploration of the language of self and others in Indonesian and English, including how language is situated within social and cultural contexts that influence its use. Differences and similarities across the languages and contexts were highlighted.

Morgan's study presented "an intercultural orientation to learning Indonesian names and pronouns, where a deliberate emphasis on understanding what pronouns say about identity and sense of self, for young learners, is foregrounded" (Morgan, 2010, p. 27). Bearing in mind the young age of the learners, the scaffolded explorations took place in English. Morgan reported that, although young, the students "were able to compare languages and cultures and reflect on their language use and enculturation, in rudimentary but significant ways" (p. 33).

Wagner et al. (2017) presented a series of "participatory action research" studies across a broad age range in several different contexts, with a view to presenting "the perspectives of experienced language teachers who have successfully integrated intercultural projects … incorporating a contemporary intercultural stance within the language curriculum" (p. x).

The Wagner et al. collection included accounts from four American primary/middle school classrooms for L2 learners where Byram's (1997) intercultural model was a criterion for teachers and their research partners as they integrated intercultural activities into their Spanish lessons. Positive intercultural outcomes perceived by the teacher-researcher partners included 6th grade (11–12-year-old) students' "growing ability to critically consider their preconceived notions" (Roher & Kagan, 2017, p. 74), and 8th grade (13–14-year-old) students moving from a focus on their own perspectives to "a point of view which also included questions and different perspectives" (Despoteris & Ananda, 2017, p. 89).

Each of the above studies reported some success with regard to the inclusion of an intercultural dimension. Wagner et al. (2017) cautioned, however, that, although most teachers believe that culture should be "an integral component" of the L2 classroom, teachers generally "lack the skills to accomplish this task [of integration] effectively." This, they suggested, indicated that "additional guidance in the area of intercultural communicative competence may empower teachers to confidently design lessons in intercultural competence (IC)" (p. x). In what follows, we consider studies that have highlighted specific challenges and issues.

2.7.2 Embedding Intercultural Explorations in School Contexts

In this section, we present several studies that illustrate challenges faced by teachers who have attempted to embed intercultural exploration into L2 classrooms. Acknowledging that *intercultural understanding* had been incorporated as one of seven General Capabilities of the Australian Curriculum (see earlier in this chapter), Díaz (2013) reported findings from a teacher professional development programme "based on focusing on a topic/linguistic aspect to be explored, [and] integrating activities aimed at fostering intercultural understanding" (p. 14). Data from interviews and observations prior to the intervention had revealed several constraints. Teachers perceived that they lacked both time and resources to integrate an intercultural dimension into their L2 teaching, struggled with how to assess their students' gains in intercultural understanding, and could not see how an intercultural emphasis could be sustained. Attempts were made to address these challenges in the programme, which included workshops and classroom-based action research projects. Díaz' findings suggested nonetheless that, despite proactive intervention, teachers continued to struggle as they attempted to translate theoretical conceptualisations into classroom practice. Díaz concluded that teachers needed to rethink the underpinning assumptions about what L2 teaching is and entails, noting that this level of critical reflection on current assumptions, beliefs and practices "lies at the core of developing, and modelling, the underpinnings of intercultural understanding" (p. 19).

Sercu (2005) investigated the extent to which Flemish secondary school-level teachers were aware of the intercultural dimension in language teaching and whether they incorporated an intercultural stance in their teaching. Her participants were teachers of English, French and German. It was found that most teachers were aware of and wanted to promote intercultural learning, but that they were unsure how to include intercultural competencies due to practical circumstances, teaching materials or their own lack of preparation.

Similarly, Castro et al. (2004) investigated language and intercultural practices and beliefs among 35 secondary teachers of English as a foreign language (EFL) in Spain. They found that most teachers perceived the learning of the language as more important than reaching cultural objectives. As a consequence, the teachers devoted around 80% of their time to language instruction. Despite a desire to include more culture in their teaching, teachers felt that curriculum requirements and time constraints made this endeavour almost impossible.

A longitudinal study involving 40 primary schools in England indicated a mismatch between the clearly articulated importance of the intercultural dimension in policy documents and statements by teachers, and teachers' actual practices (Driscoll et al., 2013). Although many schools included experiential opportunities for students to connect with other cultures by, for example, organising whole-school intercultural events or establishing international partnerships, the study found that children did not as a consequence demonstrate a greater understanding of their own lives or cultural identity and did not show heightened global awareness. The authors' explanation was that, although the activities were potentially enriching in themselves, they were not connected to each other. They concluded that cultural development needed to be included systematically and required collaborative planning and an overarching cultural framework, with links between all curricular subjects.

The study by Driscoll et al. (2013) also concluded that *incidental* teaching of intercultural aspects was insufficient to create intercultural understanding and that *explicit* teaching and reflection were necessary. Naidu (2020) came to a similar conclusion. She interviewed Indonesian language teachers at both primary and secondary levels in Australia, with the aim of establishing the teachers' understanding of "culture" and concepts of interculturality. Teachers in her study found the idea of intercultural teaching appealing, but were aware of their own limitations with regard to knowledge and understanding of Indonesian culture and queried whether they had the tools to foster intercultural learning. Naidu also encountered confusion about what culture actually was and acknowledged that teachers' uncertainties surrounding the cultural dimension in L2 teaching and how to address it could leave teachers reluctant to address the complexity of culture, avoiding it altogether and instead focusing on more straightforward linguistic aspects.

Walton et al. (2013) systematically reviewed the literature focusing on school-based approaches to developing students' intercultural understanding. Some of their key findings were that only building cultural knowledge and awareness was not enough to promote long-term changes in attitudes and that a critical approach towards cultural diversity was needed by teachers and students to develop appropriate understanding. Furthermore, the reviewed studies suggested the importance of ongoing intercultural contact. The studies also called consistently for investment in supporting the development of teachers' professional and personal intercultural capabilities, as the onus was often on the teachers to implement strategies to support intercultural understanding, with minimal support.

The research studies reviewed by Walton et al. (2013) suggested that teachers needed support to feel more confident before having complex cultural discussions and having to respond to questions or controversial cultural aspects. This notion was supported by Brunsmeier's (2017) study of 19 primary school teachers' intercultural practices in Germany. The teachers stated a need for a framework to deal with learners' cultural and intercultural questions and to help them to "trigger" age-appropriate reflection on students' own culture(s). Similarly, Toner (2010) found that primary school teachers in Australia were reluctant to discuss issues they considered too complex or controversial, even when students initiated such discussions. This is echoed in Naidu's (2020) study, where it was found that teachers avoided teaching cultural aspects when they were uncertain how to approach a topic.

Walton et al.'s (2013) review of studies highlighted that there was no or only minimal long-term effect in programmes designed to foster intercultural understanding unless a systematic and school-wide approach was implemented. This is supported by Driscoll et al. (2013) who called for a systematic implementation of intercultural learning and an overarching framework for it. Along the same lines, Ohi et al. (2019) supported the call to embed intercultural learning into broader school contexts and practices, reflected in actions and interactions across school leaders and students.

The above studies highlight how implementing an intercultural dimension in school classrooms faces a number of challenges, mostly relating to the expectations placed on the teachers of languages. A possible way forward seems to be embedding intercultural education at school- and system-levels with a concerted and coherent approach to supporting the schools in doing this.

2.7.3 Collaborations Between Teachers and Teacher Educators/Researchers

Several studies in addition to Díaz (2013) highlight collaborations to support intercultural learning, and note particular benefits. Kohler's (2015) study with three teachers of Indonesian in Australian secondary schools was framed as a collective case study involving participant action research. In the longitudinal study which took place across one school year, Kohler supported the teachers' intercultural learning through processes of collaborative planning, providing input and resources, feedback on classroom observations, and probing and questioning of what was observed. Her input was often in the form of suggestions or clarifications rather than as directives. One key component for Kohler was the exploration of how authentic L2 texts could be used as means to explore the inter-relationship between language and culture. The teachers used this emphasis in their practice. However, each mediated an intercultural perspective in their own way, depending on their individual understanding and beliefs.

Müller-Hartmann and Schocker (2018) integrated task-based language teaching (TBLT) and intercultural language teaching in a three-year action research project with secondary school-level EFL teachers in Germany. Specifically, and as we noted in Chap. 1, TBLT is a constructivist-informed learner-centred and experiential approach to L2 pedagogy. In TBLT, the role of the teacher shifts from instructor to facilitator, and language learners have a crucial level of responsibility to process language in use and work out how it functions through engagement in communicative tasks. As such, there is arguably a synergy between the theoretical impetus for task use and intercultural exploration (an issue we take up again in Chap. 8).

The project instigated by Müller-Hartmann and Schocker (2018) was designed as professional learning and development for 20 in-service secondary teachers and was based on a collaboration between teachers, researchers and teacher educators. The project had several components. Initially, the researchers presented Byram's ICC model alongside proposals for TBLT and teachers shared the kinds of language use tasks they typically used in their classrooms. In a collaborative workshop, teachers and researchers jointly reflected on these tasks and discussed how ICC might be incorporated, brainstorming different options, designing tasks, and considering how they might be trialled. Teachers then went on to trial the designed tasks in their own classrooms before the next collaborative workshop session in which all participants reflected again on the effectiveness of the tasks. Over time, the teachers set up cycles of regular collaboration, including a cyclical approach to planning and teaching, and pooling of ideas. The authors report that, as a result of the longitudinal teacher-educator-researcher collaboration, the teachers designed tasks from their learners' perspectives, involved learners in task creation, tapped into the students' own experiences, and thus turned theoretical concepts into do-able experiences for their learners. However, the authors highlighted the need for ongoing support from peers, teacher educators and researchers.

2.7.4 Promoting Explicit Teaching and Scaffolding for Intercultural Learning

In this section, we review studies where teachers embarked on carefully scaffolded intercultural learning experiences in online and face-to-face settings.

An online school exchange between school classes in England and Germany was the focus of Peiser's (2015) study. The project aimed to develop intercultural understanding through online communication over a period of four months. The activities involved asynchronous communication, text and videos, which were uploaded to websites, and posts on discussion boards. Topics involved interests, hobbies, holiday activities and school, and students asked and answered each other's questions in small-group settings to encourage discussion around observed similarities and differences.

Peiser's (2015) study raises important questions around the role of the teacher in the constructivist-informed classroom. Although it might be assumed that the teacher's role is less directive and more facilitative in telecollaborative projects between students, an increasing body of research has revealed that pedagogical involvement (i.e., teacher direction) becomes important for intercultural learning. Teachers, according to Peiser's study, needed to guide students on how to become aware of and describe their own cultures, and on how to locate and interpret information provided by the project partners in a wider cultural context. Peiser concluded that without this explicit scaffolding provided by the teacher, students' lack of intercultural understanding could easily lead to cultural misunderstandings.

Using a similar approach to Peiser (2015), Yates and Fellinger (2016) designed an 11-week telecollaboration between two groups of school learners of German, one group in New Zealand and one in the United States. The activities set up for the German language learners in both settings explicitly focused on intercultural learning, including aspects of German, US and New Zealand cultures, and included online collaboration between students communicating in German. The activities were carefully scaffolded and focused on explicit reflections on students' own and other cultures. It was found that the project was a positive experience for the students, allowing them to be creative, communicating with students from other countries, and becoming more aware of similarities and differences between cultures.

In her classroom-based research, Jäger (2011) used literary texts and drama-oriented activities in a German secondary school setting to explicitly support the development of the intercultural understanding of her EFL students. Her study showed that neither a seemingly appropriate text, for example a story of migration, nor a drama activity focusing on improvisation or role-play, automatically guaranteed or even fostered intercultural learning. While literary texts and accompanying drama activities were promising starting points, the teacher's skill was a crucial factor in challenging stereotypes, supporting in-depth reflection and creating an awareness in students that communication was culture-bound and had a performative dimension. The study concluded that students were able to portray people from different cultural backgrounds in drama activities, transferring their intercultural learning to adequate body language, gestures or facial expressions, but only once they were provided with scaffolded and explicit support relating to socio-cultural background knowledge, body language and enhancing communicative effectiveness.

In a study looking at school-wide implementation of intercultural understanding in Australian schools, Ohi et al. (2019) combined explicit teaching alongside collaboration. Their two-year project included professional learning modules and workshops on intercultural learning and pedagogies for teachers, and schools collaborated in clusters to design specific learning programmes for their schools. The study established that the explicit teaching of intercultural aspects in a language classroom was not sufficient on its own to have a long-term effect and that intercultural learning showed better results through school-wide implementation. Findings, presented as case studies, revealed the effectiveness of school-wide approaches for intercultural capabilities: school leaders developed multi-faceted approaches aimed to impact the whole school, starting with a shared understanding of intercultural learning for the entire school staff. Once core beliefs were established, they were then shared with students, parents and the wider school community. Curriculum leaders worked with the leadership team and teachers to ensure that intercultural capabilities were embedded in the school curriculum across disciplines, and teachers from all year levels collaborated to develop a strategic approach to develop students' and teachers' intercultural capabilities.

2.8 Conclusion

A recurring theme of the international literature, and in particular of prior school-level studies, is just how difficult it appears to be to integrate an intercultural dimension into L2 programmes. Despite some promising results in a handful of studies, a recent volume that has surveyed the field (López-Jiménez & Sánchez-Torres, 2021) confirms this persistent problem. In the European context, Brunsmeier (2017) spoke of the development of L2 learners' intercultural competence as "a big challenge," due to "vague theoretical conceptions" of a construct that "has not yet been clearly defined for young learners" (p. 152). In the Australian context, Kohler (2015) recognised the immense struggle that teachers encountered as they sought to integrate culture into L2 classrooms and Díaz (2013) highlighted the huge gap that exists between theory and practice. As a result, putting an intercultural orientation into practice in many L2 classrooms was, in Díaz (2013) perception, "still at a rudimentary stage," and happening at a pace that she described as "almost glacial" (p. 19).

Díaz (2013) reached the conclusion that putting the intercultural dimension into active practice required L2 teachers to deliberately change their own classroom practices, but that this possibility "remains to be explored beyond the level of passive recognition" (p. 13). This exploration is something that the study that is the focus of this book attempted to address. Before going on to present our study, we turn in the next chapter to research in the immediate context of the study—New Zealand.

References

American Academy of Arts & Sciences. (2017). *America's languages: Investing in language education for the 21st century*. Retrieved from http://www.amacad.org/multimedia/pdfs/publications/researchpapersmonographs/language/Commission-on-Language-Learning_Americas-Languages.pdf

American Council on the Teaching of Foreign Languages. (2014). *Global competence position statement*. Retrieved from https://www.actfl.org/news/position-statements/global-competence-position-statement

Australian Curriculum, Assessment and Reporting Authority (ACARA). (2011). *Intercultural understanding*. Retrieved from https://australian-curriculum.edu.au/f-10-curriculum/general-capabilities/intercultural-understanding

Australian Federation of Modern Language Teachers Associations. (2005). *Professional standards for the accomplished teaching of languages and cultures*. Retrieved from http://pspl.afmlta.asn.au/doclib/Professional-Standards-for-Accomplished-Teaching-of-Languagesand-Cultures.pdf

Barton, A., Bragg, J., & Serratrice, L. (2009). 'Discovering language' in primary school: An evaluation of a language awareness programme. *The Language Learning Journal, 37*(2), 145–164.

Beacco, J. C., Coste, D., van de Ven, P., & Vollmer, H. (2010). *Language and school subjects: Linguistic dimensions of knowledge building in school curricula*. Council of Europe. Retrieved from https://rm.coe.int/16805a0c1b

Bennett, M. J. (1986). A developmental approach to training for intercultural sensitivity. *International Journal of Intercultural Relations, 10*(2), 179–196.

Bennett, M. J. (2004). Becoming interculturally competent. In J. Wurzel (Ed.), *Toward multiculturalism: A reader in multicultural education* (2nd ed., pp. 62–77). Intercultural Resources Corporation.

Bhabha, H. K. (1994). *The location of culture*. Routledge.

Brunsmeier, S. (2017). Primary teachers' knowledge when initiating intercultural communicative competence. *TESOL Quarterly, 51*(1), 143–155.

Byram, M. (1997). *Teaching and assessing intercultural communicative competence*. Multilingual Matters.

Byram, M. (2012). Language awareness and (critical) cultural awareness—Relationships, comparisons and contrasts. *Language Awareness, 21*(1–2), 5–13.

Byram, M. (2014). Twenty-five years on—From cultural studies to intercultural citizenship. *Language, Culture and Curriculum, 27*(3), 209–225.

Byram, M. (2015). Culture in foreign language learning—The implications for teachers and teacher training. In W. M. Chan, M. Nagami, I. Walker, & S. Kumar (Eds.), *Culture and foreign language education: Insights from research and implications for the practice*. De Gruyter.

Byram, M. (2018). Intercultural competence. In C. Chapelle (Ed.), *The encyclopedia of applied linguistics*. Wiley.

Byram, M. (2021). *Teaching and assessing intercultural communicative competence: Revisited* (2nd ed.). Multilingual Matters.

Byram, M., Holmes, P., & Savvides, N. (2013). Intercultural communicative competence in foreign language education: Questions of theory, practice and research. *The Language Learning Journal, 41*(3), 251–253.

Byram, M., & Risager, K. (1999). *Language teachers, politics and cultures*. Multilingual Matters.

Byram, M., & Wagner, M. (2018). Making a difference: Language teaching for intercultural and international dialogue. *Foreign Language Annals, 51*(1), 140–151.

Canale, M. (1983). On some dimensions of language proficiency. In J. W. J. Oller (Ed.), *Issues in language testing research* (pp. 333–342). Newbury House.

Canale, M., & Swain, M. (1980). Theoretical bases of communicative approaches to second language teaching and testing. *Applied Linguistics, 1*(1), 1–47.

Castro, P., Sercu, L., & Méndez-García, M. C. (2004). Integrating language-and-culture teaching: An investigation of Spanish teachers' perceptions of the objectives of foreign language education. *Intercultural Education, 15*, 91–104.
Chan, W. M., Bhatt, S. K., & Nagami, M. (2015). *Culture and foreign language education: Insights from research and implications for the practice.* De Gruyter.
Chomsky, N. (1965). *Aspects of the theory of syntax.* MIT Press.
Cochran-Smith, M., & Lytle, S. L. (1999). The teacher research movement: A decade later. *Educational Researcher, 28*(7), 15–25.
Council of Europe. (2001). *Common European framework of reference for languages.* Cambridge University Press.
Council of Europe. (2003). *Declaration on intercultural education in the new European context.* Conference of European Ministers of Education, 21st Session. Council of Europe.
Deardorff, D. (2006). The identification and assessment of intercultural competence as a student outcome of internationalization at institutions of higher education in the United States. *Journal of Studies in International Education, 10*, 241–266.
Dellit, J. (2005). *Getting started with intercultural language learning: A resource for schools.* Retrieved from http://www.decd.sa.gov.au/curric/
Department of Employment, Education and Training. (1991). *Australia's language: The Australian language and literacy policy.* Australian Government Publishing Service.
Dervin, F. (2016). *Interculturality in education: A theoretical and methodological toolbox.* Palgrave Macmillan.
Dervin, F., Moloney, R., & Simpson, A. (2020). Going forward with intercultural competence (IC) in teacher education and training: Beyond the 'walls built by ghosts'? In F. Dervin, R. Moloney, & A. Simpson (Eds.), *Intercultural competence in the work of teachers: Confronting ideologies and practices* (pp. 3–16). Routledge.
Despoteris, J., & Ananda, K. (2017). Intercultural competence: Reflecting on daily routines. In M. Wagner, D. Perugini, & M. Byram (Eds.), *Teaching intercultural competence across the age range: From theory to practice* (pp. 60–79). Multilingual Matters.
Díaz, A. (2013). Intercultural understanding and professional learning through critical engagement. *Babel, 48*(1), 12–19.
Díaz, A. (2016). Developing interculturally-oriented teaching resources in CFL: Meeting the challenge. In R. Moloney & H. L. Xu (Eds.), *Exploring innovative pedagogy in the teaching and learning of Chinese as a foreign language* (pp. 115–135). Springer.
Driscoll, P., Earl, J., & Cable, C. (2013). The role and nature of the cultural dimension in primary modern languages. *Language, Culture and Curriculum, 26*(2), 146–160.
Fantini, A. (2006). *Assessment tools of intercultural communicative competence.* Retrieved from http://www.sit.edu/publications/docs/competence.pdf
Fantini, A., & Tirmizi, A. (2006). *Exploring and assessing intercultural competence.* Retrieved from http://digitalcollections.sit.edu/worldlearning_publications/1
Fosnet, C. T. (Ed.). (1996). *Constructivism: Theory, perspectives, and practice.* Teachers College Press.
Harbon, L., & Moloney, R. (2013). *Language teachers' narratives of practice.* Cambridge Scholars Publishing.
Hill, M., & Cowie, B. (2012). *The contribution of the teaching and learning research initiative to building knowledge about teaching and learning: A review of school sector projects, 2003–2012.* Teaching and Learning Research Initiative.
Holmes, P., & MacDonald, M. (2020). Editorial: The 'good' interculturalist yesterday, today and tomorrow: Everyday life-theory-research-policy-practice. *Language and Intercultural Communication, 20*(1), 1–5.
Hu, A. (2013). Intercultural learning. In C. A. Chapelle (Ed.), *The encyclopedia of applied linguistics* (pp. 1–7). Blackwell.
Hu, A., & Byram, M. (2009). *Intercultural competence and foreign language learning: Models, empiricism, assessment.* Gunter Narr Verlag.

Hymes, D. (1972). On communicative competence. In J. B. Pride & J. Holmes (Eds.), *Sociolinguistics* (pp. 269–293). Penguin.
Jäger, A. (2011). *Kultur szenisch erfahren*. Peter Lang.
Jokikokko, K. (2016). Reframing teachers' intercultural learning as an emotional process. *Intercultural Education, 27*(3), 217–230.
Kohler, M. (2015). *Teachers as mediators in the foreign language classroom*. Multilingual Matters.
Kolb, D. A. (1984). *Experiential learning: Experience as the source of learning and development*. Prentice-Hall.
Kramsch, C. (1993). *Context and culture in language teaching*. Oxford University Press.
Kramsch, C. (2009). Third culture and language education. In V. Cook & L. Wei (Eds.), *Contemporary applied linguistics: Vol.1, language teaching and learning* (pp. 233–254). Continuum.
Liddicoat, A. (2005). Teaching languages for intercultural communication. In D. Cunningham & A. Hatoss (Eds.), *An international perspective on language policies, practices and proficiencies* (pp. 201–214). Fédération Internationale des Professeurs de Langues Vivantes (FIPLV).
Liddicoat, A. (2011). Language teaching and learning from an intercultural perspective. In E. Hinkel (Ed.), *Handbook of research in second language teaching and learning* (Vol. II, pp. 837–855). Lawrence Erlbaum Associates.
Liddicoat, A., & Scarino, A. (2013). *Intercultural language teaching and learning*. Wiley-Blackwell.
Lo Bianco, J., Liddicoat, A., & Crozet, C. (Eds.). (1999). *Striving for the third place: Intercultural competence through language education*. Language Australia.
López-Jiménez, M. D., & Sánchez-Torres, J. (Eds.). (2021). *Intercultural competence past, present and future: Respecting the past, problems in the present and forging the future*. Springer.
MacDonald, M. (2019). The discourse of 'thirdness' in intercultural studies. *Language and Intercultural Communication, 19*(1), 93–109.
May, S. (2014). Justifying educational language rights. *Review of Research in Education, 38*(1), 215–241.
Moeller, A., & Nugent, K. (2014). *Building intercultural competence in the language classroom*. Department of Teaching, Learning and Teacher Education. Paper 161. Retrieved from http://proldanmarcos.dropmark.com/219090/4343074
Moloney, R. (2008). You just want to be like that: Teacher modelling and intercultural competence in young language learners. *Babel, 42*(3), 10–19.
Moloney, R., Harbon, L., & Fielding, R. (2015). Pre-service teachers discovering intercultural enquiry in language classroom discourse. In W. Chan, S. Bhatt, M. Nagami, & I. Walker (Eds.), *Culture and foreign language education: Insights from research and implications for the practice* (pp. 59–86). De Gruyter Mouton.
Morgan, A.-M. (2010). Me, myself, I: Developing concepts of self and identity in early years language classrooms. *Babel, 45*(2–3), 26–34.
Müller-Hartmann, A., & Schocker, M. (2018). The challenge of thinking task-based teaching from the learners' perspectives: Developing teaching competences through an action research approach to teacher education. In M. Ahmadian & M. Garcia Mayo (Eds.), *Recent perspectives on task-based language learning and teaching* (pp. 233–257). De Gruyter.
Naidu, K. (2020). Attending to 'culture' in intercultural language learning: A study of Indonesian language teachers in Australia. *Discourse: Studies in the Cultural Politics of Education, 41*(4), 653–665.
Neuner, G. (2012). The dimensions of intercultural education. In J. Huber (Ed.), *Intercultural competence for all: Preparation for living in a heterogeneous world* (pp. 11–49). Council of Europe Publishing.
Noddings, N. (2005). *Educating citizens for global awareness*. Teachers College Press.
OECD. (2016). *Global competency for an inclusive world*. Retrieved from http://repositorio.minedu.gob.pe/bitstream/handle/123456789/4561/Global%20competency%20for%20an%20inclusive%20world.pdf?sequence=1&isAllowed=y

Ohi, S., O'Mara, J., Arber, R., Hartung, C., Shaw, G., & Halse, C. (2019). Interrogating the promise of a whole school approach to intercultural education: An Australian investigation. *European Educational Research Journal, 18*(2), 234–247.

Paige, R. M., Jorstad, H., Siaya, L., Klein, F., & Colby, J. (2000). *Culture learning in language education: A review of the literature.* CARLA. Retrieved from https://carla.umn.edu/culture/res/litreview.pdf

Papademetre, L. (2000). Developing pathways for conceptualising the integration of culture-and-language. In A. J. Liddicoat & C. Crozet (Eds.), *Teaching languages, teaching cultures* (pp. 141–149). Language Australia.

Peiser, G. (2015). Overcoming barriers: Engaging younger students in an online intercultural exchange. *Intercultural Education, 26*(5), 361–376.

Perry, L. & Southwell, L. (2011). Developing intercultural understanding and skills: Models and approaches. *Intercultural Education, 22*(6), 453–466.

Piątkowska, K. (2015). From cultural knowledge to intercultural communicative competence: Changing perspectives on the role of culture in foreign language teaching. *Intercultural Education, 26*(5), 397–408.

Porto, M. (2016). Ecological and intercultural citizenship in the primary English as a foreign language (EFL) classroom: An online project in Argentina. *Cambridge Journal of Education, 46*(4), 395–415.

Rauschert, P., & Byram, M. (2018). Service learning and intercultural citizenship in foreign-language education. *Cambridge Journal of Education, 48*(3), 353–369.

Roher, P., & Kagan, L. (2017). Using the five senses to explore cities. In M. Wagner, D. Perugini, & M. Byram (Eds.), *Teaching intercultural competence across the age range: From theory to practice* (pp. 60–79). Multilingual Matters.

Rowe, G., & Wright, G. (1999). The Delphi technique as a forecasting tool: Issues and analysis. *International Journal of Forecasting, 15*(4), 353–375.

Scarino, A., & Liddicoat, A. J. (2009). *Teaching and learning languages: A guide.* Curriculum Corporations.

Sercu, L. (2005). Foreign language teachers and the implementation of intercultural education: A comparative investigation of the professional self-concepts and teaching practices of Belgian teachers of English, French and German. *European Journal of Teacher Education, 28*(1), 87–105.

Sercu, L. (2006). The foreign language and intercultural competence teacher: The acquisition of a new professional identity. *Intercultural Education, 17*, 55–72.

Sercu, L. (2010). Assessing intercultural competence: More questions than answers. In A. Paran & L. Sercu (Eds.), *Testing the untestable in language education* (pp. 17–34). Multilingual Matters.

Sercu, L., Bandura, E., Castro, P., Davcheva, L., Laskaridou, C., Lundgren, U., & Ryan, P. (2005). *Foreign language teachers and intercultural competence: An investigation in 7 countries of foreign language teachers' views and teaching practices.* Multilingual Matters.

Sinicrope, C., Norris, J., & Watanabe, Y. (2007). *Understanding and assessing intercultural competence: A summary of theory, research, and practice.* University of Hawaii Second Language Studies Paper.

Siqueira, S. (2017). Intercultural language educators for an intercultural world: Action upon reflection. *Intercultural Education, 28*(4), 390–407.

Spitzberg, B. H., & Changnon, G. (2009). Conceptualizing intercultural competence. In D. K. Deardorff (Ed.), *The Sage handbook of intercultural competence* (pp. 2–52). Sage.

Toner, M. (2010). *Other ways: Intercultural education in Australian primary schools.* Ph.D. thesis, RMIT University.

UNESCO. (2013). *Intercultural competences: Conceptual and operational framework.* Retrieved from https://en.unesco.org/interculturaldialogue/resources/132

Wagner, M., Perugini, D., & Byram, M. (Eds.). (2017). *Teaching intercultural competence across the age range: From theory to practice.* Multilingual Matters.

Walton, J., Priest, N., & Paradies, Y. (2013). Identifying and developing effective approaches to foster intercultural understanding in schools. *Intercultural Education, 24*(3), 181–194.

References

Yates, E. S., & Fellinger, P. (2016, April). *Teaching intercultural competence in the language classroom: A guide for teachers*. Paper presented at the 2016 annual meeting of the American Educational Research Association. Retrieved from the AERA Online Paper Repository. https://www.aera.net/Publications/Online-Paper-Repository

Young, J. T., & Sachdev, I. (2011). Intercultural communicative competence: Exploring English language teachers' beliefs and practices. *Language Awareness, 20*(2), 81–98.

Zhou, V. X., & Pilcher, N. (2019). Revisiting the 'third space' in language and intercultural studies. *Language and Intercultural Communication, 19*(1), 1–8.

Open Access This chapter is licensed under the terms of the Creative Commons Attribution 4.0 International License (http://creativecommons.org/licenses/by/4.0/), which permits use, sharing, adaptation, distribution and reproduction in any medium or format, as long as you give appropriate credit to the original author(s) and the source, provide a link to the Creative Commons license and indicate if changes were made.

The images or other third party material in this chapter are included in the chapter's Creative Commons license, unless indicated otherwise in a credit line to the material. If material is not included in the chapter's Creative Commons license and your intended use is not permitted by statutory regulation or exceeds the permitted use, you will need to obtain permission directly from the copyright holder.

Chapter 3
The Intercultural Dimension in the New Zealand Language Teaching Context

3.1 Introduction

In Chap. 2, we documented a range of international studies into the intercultural dimension in language education, with a particular focus on young learners of an additional language (L2). The review of the international literature highlights the reality that, on the one hand, the development of language learners' intercultural capability has become a significant focus of attention in a range of contexts across the globe. On the other hand, studies reveal the complexities involved with both defining and operationalising the intercultural dimension. In this chapter, we revisit New Zealand as the site for our own study and expand on the brief introduction to the New Zealand context that we gave in Chap. 1, including the incorporation of the intercultural into the *New Zealand Curriculum* (NZC). We then review New Zealand-based studies into the intercultural dimension of L2 learning.

3.2 A History of Language Policy Development in New Zealand

Watts (1997) provided a useful and succinct summary of the historical language situation of New Zealand, going back to the early establishment of the country as a colony of Britain in the 1840s—a situation he described as being characterised by both complexity and diversity. As Watts considered events of the past few decades, his account drew attention to a 1987 curriculum review that heralded what may arguably be described as several "watershed" moments for New Zealand with regard to language learning and the language–culture interface, beginning in the early 1990s. The 1987 review had recommended that New Zealand needed to develop a national policy for languages. A policy was needed that would address the complex language needs of a diverse population, and, in particular, issues regarding:

- English, as the dominant language in New Zealand by virtue of colonisation, and a de facto (although not *de jure*) "official" language;
- te reo Māori, the language of *tangata whenua*, the indigenous "people of the land";
- Pasifika languages, the languages of our closest Pacific neighbours, and of many people from the islands who had made New Zealand their home;
- and (last but not least) international languages, some of which had become embedded in the school system as a consequence of colonisation (e.g., French, German), and some which were becoming established as a consequence of New Zealand's position in the world (e.g., Chinese, Japanese).

The proposal, Watts (1997) made clear, was for a policy that would cover both first language (L1) and additional language (L2) contexts. It would need to be a broad-based policy, covering several sectors of society. However, the policy, if enacted, would have important implications for the compulsory schooling sector.

In 1990, and as a consequence of the review, Phil Goff, then Minister of Education in a Labour-led administration, announced the government's intention to develop and fund the policy (Goff, 1990). Goff recognised that L2 learning in New Zealand's schools had thus far developed in quite an ad hoc way, and indicated that a languages policy could become the catalyst for recommendations around how to develop more effective L2 programmes, beginning with the primary school sector (Years 1 to 6). In particular, he indicated that programme developments were necessary so that New Zealand could position itself more strongly as a global player on the world's stage.

Labour's ambitious plan, as outlined in 1990, did not get very far. A general election later that year saw a shift to a National-led (Conservative) government. Nevertheless, another significant voice in the calls to develop a national languages policy was found in Don McKinnon, who was appointed to the roles of Deputy Prime Minister and Minister of Foreign Affairs and Trade in the new government. For example, in a speech entitled "English is not enough," McKinnon (1992) is recorded as having declared, "[w]e really must learn to speak other languages" (p. 1). Building on the stance that Goff, as former Education Minister, had taken in 1990, McKinnon went on to argue:

> The curricula in New Zealand schools and courses available in universities must equip young people with language and cultural skills. ... New Zealand's ability to earn a living – our very future in fact – depends on young New Zealanders acquiring international language skills. (p. 1)

Thus, it seemed that cross-party government rhetoric of the 1990s was intended to underscore imperatives for New Zealand's younger generations to develop both linguistic and intercultural proficiency in order to help secure the country's future prosperity. The policy advocacy of the 1990s led to the publication of a document intended to provide impetus for further discussion—*Aotearoa: Speaking for Ourselves* (Waite, 1992). This important document aimed to address the diverse societal linguistic needs that Watts (1997) had identified, but acknowledged the importance of international languages for an outward-looking nation. Although the policy plan was short-lived, being abandoned by the government in 1993 (East et al., 2007), the utilitarian discourse that school students should be encouraged to learn

L2s in order to strengthen New Zealand's ability to inter-relate internationally in an increasingly globalised world did influence how languages became promoted in a document published in 1993—The *New Zealand Curriculum Framework* or NZCF (Ministry of Education, 1993).

The NZCF represented the first attempt since the 1940s to present a government-authorised "foundation policy" and "coherent framework" for teaching, learning and assessment in the New Zealand compulsory schooling sector across all curriculum areas (Ministry of Education, 1993, p. 1). With regard to the direction of the NZCF in general, both the opening and the closing pages of the document underscored a global and outward-looking focus—New Zealand needed "a work-force … which has an international and multicultural perspective" (p. 1) in a context where "[m]ore trade is occurring with the non-English speaking world" (p. 28). Furthermore, with specific regard to L2 learning, the document stated not only that "[a]ll students benefit from learning another language from the earliest practicable age," but also that students "will be able to choose from a range of Pacific, Asian and European languages, all of which are important to New Zealand's regional and international interests" (p. 10). Thus, an agenda was set that appeared to recognise the importance of skills in both languages and cultures, alongside recognition that the languages of our closest neighbours must feature prominently in that mix.

It must be acknowledged that, at the practical level, a significant problem with regard to the NZCF was that L2 learning was subsumed within a broader curriculum area—*Language and Languages*—that included English as L1. This often led in practice to the marginalisation of L2 learning because schools and students could fulfil the expectations of the learning area through the study of English.

This is not to suggest that the study of an L2 did not have a recognised place in some New Zealand's schools up to that time. As we acknowledged in Chap. 1, many secondary schools (Years 9 to 13, 13+ to 17 + years of age) had established programmes in L2 learning, taught by qualified specialist teachers, and languages were seen in a number of these schools (particularly the more academically oriented) as integral components of students' learning. Furthermore, intermediate schools (Years 7 and 8, 11+ to 12+ years of age) were beginning to introduce programmes, often designed as small-scale "taster" options that would enable students in these two school years to begin learning a new language for a short period of time (perhaps a term or a couple of terms out of four school terms per year). This was in line with a curriculum intention to encourage schools to provide opportunities for all students from Years 7–10 to study an L2.

Subsequent to the release of the NZCF, and in a bid to support the development of L2 programmes that would encourage genuine communication for real-world purposes, guidelines for a range of L2s taught in schools were published and released over a number of years between 1995 and 2002. The most recent of these documents provided the most overt indication that a Communicative Language Teaching (CLT) approach predicated on a Presentation-Practice-Production (PPP) model was being advocated (see Chap. 1). For example, the following statement is found in both the French and German documents:

> Communicative language teaching is teaching that encourages learners to engage in meaningful communication in the target language – communication that has a function over and above that of language learning itself. Any approach that encourages learners to communicate real information for authentic reasons is, therefore, a communicative approach. (Ministry of Education, 2002a, 2002b, p. 16)

The guidelines followed traditional L2 curriculum models that "divide the language into lexis, structures, notions or functions, which are then selected and sequenced for students to learn in a uniform and incremental way" (Klapper, 2003, p. 35). Thus, the primary focus of L2 programmes was on developing learners' linguistic proficiency in communicative contexts (that is, communicative competence), with a strong emphasis on accuracy of language use.

The cultural dimension of L2 learning was addressed in the guidelines, and a clear interface was drawn between language (communication) and culture (context). In the French and German guidelines, for example, teachers were presented with the following information:

> Language and culture are closely related. … Students should learn that speaking a different language involves much more than simply conveying the same message in different words. Communicating in another language means being sensitive not only to what is said (and what is left unsaid) but also to how something is said. Every language involves gestures as well as words and indirect messages as well as direct ones. As students come to appreciate this, they begin to understand the interaction between language and culture. (Ministry of Education, 2002a, 2002b) (p. 11)

Teachers were encouraged to take the cultural dimension into account as they planned their programmes and to include authentic materials that reflected and gave illustrations of the target culture, albeit modified linguistically if necessary to suit the target level of the learners. There was, however, little supporting guidance within the document regarding how exactly teachers might take account of these cultural considerations, and a default position became one that tended to focus on culture-as-artefact (Sehlaoui, 2001), separated from learning the TL.

3.3 New Zealand's 2007 School Curriculum

East (2012b) noted that the beginning of the twenty-first century marked "a significant move forward in languages-in-education planning" (p. 31). Between 2001 and 2003, a Labour government elected in 1999 began the process of reviewing the NZCF to determine its continued fitness for purpose. This led, in 2007, to the publication of a revised national curriculum for New Zealand's compulsory school system (Years 1–13)—the *New Zealand Curriculum* or NZC (Ministry of Education, 2007), with an expectation that its requirements would be enacted in all schools by the start of the academic year 2010.

As part of the process of planning for curriculum renewal, a recommendation had been made to make the learning of an L2 an entitlement (although not a compulsory requirement) for all students in Years 7–10, thus strengthening what had been suggested in the NZCF. Crucial influences on this recommendation were two international critiques of the original curriculum document, one from Australia (Australian Council of Educational Research, 2002) and the other from the UK (Le Métais, 2002), that called attention to the low priority given to L2 learning in the NZCF. Thus, for language teachers in particular, an exciting component of the revised curriculum was the introduction of a new learning area that had thus far not been present—*Learning Languages*. This new learning area created dedicated space for L2 teaching and learning, alongside an expectation that a language programme would be made available to students, at least in school Years 7–10.

The published expectation of programmes aligned to *Learning Languages* continued, and re-emphasised, the communicative agenda, that is, an agenda that the new learning area "puts students' ability to communicate at the centre" (Ministry of Education, 2007, p. 24). Achievement outcomes were benchmarked against the "can-do" statements of the Common European Framework of Reference for Languages or CEFR (Council of Europe, 2001; Koefoed, 2012; Scott & East, 2012). These suggested that, by the end of schooling (Year 13), students should be able to operate in the target language (TL) at the intermediate level B1, with more proficient students approaching B2 level. These proficiency levels were no longer tied to specific topics, language, functions and structures. As a consequence, the language-specific curriculum documents that had informed teaching programmes since the release of the original NZCF in 1993 were officially withdrawn and were no longer to be used as the basis of programme planning. Teachers were therefore free to exploit any resources to fulfil curriculum requirements.

As for the place of culture in this newly introduced learning area, there was, as we noted in Chap. 1, a three-fold expectation. Students would not only (1) "learn about culture" (learning facts about the target culture), but also about (2) "the inter-relationship between culture and language" (exploring the language–culture interface). Students would also be expected to (3) "compare and contrast different beliefs and cultural practices, including their own" so that they "understand more about themselves and become more understanding of others" (Ministry of Education, 2007, p. 24)—that is, the development of an intercultural dimension. Specific achievement objectives became aligned to these foci (Ministry of Education, 2009a) and some basic examples of what these objectives might look like in practice were provided in a *Learning Languages* curriculum guide (Ministry of Education, 2016).

The intercultural agenda for New Zealand's education system became further emphasised by the publication of three more generic (i.e., not L2 focused) documents. First, Bolstad et al. (2012), in a document designed to stimulate thinking about future developments to New Zealand's education system, argued that New Zealand's twenty-first-century citizens needed to be "educated *for* diversity—in both the people sense and the knowledge/ideas sense." This, the report's authors argued, was because "[t]he changing global environment *requires* people to engage – and be able to work – with people from cultural, religious and/or linguistic backgrounds or world views that are *very different* from their own" (our emphases). On this basis, Bolstad et al. concluded that education *for* diversity was "an essential aspect of twenty-first century citizenship" (p. 25).

A second report (Ministry of Education, 2014) encouraged the development of *international capabilities* as a cross-curricular endeavour, referring to these capabilities as "global competence," "international-mindedness," and "cross-cultural competence" (p. 4). This set of competencies was considered as socially and economically important for New Zealand, and would contribute to helping young New Zealanders to achieve success as intercultural citizens (p. 6). In a real sense, therefore, this report became a policy enactment of McKinnon's (1992) earlier rhetoric. The document encouraged a comparative and reflective intercultural stance:

> Being internationally capable includes not only the awareness of other cultures, but also the awareness of one's own culture as being particular and specific. It involves the understanding that we all experience our lives through a number of cultural and personal 'lenses', and that comprehending and accepting others' needs and behaviours rests as much on understanding ourselves as it does on understanding them. (Ministry of Education, 2014, p. 4)

The document acknowledged the special place of *Learning Languages*, and the learning of an L2 as "one of the most effective ways for students to develop cross-cultural communicative competence and an awareness of other cultures and worldviews" (p. 12). However, the recommendations were designed to operate across the curriculum, and were aligned to seven *values* and five *key competencies* that underpinned all learning areas of the curriculum (Ministry of Education, 2007, pp. 10, 12–13). As East (2012b) explained, the values emphasised "recognition and understanding of different ways of being and the development of openness towards 'otherness'." The key competencies emphasised "the learner's central role in the process of learning and the active development of independence and autonomy, and co-operation with others mediated through social interaction" (p. 32). The report made a specific link:

> *International capabilities* are how the *New Zealand Curriculum* (NZC) Key Competencies look when young people apply them in intercultural and international contexts. That is, international capabilities are the knowledge, skills, attitudes, dispositions, and values that make up the Key Competencies that enable people to live, work, and learn across national and cultural boundaries. (Ministry of Education, 2014, p. 1)

Third, and aligned to the publication of the 2014 report, Bolstad et al. (2013) presented a set of recommendations arising from an exploratory study to consider the feasibility of measuring New Zealand students' international capabilities. At the school level, small-group workshops were undertaken with 13 secondary school staff and 21 senior secondary students (Years 12 and 13). Additional views were solicited from ten adults who had relevant expertise and perspectives on what the international capabilities might mean in post-school contexts. Workshops with teachers indicated that *Learning Languages* was seen as a useful catalyst for the development of the capabilities, alongside school-wide emphases on celebrating and recognising cultural and linguistic diversity, trips overseas and hosting international students. The students themselves recognised the value of "the highly multicultural social interactions and friendship groupings they experienced in their schools," which "seemed considerable in terms of how internationally minded, or comfortable with diversity and difference, they believed themselves to be" (p. 36). The report argued that measuring

New Zealand students' international capabilities might enable better understanding of how the schooling system could help with increasing young New Zealanders' knowledge and skills so that they could operate more effectively across cultures. The study focus was, however, restricted to senior secondary students. It took no account of what such capabilities might look like, or how they might be assessed, at more junior school levels.

3.4 Te reo Māori

At this juncture, it is important to acknowledge te reo Māori, which, as we stated at the start of this chapter, holds a distinctive place in New Zealand as the language of *tangata whenua*. At the time of colonisation, te reo Māori was the predominant language in New Zealand. However, colonisation precipitated a decline such that, by the early 1860s, *Pākehā* (European New Zealanders) became the majority, English became the dominant language, speaking te reo Māori was strongly opposed, and the language was progressively limited to Māori communities living separately from Pākehā.

By the mid-twentieth century, and after decades of suppression, it was acknowledged that te reo Māori was endangered. From the 1970s, many Māori people began to reaffirm their identity as Māori, and, from the 1980s, major initiatives pushed for a revival of the language. The Māori Language Act (1987) gave the language official status. The curriculum and policy debates of the late 1980s and early 1990s must be seen against these crucial developments.

Te reo Māori is thus protected in law as an official language of New Zealand (unlike the English language which, as we previously stated, has de facto rather than *de jure* status). One of the many consequences of this has been the establishment of primary and secondary *Kura Kaupapa Māori* (Māori language immersion schools). These schools operate on the basis of their own curriculum document (Te Karauna, 2008) which parallels (but is distinct from) the NZC.

In the English-medium schooling sector, governed by the NZC, te reo Māori is theoretically one of the languages that may be offered in schools as part of *Learning Languages*, and is one of a range of languages (including Pasifika languages) that, in that context, hold a "special place" (Ministry of Education, 2007, p. 24). In practice, in many English-medium schools, departments for languages operate independently from departments for te reo Māori, and the option for students to study te reo Māori may also be offered independently of the learning area.

Support for te reo Māori in English-medium contexts is made available through published curriculum guidelines (Ministry of Education, 2009b) that, in contrast to the withdrawal of guidelines for other languages, still remain in operation. The encouraged pedagogical approach is framed as communicative, and draws on arguments in this respect reminiscent of those presented, for example, in the former French and German documents (Ministry of Education, 2002a, 2002b).

Crucially, however, the teaching and learning of te reo Māori provides particularly rich opportunities to explore the language–culture interface due to strong interweaving of language and culture. The curriculum guidelines acknowledge that, for *all* languages, "[t]here is an inherent connection between language and culture" and that "language is embedded in culture and also expresses culture" (Ministry of Education, 2009b, p. 22). For Māori in particular, "[t]e reo Māori and *tikanga Māori* [Māori values and practices] are intertwined, and so learning te reo Māori gives students access to *te ao Māori* (the Māori world) and to Māori world views." For students, learning the language will therefore "enrich and broaden their understandings of the uniqueness and complexity of te ao Māori" and "the central roles that language, culture, place, and heritage play in shaping identity and in giving direction and meaning to life," alongside "the important role that indigenous languages and cultures play in New Zealand and throughout the world" (p. 13).

3.5 Supporting Enactment of the *Learning Languages* Learning Area

As we pointed out in Chap. 1, *Learning Languages* in the NZC comprises three components or "strands":

1. The core *communication* strand;
2. The supporting *language knowledge* strand;
3. The supporting *cultural knowledge* strand.

Effective communication in the TL is therefore the overarching goal of L2 programmes in schools. Language knowledge (grammar focus) and cultural knowledge (culture focus) are seen as equal strands that support effective communication.

A range of support initiatives was put in place to support teachers as they began to understand and engage with the expectations of the revised school curriculum and the three-strand model. Crucial among these were two documents additional to the NZC (Ministry of Education, 2007). These were literature review documents, commissioned by New Zealand's Ministry of Education, that were intended to provide teachers with a solid, theoretical, literature-informed basis for the different strands of the NZC—Ellis (2005) and Newton et al. (2010).

3.5.1 The Ellis (2005) Report

The so-called Ellis report proposed ten principles for second language acquisition (SLA) in the instructed context (pp. 33–42), emerging from a review of the international literature on instructed SLA. Essentially, it was proposed that effective instruction in the L2 classroom needed to ensure that:

1. there is a balance between fluency and accuracy, with a particular focus on fluency or communication, and the development of implicit grammatical knowledge for purposes of effective communication (Principles 1 to 4);
2. learners should be given opportunities to process language input, create language output, and interact in the TL (Principles 6 to 8);
3. learners' individual differences should be respected (Principles 5 and 9);
4. and, finally, proficiency evidence, for assessment purposes, should be collected from both free and controlled production (Principal 10).

The ten principles were thus designed to support teachers as they aimed to ensure a communicative focus in their programmes in line with the NZC's core *communication* strand, but also enabled teachers to address the supporting *language knowledge* strand.

Parallel to Ellis (2005) was an account of classroom-based research which had investigated L2 teachers' beliefs and practices (Erlam & Sakui, 2006). A key aim of the research was to establish the extent to which teachers' beliefs and practices aligned with the ten principles. Accounts were published about two teachers of French and two teachers of Japanese (representing at that time the two most popular international languages taught in New Zealand secondary schools). These teachers had not been informed prior to the studies what the ten principles were so that they could not adapt their classroom practices to the focus of the research. A positive finding was that teachers' beliefs and practices were generally in line with the communicative expectations of the curriculum support documents that were then in force (Ministry of Education, 1998, 2002a). Furthermore, when the teachers had the opportunity to review the ten principles, enthusiasm about their potential impact was expressed. As one teacher of French noted:

> Reading the principles of effective second language teaching made me really think about what I'm doing and where my approach comes from. … Reading the report made me want to investigate more and get involved in producing teaching resources that will make it easier for teachers to put these principles into action. I think current resources do that very poorly indeed. (p. 17)

Ellis (2005) and Erlam and Sakui (2006) provided two complementary documents (the first largely theoretical, and the second markedly practical) that, taken together, could inspire teachers' reflections on their own beliefs and practices. All primary and secondary schools in New Zealand received one hard copy of both reports, and both were also accessible online. Furthermore, appendices in the Erlam and Sakui report provided observation and reflection questions for each of the ten principles, and teachers were encouraged to use the principles and the case studies to help them carry out investigations into their own teaching.

It is important to note that the focus of Ellis (2005) was on principles that would support only two of the published strands of the NZC—*communication* and *language knowledge*. Ellis made only passing reference to "culture learning"—conceptualised in an isolated and facts-based way as "the teaching of cultural/ceremonial topics" (p. 5). There was no dialogue about the place of cultural knowledge in SLA, and no discussion of the integration of language and culture and the role of critical reflection across cultures. A separate Ministry-funded initiative was established to consider the cultural dimension, and the *cultural knowledge* strand became the focus of an entirely independent report (Newton et al., 2010).

3.5.2 The Newton et al. (2010) Report

As we stated in Chap. 1, the Newton et al. (2010) report proposed six principles to support an exploration of the intercultural in the context of a communicative approach to language teaching (p. 63). These propose that intercultural exploration:

1. integrates language and culture from the beginning;
2. engages learners in genuine social interaction;
3. encourages and develops an exploratory and reflective approach to culture and culture-in-language;
4. fosters explicit comparisons and connections between languages and cultures;
5. acknowledges and responds appropriately to diverse learners and learning contexts;
6. emphasises intercultural communicative competence rather than native speaker competence.

The intention of the first principle (aligned to the second intercultural expectation of the NZC *cultural knowledge* strand, i.e., the inter-relationship between culture and language) was to highlight how culture is inextricably bound to language users' everyday lives and interactions. This was designed to promote an initial integration between culture and language, and an expectation was promoted that teachers would help students to build conceptual bridges between language and culture right from the start of the language learning process. This was perceived as being relatively easily achieved by highlighting the rich cultural content embedded in seemingly simple samples of language, such as greetings. Learners were to be encouraged to *notice* and make *connections* between their own L1 and the TL. As East et al. (2017) explained:

> This principle encourages teachers to lead discussion around how the culture informs the language and the language informs the culture, for example, how culture can be seen in language/grammar structures, vocabulary, conventions of use, and so on, and how language structures and use can be seen in the enactment and lived experience of culture. (p. 26)

Principle 2 reflected the NZC key competency of *relating to others*, a competency designed to enhance skill in "interacting effectively with a diverse range of people in a variety of contexts" (Ministry of Education, 2007, p. 12). Teachers were encouraged to utilise any interactions in the TL as opportunities to "notice and explore culture-in-language and to develop communicative awareness" (Newton et al., 2010, p. 67). Teachers were also encouraged to facilitate opportunities for explicit focus on cultural comparisons, which might largely take place in students' L1. These instances were designed to raise learners' awareness of their own ways of interacting with others as well as those of others in the class and TL speakers.

The third principle promoted learner exploration of both visible and invisible elements of culture. In this regard, Newton et al. (2010) acknowledged that factual information about different cultures has a place (in line with the first intercultural expectation of the *cultural knowledge* strand, i.e., learning about culture). More importantly, however, this information needed to be interrogated and critiqued by learners. The starting point for such interrogation would usually be learners' exploration of their own culture and cultural identity, and "through this lens of self-awareness, examination of their attitudes towards the target language and culture" (p. 68). The purpose of such critical reflection would be to enable learners to step beyond stereotypical "us and them" conceptualisations, and to move towards "more empathetic and self-aware perceptions and attitudes" (p. 69).

Building on Principle 3, Principle 4 was designed to encourage and promote comparison across languages and cultures (as an outworking of the third intercultural expectation of the *cultural knowledge* strand, i.e., comparing and contrasting different beliefs and cultural practices, including learners' own). This was not, however, framed as an exclusively L1-TL cross-cultural comparison. Rather, Newton et al. (2010) recognised the linguistic and cultural diversity that already existed in the New Zealand L2 classroom, and built on the recognition that diversity and difference must be "central to the classroom endeavour" (Alton-Lee, 2003, p. 6), with a view to creating "caring, inclusive, and cohesive learning communities" (p. 22) and quality teaching that "respects and affirms cultural identity" (p. 32). Newton et al. thus argued that "comparisons and connections can be multi-faceted, as learners explore and share each other's cultures, while cooperatively exploring a new culture and learning a new language" (p. 69). This, they acknowledged, is a process designed to facilitate learners' movement into "a third place" (see Chap. 2)—"an intercultural position between cultures," and "a position from which the learner can negotiate differences and interact comfortably across cultures" (p. 70).

Following on from Principle 4, Principle 5 acknowledged and celebrated the linguistic and cultural diversity of many New Zealand classrooms—a diversity which can engender rich intercultural comparisons and contrasts beyond the TL. Principle 6 emphasised the reality that the goal of L2 programmes is no longer to achieve an L1 norm of competence, but to recognise that there will always be more to learn—not only about the target language, but also about the target culture, and language users' interactions with that culture.

3.6 Supporting Teachers with Enacting the Strands

With regard to the ten Ellis (2005) principles, significant professional development took place, particularly in the initial five-year period following their publication. In 2005, the principles were shared with teachers via a series of "language seminars" or LangSems. These are one-day professional development opportunities organised on a biennial basis in different regions of the country by the New Zealand Association of Language Teachers (NZALT), a professional association of which many teachers of L2 in New Zealand are members. In each venue, Erlam presented a plenary address on the principles. Additional presentations and workshops followed.

Furthermore, a Ministry of Education funded one-year professional development initiative—the Teacher Professional Development Languages (TPDL) programme, piloted in 2005 and 2006, and running in subsequent years until 2018—placed particular emphasis on exploring the ten principles with teachers. There was an initial focus on supporting teachers at the intermediate school level (Years 7 and 8) who, as we noted in Chap. 1, were not subject specialists, and often had limited proficiency in the TL. One part of the programme enabled participants to upskill in the language they were teaching. In another part, participants were expected to undertake a teaching as inquiry project (see Chaps. 1 and 4) in which participants, drawing on aspects of the ten principles, planned and investigated a classroom intervention and reported on learning outcomes.

Thus, it seemed that the ten principles were being taken up seriously by both curriculum leaders and the Ministry of Education. At least theoretically, all L2 teachers in New Zealand would have been exposed to the principles in one way or another—whether through publications or professional development.

Promotion and dissemination of the six Newton et al. (2010) principles stand in stark contrast. Although the Ministry of Education supported the promotion of the Newton et al. report through workshops, classroom visits and national advisors as "cultural experts," this was predominantly only picked up by specialist secondary teachers, and the principles were not subject to anything like the level of exposure that Ellis (2005) received. The Newton et al. report was not disseminated to all schools in hard copy; no parallel practice document was produced; NZALT did not take up the principles in targeted professional development; and although the TPDL programme provided some space for an exploration of the Newton et al. principles, this was limited in comparison with a major focus on Ellis (2005).

East (2012a) explained what might have happened. On the one hand, the fact that the Ellis (2005) report was released well ahead of the publication of the NZC and was widely disseminated meant that it quickly came to shape thinking and practice in schools. On the other hand, the Newton et al. (2010) report, due to be published at some time in 2009, was delayed, and was therefore only accessible to teachers well after the NZC had been launched (and, as we have noted, was not widely distributed). East concluded, "[t]he publication and widespread dissemination of Ellis has meant that in practice its recommendations have become quite embedded into many teachers' thinking." By contrast, the much later publication of Newton et al. meant that teachers did not have any extensive opportunities to engage with the six intercultural principles. These contrasting trajectories, East argued, "raise questions about how teachers were beginning to integrate Strand 3 [*cultural knowledge*] into their practices" (p. 61).

A disconcerting reality emerges. Two crucial support documents (Ellis, 2005; Newton et al., 2010) arguably should have been equally foundational in shaping teachers' thinking and practices in the L2 classroom. The vastly different paths taken as these documents were produced and disseminated might leave us with the impression that Newton et al. is less significant, and less defining for practice, than Ellis. In turn, this might be taken to suggest that the *intercultural* dimension is seen as peripheral to the language learning endeavour, and may be treated as less necessary than learning the L2 per se. As we indicated in Chap. 1, a cultural focus is potentially reduced to "something to talk over if there are a few minutes free from the *real* business of language learning" (Byram, 1991, pp. 17–18, our emphasis).

As we also noted in the opening chapter, and explored in more detail in Chap. 2, prior studies beyond New Zealand have demonstrated teachers' uncertainty about how to implement intercultural language teaching. The New Zealand situation, which is no exception to this challenging uncertainty, is arguably exacerbated by the relative obscurity of Newton et al. (2010) in comparison with Ellis (2005). Furthermore, and as we signalled in Chap. 1, at the time of the publication of the NZC in late 2007, L2 programmes were already quite well established in secondary schools, and taught by specialist teachers. Up to that time, these programmes had been influenced by specific and language-focused curriculum guidelines. The NZC requirement to provide L2 programmes in Years 7 and 8 gave additional impetus for schools at the intermediate level to introduce such programmes. This has led in practice to the phenomenal growth of L2 programmes in the intermediate sector (East, 2021). A challenge, however, was (and is) that these programmes were (and still are) often delivered by non-specialist staff who may themselves only have a minimal level of proficiency in the TL (Scott & Butler, 2007).

With regard to resourcing, examples of how the six Newton et al. (2010) principles may be realised in practice (although potentially useful) are largely limited to what might happen in the senior secondary school, Years 11–13 (Ministry of Education, 2016). One useful initiative to provide support materials for teachers and students in the intermediate Years 7 and 8 who are new to learning the TL was the *Learning Languages Series* (LLS). This series contains a progression of lessons accompanied by worksheets and video resources, and a range of languages is supported (Ministry of Education, n.d.). However, having been produced prior to the publication of the NZC, there is a strong language focus which favours the teacher's role in classroom delivery. Also, the resources are now technologically quite outdated, utilising, for example, CDs and analogue videos; no online or digital resources are provided. Thus, teachers at the intermediate level are also faced with significant resourcing challenges.

The study presented in this book was one means of investigating and addressing the challenges. However, before moving on (in subsequent chapters) to present the study, in the remainder of this chapter we review a number of earlier studies that have taken place in the New Zealand context to investigate teachers' and students' intercultural development. Each study was influenced, in one way or another, by a consideration of the six Newton et al. (2010) principles. In what follows, we outline the findings of these studies, highlighting challenges with implementation of the principles.

3.7 Studies into the Intercultural in the New Zealand Context

Earlier in this chapter, we noted the importance for professional learning and development of New Zealand's year-long TPDL programme, which ran from 2005 to 2018. With regard to the specific *language learning* aims of the programme, Erlam and Tolosa (2022) documented the findings of a valuable study. However, the *cultural/intercultural* dimension has been a strong focus of one earlier series of studies. Conway et al. (2010, 2012) presented findings from an official evaluation of the TPDL programme in 2008, as reported in Harvey et al. (2009). The researchers were interested in the development of both the *language knowledge* and *cultural knowledge* strands of *Learning Languages*, and a key focus of their evaluation was expressed in these words:

> Given the development of teachers who may have limited TL proficiency, and the significant shift in the curriculum which necessitates a new intercultural teaching pedagogy, the question needs to be asked: How effective is the [TPDL] programme in building capability? (Conway et al., 2012, pp. 163–164)

Data were collected at three points throughout the year from participant surveys ($n = 25$) alongside observations and face-to-face interviews with a subset of teachers ($n = 7$). This subset was selected to ensure representation from a range of geographical areas, school types, teaching experience and language ability. Programme documents and milestone reports submitted to the funder (New Zealand's Ministry of Education) by the professional development organiser were used as additional data sources.

Conway et al. (2010, 2012) found that a focus on the ten Ellis (2005) principles enabled the participating teachers to increase their understanding of how to enhance learners' SLA, due to the programme's "deep principled knowledge base" (2010, p. 449). Indeed, it was noted that teachers "constantly mentioned 'the Ellis principles' and how understanding these was helping them to know more about their learners" (2012, p. 172). By contrast, there was less apparent success in improving teachers' understanding of cultural knowledge due to a contrasting lack of a sufficiently robust knowledge base. In the researchers' view, "[w]hile observation data indicated the [TPDL] programme had a clear positive impact on the teachers' provision for learners to develop language knowledge, the results were less positive for the development of learners' cultural knowledge" such that "[b]y the end of the course, there was limited evidence of teachers encouraging learners to develop this knowledge strand" (2010, p. 453). In particular, "limitations were most noticeable in the areas of explicitly encouraging learners to view their world through the eyes of others and to cross cultural boundaries and interact appropriately in the target language" (2012, p. 173).

It is important to acknowledge that, at the time of Conway et al.'s data collection, Newton et al. (2010) had not been released. It was therefore, as the researchers put it, "not surprising that there was limited attention to culture in the observed lessons since teachers made no mention in the interviews of any sustained intention to provide opportunities to develop cultural knowledge" (Conway et al., 2010, p. 455).

3.7 Studies into the Intercultural in the New Zealand Context

The researchers concluded that further data might be more illuminating, and noted (Conway et al., 2012) that, subsequent to the release of Newton et al. (2010), several steps were taken within the TPDL programme to address the imbalance towards the Ellis (2005) principles, including dissemination of the Newton et al. report to teacher participants.

Two further studies by Conway and Richards (2014, 2018) presented findings from an extension to their research, continuing a specific emphasis on the intercultural language teaching practices of New Zealand L2 teachers, but moving beyond TPDL participants. A teacher survey in 2013 ($n = 65$) collected data on teachers' understandings and implementation of the Newton et al. (2010) principles, and elicited a snapshot of teachers' reported beliefs, practices, skills and knowledge. A particular focus of the investigation was on reflection (i.e., Newton et al. Principles 3 and 4). Semi-structured interviews were subsequently conducted with a subset of 12 case-study teachers. These covered a range of languages, school locations and school types, catering for different groups of students between Years 7 and 13.

Survey results appeared to be quite positive. Twenty respondents (31%) indicated that they "often" or "always," and 35 (54%) that they "sometimes," asked their students to reflect. Of the remainder, ten respondents (15%) noted that they "rarely" or "never" did this. The majority were therefore reporting that, to different extents, they were encouraging intercultural reflection in the context of language learning (Principle 3). Furthermore, 56 teachers (86%) reported that they encouraged their students to reflect not only on their own culture and experiences, but also on the culture and experiences of the target population, leading to an element of comparison and contrast (Principle 4).

Nevertheless, the case-study interviews indicated that reflection appeared to these teachers to equate to comparison, and that over half of the 12 teachers reported reflection in terms of learners' noticing of similarities and differences. That is, learners "may have noticed something contrary to their expectations when comparing. However, teachers did not report scaffolding their learners to reflect or provide examples of learner reflection" (Conway & Richards, 2018, p. 380). Interestingly, Conway and Richards (2018) reported that language proficiency, experience of the target culture and professional development (although important contributors to enhanced practice in some cases) did not always appear to be factors influencing practice.

Oranje (2016) investigated teachers' understandings of the Newton et al. (2010) principles at the secondary school (Years 9–13) level, and added an experiential dimension in the form of an interculturally oriented classroom intervention. In Phase I (conducted in 2013), also reported in Oranje and Smith (2018), a survey was administered to ascertain secondary school language teachers' beliefs regarding culture in the language classroom. Of 74 responses to a question designed to elicit how familiar teachers were with the specific concept of *intercultural* CLT (ICLT), it was found that 23 teachers (31%) reported familiarity with the concept and aimed to put its principles into practice. However, five (7%) did not practice ICLT even though they reported a level of familiarity with it, 15 (20%) had heard of it, but were unfamiliar with its main precepts, and 31 (42%) had not heard of ICLT. Thus, the majority were reporting no or minimal awareness or understanding of ICLT.

Phase 2 of Oranje's (2016) study, aspects of which were also reported in Feryok and Oranje (2015), was an in-class intervention involving teachers and students in three secondary school language classes (2 × German, 1 × French). These classes participated in term-length (up to 10-week) student-centred activities which Oranje labelled as cultural portfolio projects (CPPs). The CPPs embodied principles of ICLT and were designed to demonstrate the Newton et al. (2010) principles in practice.

Although there was some week-to-week flexibility with how the projects unfolded, and teachers had autonomy over the number of lessons devoted to the CPP project and the level of the researcher's involvement in class activities, four components were fixed for each project. Firstly, the class generated statements about their existing understanding about the target culture. The students each then chose one statement and explored its validity through a range of sources. The statement was then reformulated in relation to the students' own culture and the validity was retested. Finally, the findings were presented to the class, so all students were exposed to the range of perspectives explored (Oranje, 2016).

The participant teachers held different perspectives on the balance to be maintained between L1 and TL as students undertook the projects, but recognised scope for TL use as students engaged with authentic resources. Furthermore, the fourth stage (findings) could be presented in the TL, with the presentation contributing to students' formal assessment in the TL.

Qualitative data on the impact of the CPPs were gathered from observations, interviews and group discussions. It was found that the teachers in Phase 2 acknowledged the importance of culture, but their practices did not always align with this acknowledgement. There was, rather, "a pervading perception that the elevation of culture in the curriculum required *only* greater incorporation of culture into lessons" (p. 299, our emphasis), that is, there was both a perceptual and a practical divide between language and culture, rather than an understanding of inter-relatedness and an attempt to develop an *intercultural* positioning.

To some extent, Oranje (2016) blamed the NZC document for a language–culture divide. That is, "[t]he curriculum asserts the *equivalence* of language and culture and their *joint* role in communication," but the support materials available to teachers "do little to guide teachers in the *practice* of the cultural dimension" (p. 299, our emphases). Essentially, Oranje's study supported the conclusions reached by Conway and Richards (2014, 2018)—teacher understanding and implementation of the Newton et al. (2010) principles continued to be quite restricted. Oranje's argument also underscores the impact of the different trajectories taken with regard to Ellis (2005) and Newton et al., as noted by East (2012a). As Oranje concluded, "[a]dvances are being made in the practice of ICLT elsewhere in the world." She went on to argue, "New Zealand teachers must be better supported in the practice of ICLT; otherwise, they will be forever playing catch up" (p. 325). In summing up a key factor for success with regard to the intercultural based on her findings, Oranje (2021) argued that "insufficient emphasis on reflection on one's own cultural viewpoint is a defining feature of teachers who do not practice intercultural teaching, even if they report cognitions that support the approach" (p. 143).

3.7 Studies into the Intercultural in the New Zealand Context

Two further largely observation-based and non-interventionist studies in New Zealand school L2 classrooms were reported by Kennedy (2016, 2020) and Ramírez (2018a, 2018b). In both cases, the six Newton et al. (2010) principles provided the theoretical framework through which the findings were analysed and interpreted.

Kennedy (2016) presented a small-scale qualitative case study of one teacher and three students in a Year 11 class where Mandarin was the TL. The teacher, an L1 speaker of Mandarin, had taught in New Zealand for 15 years. Since the teacher did not report any prior knowledge of an ICLT approach, the researcher was interested in noting any naturally occurring (i.e., unplanned) incidents of intercultural exploration over a four-month period during 2015. During the first five weeks, she observed one class per week to enable the students and teacher to get used to her presence, with formal data collection beginning after that point. In addition to observations, data were elicited through stimulated recall based on prompts from audio-recordings of the class, field notes, unstructured and semi-structured interviews and a final written reflection from the students.

Kennedy (2016) found that some intercultural incidents did emerge naturally. However, no explicit focus on the intercultural dimension was apparent, and opportunities for students to develop the skills and attitudes that contribute to intercultural capability in the language classroom were lacking. Kennedy speculated, however, that the cultural activities she observed in class could be transformed into more powerful incidents by the addition of regular comparative and reflective opportunities on the part of learners.

Two key conclusions drawn by Kennedy (2016) were that teacher awareness and understanding of ICLT need to be developed, and that intercultural reflection and comparison need to be regularly included in language classes. As a follow-up, and working with two Year 10 Mandarin classes, Kennedy (2020) described a five-week intercultural project which she designed to focus on school life as a component of a ten-week unit on school. The classes worked together with Years 10 and 11 English Language classes which were timetabled at the same time and contained a high number of Chinese international students. The project thus enabled comparison and contrast about school life through authentic interaction with TL speakers and facilitated the use of both Mandarin and English. Kennedy concluded, "provision of explicit time and focus for intercultural comparison and reflection in class did enable students to decentre and develop critical awareness of oneself and of others" (p. 440).

A larger-scale observational project was reported by Ramírez (2018b) who, in the course of 2015 and early 2016, collected data from 16 teachers of Chinese, Japanese, French and Spanish (four of each), who were working with students in Years 8 and 9. The study was carried out in two stages, each involving eight teachers. Ramírez recognised from previous studies that she would encounter wide variability in teachers' knowledge and understanding of the intercultural dimension, including the Newton et al. (2010) principles. Her study was therefore designed to investigate current teachers' conceptualisations and practices, using the principles as an interpretive lens. She also considered whether professional development and proficiency in the TL made a difference to teachers' conceptualisations and practices. To achieve this, an online test was used to place participants into two groups: high proficiency

(CEFR B2 to C2) and low proficiency (CEFR A1 to B1). In each of the two six-month stages, qualitative data were gathered from each of the teachers through a preliminary interview, two cycles of classroom observation followed by teacher reflections, and a concluding interview.

Ramírez' (2018b) findings indicated that teachers demonstrated an initial level of awareness of the six Newton et al. (2010) principles, and showed what she described as "a potential for intercultural teaching" (p. 155). However, this potential was variable, and there was an inconsistent relationship between conceptualisations and practices. It was found that TL proficiency did not appear to play a consistent role in teachers' ability to conceptualise or operationalise an intercultural dimension, although low proficiency did seem to be a factor in not aligning practices with the principles. Furthermore, there was no evidence to suggest that the TL was a determinant in more articulated or developed intercultural conceptualisations and practices—it did not seem to matter what language was being taught.

Ramírez (2018b) found some evidence of the efficacy of teacher professional development. However, this appeared to be particularly the case when that professional development was deliberately targeted at the intercultural dimension. In this regard, Ramírez commented that, despite changes that had occurred within the TPDL programme since Conway et al.'s original (2010, 2012) study, an exploration of the intercultural within this programme still appeared to have been insufficiently developed. As Ramírez noted, those participants in her study who had completed the TPDL programme "demonstrated a *slightly* higher level of awareness/knowledge of the theory behind the iCLT principles, but did *not* demonstrate more developed *practices* of iCLT" (p. 162, our emphases). This, in her view, was not surprising, given a continued stronger focus on the ten Ellis (2005) principles within that programme.

Ramírez came to the conclusion that the implementation of the Newton et al. (2010) principles in New Zealand L2 classrooms, as also identified by Oranje (2016), was "inadequate" (Ramírez, 2018b, p. 183), due to the persistence of "an iCLT theory–practice gap" (Ramírez, 2018a, p. 26).

3.8 Conclusion

In summary, the development of intercultural capability, both in and beyond the context of L2 learning, has been identified as a priority for New Zealand, at least since the early 1990s. In the context of a new learning area for L2 learning within a revised school curriculum and its focus on effective communication, cultural knowledge features in the NZC as a strand of knowledge that is equally as important as language knowledge.

The findings of recent New Zealand studies indicate that, despite apparent awareness of the need to incorporate an intercultural dimension into L2 classrooms, there is no widespread evidence of understanding what that dimension entails, and an intercultural dimension is frequently limited or absent in L2 classrooms, even among more experienced and specialist teachers. In other words, positive stances towards culture are in evidence, alongside some level of theoretical understanding, but there is limited application of theory to practice. It seems that New Zealand language teachers are generally insufficiently aware of, or unsure how to practise and interpret, both the Newton et al. (2010) principles and the expectations of the *cultural knowledge* strand of the curriculum. The study we report in the remainder of this book represents a further attempt to explore the intercultural in the L2 classroom.

Although published after our own study had been completed, Conway and Richards (2018, p. 380) raised several points regarding teacher support that align with the factors we took into account in the framing of our own study:

- Professional development may be a useful catalyst in moving teachers' practices forward, but such PD "needs to include robust discussion on what it means to be intercultural, what reflection means, and strategies needed to encourage learners to reflect and expand their perspectives."
- Furthermore, classroom-based experiential learning "could extend teacher understanding of how comparing and contrasting with 'the other' leads to reflection, and exposure to a more responsive pedagogy may help teachers to be more confident in working with learners' unpredictable responses as they reflect on culture."
- Additionally, or simultaneously, there is "a need for research that involves researchers, teachers and learners working together." Co-constructive studies "may reveal factors that can foster teachers' ability to provide learner opportunities for reflection and more of the underlying complexities for teachers' decisions on how they develop IC [intercultural competence] and their processes for fostering learner reflection on both language and culture."

In the next chapters, we turn to our own study into the development of interculturality among young language learners in New Zealand.

References

Alton-Lee, A. (2003). *Quality teaching for diverse students: Best evidence synthesis*. Ministry of Education.
Australian Council of Educational Research. (2002). *Report on the New Zealand national curriculum*. ACER.
Bolstad, R., Gilbert, J., McDowall, S., Bull, A., Boyd, S., & Hipkins, R. (2012). *Supporting future-oriented learning and teaching: A New Zealand perspective (report prepared for the Ministry of Education)*. New Zealand Council for Educational Research.
Bolstad, R., Hipkins, R., & Stevens, L. (2013). *Measuring New Zealand students' international capabilities: An exploratory study*. Ministry of Education.
Byram, M. (1991). Teaching culture and language: Towards an integrated model. In D. Buttjes & M. Byram (Eds.), *Mediating languages and cultures: Towards an intercultural theory of foreign language education* (pp. 17–30). Multilingual Matters.
Conway, C., & Richards, H. (2014). Intercultural language learners: Are you providing opportunities for your students to reflect? *Polyglot (Publication of the NZALT), 39*, 23–25.

Conway, C., & Richards, H. (2018). 'Lunchtimes in New Zealand are cruel': Reflection as a tool for developing language learners' intercultural competence. *The Language Learning Journal, 46*(4), 371–383.

Conway, C., Richards, H., Harvey, S., & Roskvist, A. (2010). Teacher provision of opportunities for learners to develop language knowledge and cultural knowledge. *Asia Pacific Journal of Education, 30*(4), 449–462.

Conway, C., Richards, H., Harvey, S., & Roskvist, A. (2012). Professional development for language teachers: Response to a change in learning languages policy. In B. Boufoy-Bastick (Ed.), *Cultures of professional development for teachers: Collaboration, reflection, management and policy* (pp. 159–182). Analytrics.

Council of Europe. (2001). *Common European framework of reference for languages.* Cambridge University Press.

East, M. (2012a). Addressing the intercultural via task-based language teaching: Possibility or problem? *Language and Intercultural Communication, 12*(1), 56–73.

East, M. (2012b). *Task-based language teaching from the teachers' perspective: Insights from New Zealand.* John Benjamins.

East, M. (2021). Language learning in New Zealand's schools: Enticing opportunities and enduring constraints. In U. Lanvers, A. Thompson, & M. East (Eds.), *Language learning in Anglophone countries: Challenges, practices, ways forward* (pp. 19–36). Palgrave Macmillan.

East, M., Howard, J., Tolosa, C., Biebricher, C., & Scott, A. (2017). Isolated or integrated? Should the development of students' intercultural understanding be separated from, or embedded into, communicative language use? *Babel, 52*(2/3), 25–31.

East, M., Shackleford, N., & Spence, G. (2007). Promoting a multilingual future for Aotearoa/New Zealand: Initiatives for change from 1989 to 2003. *Journal of Asian Pacific Communication, 17*(1), 11–28.

Ellis, R. (2005). *Instructed second language acquisition: A literature review.* Ministry of Education.

Erlam, R., & Sakui, K. (2006). *Instructed second language acquisition: Case studies.* Ministry of Education.

Erlam, R., & Tolosa, C. (2022). *Pedagogical realities of implementing task-based language teaching.* John Benjamins.

Feryok, A., & Oranje, J. (2015). Adopting a cultural portfolio project in teaching German as a foreign language: Language teacher cognition as a dynamic system. *The Modern Language Journal, 99*(3), 546–564.

Goff, P. (1990). *Speech presented to living language in Aotearoa, the 2nd community languages and ESOL (CLESOL) conference, 28th August.* Wellington College of Education.

Harvey, S., Conway, C., Richards, H., & Roskvist, A. (2009). *Evaluation of Teacher Professional Development Languages (TPDL) in years 7–10 and the impact on language learning opportunities and outcomes for students.* Ministry of Education.

Kennedy, J. (2016). *Exploring opportunities for developing intercultural competence through intercultural communicative language teaching (ICLT): A case study in a Chinese as a foreign language classroom in a New Zealand high school* [Masters dissertation, Victoria University of Wellington, New Zealand].

Kennedy, J. (2020). Intercultural pedagogies in Chinese as a foreign language (CFL). *Intercultural Education, 31*(4), 427–446.

Klapper, J. (2003). Taking communication to task? A critical review of recent trends in language teaching. *Language Learning Journal, 27*, 33–42.

Koefoed, G. (2012). Policy perspectives from New Zealand. In M. Byram & L. Parmenter (Eds.), *The common European framework of reference: The globalisation of language education policy* (pp. 233–247). Multilingual Matters.

Le Métais, J. (2002). *New Zealand Stocktake: An international critique.* National Foundation for Educational Research.

Māori Language Act. (1987). https://www.legislation.govt.nz/act/public/1987/0176/latest/whole.html

References

McKinnon, D. (1992). *Speech presented to the Asia 2000 'Realising the Opportunities' Seminar, May 1992*. Press release from the office of the Minister of External Relations and Trade.

Ministry of Education. (n.d). *Learning languages series*. https://learning-languages.tki.org.nz/Learning-Languages-in-the-NZ-Curriculum/Learning-Language-Series

Ministry of Education. (1993). *The New Zealand curriculum framework*. Learning Media, Ministry of Education.

Ministry of Education. (1998). *Japanese in the New Zealand curriculum*. Learning Media.

Ministry of Education. (2002a). *French in the New Zealand curriculum*. Learning Media.

Ministry of Education. (2002b). *German in the New Zealand curriculum*. Learning Media.

Ministry of Education. (2007). *The New Zealand curriculum*. Learning Media.

Ministry of Education. (2009a). *Curriculum achievement objectives by learning area*. http://nzcurriculum.tki.org.nz/The-New-Zealand-Curriculum

Ministry of Education. (2009b). *Te Aho Arataki Marau mō te Ako i Te Reo Māori - Kura Auraki / Curriculum guidelines for teaching and learning Te Reo Māori in English-medium schools: Years 1–13*. Ministry of Education.

Ministry of Education. (2014). *International capabilities*. Ministry of Education.

Ministry of Education. (2016). *Learning languages curriculum guide: Version 4*. http://seniorsecondary.tki.org.nz/Learning-languages

Newton, J., Yates, E., Shearn, S., & Nowitzki, W. (2010). *Intercultural communicative language teaching: Implications for effective teaching and learning—A literature review and an evidence-based framework for effective teaching*. Ministry of Education.

Oranje, J. (2016). *Intercultural communicative language teaching: Enhancing awareness and practice through cultural portfolio projects* [Doctoral thesis, University of Otago, New Zealand].

Oranje, J. (2021). Intercultural language teaching: On reflection. In M. D. López-Jiménez & J. Sánchez-Torres (Eds.), *Intercultural competence past, present and future* (pp. 143–161). Springer.

Oranje, J., & Smith, L. (2018). Language teacher cognitions and intercultural language teaching: The New Zealand perspective. *Language Teaching Research, 22*(3), 310–329.

Ramírez, E. (2018a). Intercultural communicative language teaching (iCLT): A selection of practical points of departure. *The New Zealand Language Teacher, 44*, 18–30.

Ramírez, E. (2018b). *The intercultural dimension in language classrooms in Aotearoa New Zealand: A comparative study across languages and teachers' levels of proficiency* [Doctoral thesis, University of Auckland, New Zealand].

Scott, A., & Butler, P. (2007). My teacher is learning like us: Teachers and students as language learners. *The New Zealand Language Teacher, 33*, 11–16.

Scott, A., & East, M. (2012). Academic perspectives from New Zealand. In M. Byram & L. Parmenter (Eds.), *The common European framework of reference: The globalisation of language education policy* (pp. 248–257). Multilingual Matters.

Sehlaoui, A. S. (2001). Developing cross-cultural communicative competence in pre-service ESL/EFL teachers: A critical perspective. *Language, Culture and Curriculum, 14*(1), 42–57.

Te Karauna. (2008). *Te Marautanga o Aotearoa*. Te Karauna/Ministry of Education.

Waite, J. (1992). *Aoteareo: Speaking for ourselves. Part A: The overview; Part B: The issues*. Ministry of Education.

Watts, N. (1997). Language policy and education in New Zealand and the South Pacific. In R. Wodak & D. S. Corson (Eds.), *Encyclopedia of language and education* (Vol. 1, pp. 189–197). Springer.

Open Access This chapter is licensed under the terms of the Creative Commons Attribution 4.0 International License (http://creativecommons.org/licenses/by/4.0/), which permits use, sharing, adaptation, distribution and reproduction in any medium or format, as long as you give appropriate credit to the original author(s) and the source, provide a link to the Creative Commons license and indicate if changes were made.

The images or other third party material in this chapter are included in the chapter's Creative Commons license, unless indicated otherwise in a credit line to the material. If material is not included in the chapter's Creative Commons license and your intended use is not permitted by statutory regulation or exceeds the permitted use, you will need to obtain permission directly from the copyright holder.

Chapter 4
Introducing the Two-Year Study

4.1 Introduction

The previous two chapters have provided important overviews of the intercultural dimension by way of laying a foundation and rationale for the study we report in this book. In Chap. 2, we focused on key aspects of the international literature on the intercultural dimension, both in education more broadly, and in the teaching and learning of additional languages (L2) in particular. We also presented the findings of a range of studies into the intercultural in educational contexts. In that chapter, we continued the discourse we had begun in the opening chapter that essentially problematises the notion of intercultural competence. In the face of a construct that is hard to pin down, we explored the challenges that teachers face. We concluded that a recurring theme of the international literature and prior studies is just how difficult it seems to be, especially at the level of programmes in schools, to integrate an intercultural dimension into L2 programmes.

In Chap. 3, our focus turned to the New Zealand context. We looked in particular at how L2 teaching and learning is currently framed in this context, and went on to discuss a number of studies into the intercultural that have taken place in New Zealand. We concluded the chapter with several of the key issues raised by Conway and Richards (2018). They suggested, first, that professional learning and development (PLD) would provide a useful (indeed, crucial) means of moving teachers' practices forward. However, this PLD needed to incorporate solid introductions to, and discussion of, how the intercultural is to be understood in the context of L2 learning, alongside the importance of reflection and strategies that might help L2 learners to reflect on and develop their own intercultural perspectives. Second, classroom-based experiential learning was seen as an important catalyst for facilitating comparison, contrast and evaluation of cultural similarities and differences. Third, Conway and Richards perceived a need for researchers to work alongside teachers in co-constructive studies that might help take both theory and practice further.

Thus, Chap. 3 (alongside Chap. 1) has examined the New Zealand educational context and the place of *Learning Languages* in the *New Zealand Curriculum* (NZC) (Ministry of Education, 2007) that set the stage for our own study to take place. The purpose of this chapter is to outline the methodological underpinnings and the research procedures of the project. The first part of the chapter addresses the approaches and methodologies relevant to the research questions we posed, followed by a discussion of our chosen data collection methods and a consideration of related ethical issues. The next part of the chapter provides a full description of the participants and the research procedures.

4.2 Background

The two-year study we report in the remainder of this book builds on the recommendations proposed by Conway and Richards (2018). In particular, we sought to find out how New Zealand primary/intermediate school teachers teaching languages could be supported to help their learners to develop their intercultural competence in the context of learning an L2. We explained in Chap. 1 that, at the outset, we made the decision to frame this competence in terms of *intercultural capability*. The *Merriam-Webster Thesaurus*, for example, defines *competence* as "the physical or mental power to do something," and *capability* as "a skill, an ability, or knowledge that makes a person able to do a particular job."[1] Although this thesaurus also suggests that *capability* can be regarded as a synonym of *competence*, and presents the *competence* definition as a secondary definition for *capability*, our perspective was that *capability* was the more apposite word in the context. Additionally, we considered that learners would develop several capabilities. That is, we were interested in exploring the extent to which, through L2 learning, learners could develop *skills, abilities and knowledge* that might inform successful intercultural interactions (as opposed to more generally developing the *physical or mental power* to undertake such interactions).

Furthermore, and in line both with the published expectations of the NZC and the recommendations of Conway and Richards (2018), we were interested in exploring the extent to which learner-centred and experiential classroom experiences, as operationalised through specific inquiries, would facilitate the development of intercultural capability. As we noted in Chap. 1, at the outset of the project we posed the following overarching research question: can a teaching as inquiry process in the context of learning an L2 enhance intermediate school learners'[2] intercultural capability?

As we explain in more detail later, this was a four-phase project over two years whose essential components were as follows:

---

[1] https://www.merriam-webster.com/thesaurus.

[2] That is, learners in school years 7 and 8 (11+ to 12+ years of age).

Phase I (Year 1 first half): collect baseline data.
Phase II (Year 1 second half): co-construct the first of two inquiry cycles.
Phase III (Year 2 first half): co-construct the second of two inquiry cycles.
Phase IV (Year 2 second half): consolidate and write up the findings.

In terms of the aspects of the study we report in this and the following chapters, we look back at the whole project from the perspective of its various stakeholders (students, teachers and ourselves as researchers/teacher educators), and address the following two questions:

1. How do stakeholders' understandings about enhancing language learners' intercultural capability change and develop over time?
2. What are the implications for language education going forward?

4.3 Research Framework

This research was situated within an interpretivist research paradigm (Lincoln & Guba, 1985) and utilised a qualitative, multiple case-study approach (Creswell & Plano Clark, 2011; Yin, 2014). Interpretivism was chosen for this study as it is a perspective that helps us to explain human and social reality. As Crotty (1998) argued, an interpretivist approach "looks for culturally derived and historically situated interpretations of the social life-world" (p. 67). In the context of this study, the social reality we sought to explain was that of the non-specialist primary/intermediate language teacher attempting to enhance the intercultural capabilities of learners through the study of an L2.

The interpretive worldview allows for a combination of data types alongside the multiple realities of the various participants and the interpretations of the researchers (Creswell & Plano Clark, 2011). Since this study focused on five teachers and their students' learning in four schools (i.e., multiple realities and various participants), a qualitative approach was applicable. It was appropriate to frame the study as multiple case studies, as each of the five teachers and their students represented individual cases. This approach aligns with Stake's (2006) contention that the complex meanings of a wider phenomenon are better understood when the particular activities and contexts of each case are considered. More broadly, the qualitative case-study approach supported our investigation of "a contemporary phenomenon in depth and within its real-life context" (Yin, 2014, p. 18).

4.3.1 Inquiry-Based Approaches

The impetus for the project documented in this book was our interest in better understanding the complexities of implementing the intercultural dimension in L2 programmes in intermediate schools in New Zealand, where, as we noted in Chap. 1, teachers are often non-specialists in the language they teach and may also be learning the language alongside their own students (Scott & Butler, 2007). This focus was deliberate for several reasons.

First, earlier studies in New Zealand have indicated that, even in contexts where teachers may have received prior teacher education and may be regarded as "specialists" in the language they teach, the intercultural dimension remains substantially under-developed (Kennedy, 2016; Oranje, 2016; Ramírez, 2018). Second, the NZC has placed a specific requirement on schools to be planning for the implementation of L2 programmes in Years 7–10, which includes the two primary/intermediate years (7 and 8). Schools with students in these years must at the very least be thinking about how they will address L2 learning. Third, and as we made clear in Chap. 3, the delivery of L2 programmes in New Zealand is informed by two different and largely mutually exclusive literature review reports (Ellis, 2005; Newton et al., 2010), with the second of these (which focuses on the intercultural dimension) being published subsequent to the release of the NZC and subject to less extensive dissemination. These three intersecting issues make the New Zealand primary/intermediate context a particularly interesting one for an investigation into the intercultural in L2 programmes.

We approached our investigation as the co-construction of new understandings and the development of "theories that are grounded in the problems and perspectives of educational practice" (Carr & Kemmis, 1986, p. 122). Therefore, the five teacher participants contributed their knowledge of practice and the five research partners (the authors) supported the teachers in evidence-based research through what we labelled as "inquiry cycles" (see Chap. 1).

The study involved working at three different levels of inquiry: *inquiry learning* as a disposition that the school students engaged in (as operationalised in the ways we document in Chap. 5); the *teaching as inquiry* cycles that the teachers designed as part of the project (see Chaps. 5 and 6); and the *collaborative inquiry* established between the researchers and the teachers (see Chap. 7). We made a deliberate decision of positioning the participants in the project as reflective partners and in reciprocal relationships, drawing on the Māori concept of *ako* (reciprocal shared learning) whereby the researchers and teachers were teaching and learning from each other, and the teachers took responsibility not only for the learning of students but also for their own learning while working with and alongside each other. Thus, teaching and learning cycles were anticipated across the intersections between the different partners.

4.3.2 Inquiry Learning

As introduced in Chap. 1, and in line with the learner-centred and experiential philosophy of the NZC, the reflective approach of inquiry learning focuses on the learners. The students' engagement in the intercultural inquiries their teachers facilitated for them enabled their learning through curiosity and discovery throughout the project.

As such, engagement with interculturality aligned well with the inquiry learning approach which encourages students to:

- ask thought-provoking questions
- investigate widely and deeply
- make sense of information to build new knowledge
- develop a solution or formulate opinions
- present or share their new understanding with others
- have a valuable learning experience that leads to taking some form of action
- reflect on what they learned and how they learned it (National Library of New Zealand, n.d., para. 4).

4.3.3 Teaching as Inquiry

At the core of the project, the second level of inquiry focused on the teachers as they planned, and then reflected on the effectiveness of, the teaching and learning interventions they facilitated in the classrooms during Phases II and III of the project (including, as appropriate, their students' learning inquiries). One way of helping teachers, whether novice or experienced, to evaluate the implications of innovation in their practices is to support them in engaging in a process of reflection. The project therefore drew on the teaching as inquiry model in which the teachers utilised "the skills of reflective practice to improve their own situations" (Ferguson, 2012, p. 6). As we pointed out in Chap. 1, this is essentially an action research model which facilitates "a process for enhancing reflective practice and professional growth and development" (Burns, 1999, p. 24), typically addressing educational issues that are practical and have theoretical interest to practitioners.

The teaching as inquiry model presented in the NZC represents an important means of developing teachers' skills in reflective practice, encouraged on the basis that "effective pedagogy requires that teachers inquire into the impact of their teaching on their students" (Ministry of Education, 2007, p. 35). The model was originally developed in the New Zealand context by Aitken and Sinnema (2008), and its aim is to address the fundamental question: what teaching approaches enhance outcomes for diverse learners? The model is designed to generate evidence of classroom learning "underpinned by a set of attitudes towards teaching and learning" (p. 54). Open-mindedness is seen as a core component, and represents "a willingness to consider teaching approaches that may be unfamiliar or that may challenge one's beliefs about the best ways to teach," alongside openness to "what the evidence shows about the effects of teaching on student learning" (p. 54).

Aitken and Sinnema (2008) also recognised fallibility and persistence as crucial elements of the model. Fallibility takes into account that learning outcomes are context-specific, and that different groups of students may respond differently to a particular pedagogical approach or intervention. With that in mind, persistence represents the willingness of teachers to continue to inquire into their own practices as part of an ongoing cycle.

Table 4.1 The teaching as inquiry model

Inquiry component	Inquiry requirement	Link to action research
Focusing inquiry	Establishes student learning goals in a specific area and leads to teacher decisions about what is important for the students with regard to their learning at the stage they have currently reached	Identify and contextualise the issue from the perspectives of theory and past research
Teaching inquiry	Draws on evidence from other contexts (e.g., theoretical frameworks; examples of effective practice) to design and carry out a teaching and learning cycle	Investigate the issue
Learning inquiry	Looks at the outcomes for learners, and considers next steps for future learning	Draw conclusions from findings

The cycle of inquiry proposed by the NZC has three components, as illustrated in Table 4.1.

Each of the components of the model reflects important elements of effective action research, and the cyclical process of "focusing—teaching—learning" can be carried out again at a later time and/or with a different group of learners.

For the purposes of our study, the development of intercultural capabilities was designated as the *focusing inquiry*. The research team supported the participant teachers to facilitate, co-construct and undertake context-specific, theory- and research-informed teaching as inquiry cycles in their selected L2 classroom. At the end of each cycle, the teachers and researchers examined the outcomes for learners as part of the *learning inquiry*. The teaching as inquiry cycles were used to encourage three components of reflective practice as articulated by East (2014):

1. reflection-*in*-action, that is, reflection *during* lesson delivery which may lead to immediate changes to practice;
2. reflection-*on*-action, that is, reflection *after* lesson delivery which may lead to subsequent practice modifications (Schön, 1983, 1987);
3. reflection-*for*-action (Killion & Todnem, 1991), that is, the opportunity for *future-focused* reflection, both before a teaching cycle has begun and after the cycle has been completed (p. 263).

4.3.4 Collaborative Inquiry

The third level of inquiry present in our project is *collaborative inquiry*, where the researchers established a partnership with the participant teachers (as detailed in Chap. 7). Collaborative inquiry (Butler & Schnellert, 2012) draws on conceptions of inquiry and collaboration offered across the literatures on collaborative action research (Burns, 1999), teacher practitioner research (Baumfield et al., 2012; Cochran-Smith & Lytle, 2009), and exploratory practice (Allwright & Hanks, 2009), most of which trace their origins to action research (see recent reviews by Burns, 2019; Manfra, 2019). As Loughran (2010) argued, linking collaboration and inquiry is "crucial to shaping ways in which changes in practice might not only be initiated, but also sustained" (p. 403). Collaboration is considered an effective approach in meeting educational goals as resources are pooled together and participants share their knowledge and expertise in their contexts of practice (Muijs et al., 2014). Establishing a shared purpose and developing mutual understanding and collegiality are considered central to this process (Loughran, 2010).

In New Zealand, collaborative inquiry is encouraged for groups of teachers working together, often with other members of a professional learning community (TKI, n.d.). In our project, the collaborative inquiry was initiated by the research team who anticipated limitations on the part of the teachers regarding their prior knowledge of intercultural language teaching and learning. We did not see our role as one in which we would direct and tell the teachers what to do; rather, our role was to clarify and suggest without imposing any preconceived conceptualisation onto the teachers about what their intercultural explorations should look like. We were keen to see what could be achieved interculturally as the teachers in our project inquired into their own practices. In turn, we hoped that what we would find out would be useful for other primary/intermediate school teachers for whom the intercultural may be an unknown concept, and would provide some guidance about how other teachers might enhance their own practices.

4.4 Data Collection Methods

The study used a number of research methods to capture the three levels of inquiry described above. Quality assurance measures were implemented throughout the project to help ensure consistency across the research team for each data source. This included establishing protocols for the data collection methods, and joint construction of indicative schedules for individual and focus group interviews.

4.4.1 Student Data

Giving voice to the students' perspectives was considered to be an essential part of this project, particularly since much of the research on intercultural language education has prioritised adult voices (those of teachers and researchers), and, further, because teachers can be predisposed to observe only what they have expected to perceive in their classrooms (Cook-Sather, 2008). In the New Zealand context,

Bolstad et al. (2013) have stressed the need to address this imbalance by providing opportunities for students to give expression to their experiences and insights.

In order to capture evidence of learners' intercultural outcomes, we held focus group interviews with small groups of students from the participant teachers' L2 classrooms. These interviews, which took place towards the end of the inquiry cycles in Phases II and III of the project, aimed to capture the students' perspectives on the intervention that was the focus of their teacher's inquiry, and—more broadly—their perceptions of language learning, and of gains in motivation, language proficiency and the development of intercultural capability. We chose to use focus groups for this purpose because they can be less stressful than individual interviews, and had potential to provide additional depth in the data due to the possibilities for interaction and reaction between the students (Bagnoli & Clark, 2010). Each of the focus group discussions was audio-recorded and transcribed.

4.4.2 Teacher Data

We used five methods to collect data from the teachers: questionnaires, interviews, observations, reflective journals and guided reflective exercises.

4.4.2.1 Questionnaires

Each teacher completed a questionnaire at the beginning of the project. This was designed to gather demographic information and background data related to the participants' level of proficiency in the TL and level of teaching experience, as well as contextual information about their current teaching position and involvement in the *Learning Languages* programme in their school.

4.4.2.2 Interviews

We conducted three types of interview with the teachers, each of which was framed as a semi-structured professional conversation, thus allowing discussion threads to develop and lead to follow-up questions. As with the student focus groups, these were all audio-recorded and transcribed. The teachers were invited to review transcripts of their interviews at a number of points during the project.

1. The initial interviews, conducted at the outset of the project during Phase I, had an overarching focus on the teachers' understandings of effective language teaching and learning and their own practices. Interview schedules contained broad areas for discussion to ensure we were collecting comparable data with all teachers while allowing flexibility in the conversations with each teacher. At this juncture, we also sought to gauge participants' current knowledge and

4.4 Data Collection Methods

understanding of the ten Ellis principles (Ellis, 2005) and the six Newton et al. principles (Newton et al., 2010).

2. After each observed lesson, we held debriefing conversations with the teachers to provide an opportunity for immediate reflection on what had transpired in each lesson. In the teacher interviews in Phases II and III we also guided the teachers in their planning for their upcoming teaching.
3. At the end of each phase of the study, we also conducted summative interviews with each teacher. The Phase I summative interview captured initial insights into the teachers' language teaching practices and goals. In Phases II and III, the final interviews guided broader reflection on the effectiveness of the inquiries the teachers had undertaken and any themes that arose out of the data from lesson observations.

4.4.2.3 Observations

An important component of not only supporting the teachers in their inquiries but also of gathering complementary evidence of intercultural learning gains through inquiry was to see the teachers in their classrooms, observe their language teaching and try to capture the unique contextual realities of their teaching. The observers were non-participants in the events of the lessons being observed. We audio-recorded the lessons to capture the specific language and cultural events, took field notes to provide background to transcriptions of the recordings, and occasionally took photos to document the context and the learning activities.

4.4.2.4 Reflective Journals

We encouraged the teachers to keep a continuing record of their own reflections on the inquiries in folders we set up for them in Google Drive, where they could additionally archive material relevant to their inquiries. The reflective journals also presented the opportunity for asynchronous dialogue with the research team, and contributed to our aim of promoting a culture of ongoing reflection and sharing among the project's participants.

4.4.2.5 Guided Reflective Exercises

The teachers engaged in guided reflective exercises at different stages of the project. These aimed to provide additional avenues for the teachers to reflect on specific aspects as the project proceeded. The reflective exercises included: responses to relevant readings, preparing brief presentations to the entire group (teacher partners and researchers) with individual updates on the project and how it was unfolding, completing a survival memo (Brookfield, 1995) and writing a vignette with their story of the project which would contribute to a published resource for other teachers.

4.4.3 Researcher Data

The collaborative inquiry led by the researchers was documented extensively in different ways. Our careful documentation of the two-year project was not initially planned as a data source. However, as part of the reflective processes of the researchers, the organised archives that we had set up proved to be valuable. These diverse data sources included project documents such as the milestone reports we were required to send to the funders on a quarterly basis; audio recordings and transcriptions of meetings of the research team and meetings with the researchers and teachers; email archives and notes from discussions involving different members of the group; and the data from our work with the teacher partners.

4.5 Ethical Considerations

Collecting data from the participants in this project required two key ethical considerations. First of all, it is acknowledged that special ethics attention is required for any research conducted in schools and with school-aged children, and additionally when teachers are working with their own students. With this in mind, we were particularly attentive to the need for fully informed voluntary consent, clear understandings regarding rights to not participate in or to withdraw from the study, permissions pertaining to classroom observations and the potential power differential between teachers and students. In addition to getting informed written consent from the school principals and teacher participants, we ensured that the students were clearly informed of the purposes of the study and its procedures, with age-appropriate supporting documentation and opportunities for questions, prior to inviting them to participate and gaining written assent. Written consent was also obtained from the participating students' caregivers.

Secondly, since the participating teachers in this study were also researcher-partners, establishing relationships of trust was crucial for the co-construction of the inquiries and the open discussion of all aspects of the project. We were mindful that although we had positioned the teachers as partners, there was a further possibility of power imbalances. Hence, all efforts were made to communicate to the teachers with transparency and consider their voices when making decisions.

4.6 Teacher Participants

As previously stated, our team of five researchers worked in partnership with five teachers from four New Zealand schools with intermediate-level students (Years 7 and 8). Each of the schools was urban, being located in or near a major New Zealand city. The student participants were between 11 and 13 years old. The classes had between 20 and 32 students, almost all of whom were beginners in the language they were learning.

We used convenience sampling initially to select the schools, based on relationships that we already had either with the teachers or with the schools (e.g., through contact when we mentored students undertaking professional practicum placements or through prior research connections), the schools' proximity for the research partners, and geographic and demographic diversity. The teacher partners were then selected with input from the consenting school principals. The number of teacher participants was fixed at five to enable a range of perspectives to be obtained within the parameters of the close teacher-researcher partnerships which characterise this study. However, a professional inevitability of the intermediate school sector can be the transitory nature whereby teachers, for a variety of reasons, move on to new positions in new schools. Some of the initially recruited teachers were unavailable by the time the project began. The final project as reported here included the five teachers we introduce below—Lillian (Chinese heritage); Kelly, Kathryn and Mike (New Zealand European); and Tamara (New Zealand-born, of Māori-Samoan ancestry).

The five teachers were representative of most generalist teachers in Year 7 and Year 8 classes in New Zealand, in that many teachers at this level have minimal fluency in the language they teach and limited experience of the associated cultures. Further, language teaching pedagogy was not part of their initial teacher education programmes. However, subsequent to their initial training, most of the teacher partners had undertaken some type of professional learning for language teaching,[3] and they all embarked on this project with a strong interest in ongoing development of their language teaching practices.

4.6.1 Lillian

Lillian was an L1 speaker of Mandarin and taught Mandarin in an intermediate school that delivered the International Baccalaureate Primary Years Programme, underpinned by the NZC, to students from 34 different nationalities. In keeping with the International Baccalaureate emphasis on internationalisation and developing intercultural understanding, languages had an important place in the school's curriculum. Each student was required to select from one of five languages offered and to continue studying the same language with three 20-min lessons a week through both Years 7 and 8.

Lillian learnt English after moving from Taiwan to New Zealand as a child, while continuing to speak Mandarin at home. She also learnt Japanese at secondary school, and went on to major in Japanese at university. Lillian did not undertake any teacher education specifically focused on language teaching and had not undertaken any professional development in language pedagogy prior to this project. She had

---

[3] This included, for example, the Teacher Professional Development Languages (TPDL) programme (see Chap. 3).

taught Mandarin at a private school in New Zealand before moving to her current intermediate school where she was the lead teacher for languages.

During the project, Lillian had approximately 20 students in her Mandarin classes—a Year 7 class in the first year (Phase II) and a Year 8 class (the same students as in Phase II) in the second year (Phase III). Approximately half of the students were from a range of Asian backgrounds, and the remainder were predominantly from New Zealand European backgrounds. The students had already encountered aspects of Asian culture and had been in contact with L1 speakers of Mandarin, both in the classroom and within the wider school community. Lillian's first two 20-min language classes each week were co-taught with a Mandarin Language Assistant who was assigned to the school each year. These lessons had a specific language focus. As Lillian progressed with the project she elected to use the third lesson each week by capitalising on the school being a "Bring Your Own Device" and a "Google-School," to facilitate student inquiries with an intercultural focus.

4.6.2 Kelly

Kelly was an L1 speaker of English, who taught Mandarin as part of her mainstream classroom programme. Kelly had learnt French at school, but did not enjoy it. Instead, she began a self-study mission to learn Mandarin. Language teaching pedagogy was not part of Kelly's initial teacher education programme, but since beginning teaching she had undertaken professional learning and development (PLD) in this area, including the year-long Teacher Professional Development Languages (TPDL) programme alongside her teaching (see Chap. 3). She had also experienced life in China as part of a three-week immersion scholarship, and continued to learn Mandarin through evening classes. Kelly rated her ability in Mandarin as at intermediate level.

In the course of this project, Kelly taught in two very different full primary schools (Years 1–8). In the first school (in Phase II of the project), the majority of the students spoke more than one language. Approximately 12% were Māori and 81% were of Pasifika heritage. The school did not have a structured approach for teaching additional languages; rather, the approach was driven by individual teachers' own interest and ability. Kelly taught a combined Year 7/8 class of 28 students, teaching all areas of the NZC. This included a 45-min Mandarin lesson each week. Some of Kelly's students knew some Mandarin already, from having had her as their teacher the previous year.

In Kelly's school in the second year of the project (Phase III) the students were mostly from New Zealand European and Asian backgrounds. As part of the school's additional language policy, every Year 5 to Year 8 classroom teacher was expected to teach Mandarin for 30 min per week. The teachers were offered professional development opportunities for teaching and learning Mandarin, and were supported by a Mandarin Language Assistant. Kelly taught her Year 7 class Mandarin for at least 30 min weekly, and aimed to integrate Mandarin into some of her classroom routines.

4.6.3 Kathryn

Kathryn taught at an intermediate school that had a tradition of teaching a range of languages. This practice was further consolidated when the school recently gained accreditation to deliver the NZC through the International Baccalaureate Primary Years Programme. All the teachers at Kathryn's school were expected to teach te reo Māori at a basic level. Those with some proficiency in an international language also taught that language as part of an arrangement where students rotated through 30-min slots of languages, physical education and ICT once every six days. In so much as there were no predetermined outcomes for the different L2 programmes, and no planned articulation between Year 7 and Year 8, these language courses functioned as "tasters" for the students prior to high school.

Kathryn was an L1 speaker of English. She had been teaching in the intermediate sector for 18 years, and began teaching Japanese six years ago at the request of her principal. At that time, she had not undertaken any teacher education specifically focused on language teaching, but she had subsequently had in-school support from a locally based language adviser. She studied Japanese at high school and university, but rated her L2 proficiency as low-intermediate and acknowledged feeling somewhat insecure about her cultural knowledge, as well as her L2 ability because she had "not used the language for over 25 years." At the time of the project, Kathryn taught Japanese to a large mixed Year 7/8 "team," which was divided into four separate classes with approximately 32 students in each. Kathryn had 30 min with each class every six teaching days.

4.6.4 Mike

Mike was an L1 speaker of English, and a teacher of French. As with Kathryn, he rated his French proficiency as low-intermediate. At the beginning of the project, Mike had 15 years' experience as a primary school teacher, with ten of those teaching Year 7 and Year 8 classes at a state intermediate school. Mike's school was traditional in its organisation, with each teacher working in their own classroom with 25–30 students. All the teachers were expected to teach a language other than English as part of their mainstream programme, but beyond that expectation, they had complete autonomy regarding which language(s) they taught and how. As such, the L2 programmes were based on the teachers' own interest and expertise (with accommodation in the form of a visiting language teacher for classes where the teacher had no knowledge at all of an additional language). This resulted in wide variability in the languages taught and the approaches used.

After disliking language learning when he studied French briefly at high school, Mike recalled in his initial interview that he "had little skill, experience, or enthusiasm" for teaching French when he started. However, he developed an interest in languages education when it became a learning area in its own right in the NZC in 2007 (see Chap. 3). After taking advantage of a range of professional learning opportunities to expand his pedagogical knowledge for teaching languages (including completing the TPDL programme and a Master's degree in Computer Assisted Language Learning), Mike considered French at the time of the project to be "a major focus and strength" of his classroom programme. Despite this and sporadic ongoing language learning, Mike reported that he still lacked confidence in speaking French.

Mike credited prior professional learning with having heightened his awareness of the interconnectedness between language and culture, but reported being nervous about introducing a cultural element into his language teaching, due to concerns regarding time being taken away from learning the language itself, combined with reservations about his own knowledge of French culture which was mostly second-hand. At the beginning of the project, Mike described his approach to language teaching as "pretty eclectic," with a goal of maintaining a good balance between traditional and communicative approaches during the one hour he spent most weeks teaching his class French.

4.6.5 Tamara

Tamara[4] taught at the same intermediate school as Mike, where she was in her third year of teaching. She was an L1 speaker of English. Tamara identified strongly with *te reo me ōna tikanga Māori* (Māori language and its cultural practices) from her father's heritage, although her skills in te reo Māori were developed primarily through cultural activities at her school, and then much later through part-time study with an indigenous tertiary education provider. Rating her proficiency in te reo Māori as low-intermediate, Tamara was aware of the challenges of teaching a language and culture that she was still learning herself. However, despite not being an expert, she was enthusiastic about integrating Māori across all the learning areas in her Year 8 class programme. Tamara stressed that a key for her in becoming a partner in the project had been to acknowledge her own limitations and seek expertise beyond the school so she could continue developing both her own and her students' knowledge of *te ao Māori* (the Māori world view).

In addition to Māori, Tamara also knew some basic French (from high school), Samoan (her mother's heritage), and New Zealand Sign Language, and used smatterings of all these languages as she taught. At the time of the study, she was also

---

[4] Tamara took part in just one inquiry cycle (Phase II of the project) because she moved to a different school at the time of the second inquiry cycle.

learning Korean alongside her students during a 40-min class each week with an L1 speaker, and she used this L2 at times in her own class. Having very limited exposure to language teaching pedagogy when she undertook her teacher education, Tamara's approach to integrating languages across the curriculum was based on her own beliefs, rather than any particular language teaching theory. With regard to enhancing intercultural appreciation, Tamara was mindful of the diversity in her students' backgrounds and ethnicities and saw these as a valuable and valued resource.

4.7 Researchers

The research team consisted of five experienced language teacher educators with various cultural and linguistic backgrounds—the five authors: Martin (UK); Constanza (Colombian); Jocelyn (New Zealand European); Christine (German); and Adèle (New Zealand European). At the time of the project, each member of the research team was directly involved with school-level language teaching and learning, and each of us therefore brought to the project experience and close familiarity with the New Zealand context for L2 teaching and learning. This included direct involvement with pre-service language teacher education (Martin, Constanza and Jocelyn), in-service language teacher education and professional learning and development (Christine and Jocelyn), and oversight for *Learning Languages* programmes in the Correspondence School, New Zealand's major provider of online and distance learning, alongside prior work in language teacher education (Adèle). We considered that this balance of expertise, with particular strength in teacher education, provided a robust and suitably qualified team to lead and facilitate the project.

Martin, as Principal Investigator, had overall responsibility for the project, but the team worked collegially at all points. Both Martin and Constanza had experience with addressing the Newton et al. (2010) principles directly in their work among pre-service secondary school teachers of languages, and Constanza and Christine additionally contributed this knowledge to the TPDL programme for teachers of languages. Christine's work at that time in a Ministry of Education funded programme to support language learning and teaching in New Zealand—International Languages Exchanges and Pathways—involved direct exploration of the Newton et al. principles with teachers. The Newton et al. principles were also components of the theoretical underpinnings Jocelyn covered in courses on additional languages education with pre-service primary school (and, therefore, generalist) teachers. Adèle brought her teacher education and doctoral research experiences to the team—the former gave particular support to the hui, and the latter (Scott, 2014), with its focus on the role of teachers of languages at the primary/intermediate level of schooling, evidenced considerable research-informed insight into the particular needs of teachers operating at this level in New Zealand.

4.8 Research Procedures

As noted at the start of this chapter, the project was conducted in four phases over a two-year period (2016–2017). Prior to that, in the second school term of 2015, we had conducted a pilot study with one composite (Years 4–8) class (see Howard et al., 2015). The piloting had allowed us to evaluate (and subsequently make small adjustments to) the proposed methods and logistics, including ethics processes, the initial teacher questionnaire, interview schedules, observation procedures and focus group protocols.

In planning for the pilot study and collaborating on a funding application for the larger project, we established a strong community of practice as a group of five researchers as we developed shared goals and established roles within the team. As we advanced the design and timeline for the project, we met with the school principals and the teachers in the second half of 2015 to discuss the study, complete the initial consent processes, and plan for Phase I of the project at the beginning of the 2016 school year. Within this larger collaborative inquiry team, we established five teacher-researcher pairs: Lillian and Martin, Kelly and Christine, Katherine and Constanza, Mike and Jocelyn, and Tamara and Jocelyn.[5] Adèle was not directly involved in data collection in schools, but contributed to other aspects of the project, such as guiding aspects of teachers' reflections (see Chap. 7).

Throughout the project, funding was provided to each of the schools so that the participating teachers could be released from some of their teaching. This was to provide time to attend meetings, take part in post-observation interviews and undertake background reading, planning and written reflections.

In what follows, we describe the organisational and procedural aspects of each of the four phases of the study.

4.8.1 Phase I (February 2016–June 2016)

The aims for Phase I were: (a) to establish rapport and develop the relationship of the research pairs; (b) to collect baseline data about the schools, their approach to teaching languages, and the teachers' background, including their knowledge about language teaching pedagogies, such as ICLT (see Chap. 3) and the teaching as inquiry process; and (c) to observe the teachers' current language teaching practices. As we noted earlier, in particular, we wanted to find out what the teacher partners already knew and understood about the two key sets of principles (Ellis, 2005; Newton et al., 2010), and the opportunities (if any) that the teachers were already creating for intercultural exploration. After completing the background questionnaire, each teacher met with their research partner for an initial 30–60 min interview, followed by

---

[5] Since Mike and Tamara were located in the same school, it made sense for the two teachers to work with one researcher.

two (or more) separate classroom observations and subsequent 20–40 min debriefing conversations. A final summative interview enabled the teachers to further *reflect-on-action* in relation to their teaching during Phase I.

4.8.2 Phase II (July 2016–December 2016)

Phase II began with a two-day workshop meeting of all the participants (five teachers and five researchers). We referred to this meeting as a *hui*, using a Māori word that has been adopted into mainstream use in New Zealand to denote any kind of assembly or congregation or meeting for purposes of discussion.

An important aim of the first hui was for all members of the research team to share their experiences from Phase I, and review the emerging findings. The data at that point indicated that, in line with the recommendations of Ellis (2005), all of the teachers viewed language teaching and learning primarily from a communicative perspective. With regard to developing intercultural capability, the teachers were not aware of the Newton et al. (2010) principles or the intercultural expectations embedded in the curriculum, and an intercultural focus was not evident in their practice (Howard et al., 2016). In line with the background we presented in Chap. 3, this finding was not unanticipated, and the intercultural dimension became a specific focus for the remainder of the two days.

We held workshops to introduce the teachers to the six Newton et al. (2010) principles and to facilitate understandings of the distinction between cultural knowledge and an intercultural dimension in language teaching. This included background reading to introduce the teacher participants to the key messages of the Newton et al. report. It also included short presentations by two people who had undertaken prior research into the intercultural in New Zealand—Kennedy and Ramírez—who shared aspects of their own studies and findings (as reported in Chap. 3). We also reviewed with the teachers the teaching as inquiry cycle proposed by the NZC, and began to explore foci that each teacher could use for the intercultural learning opportunities they would undertake with their own classes over the following two school terms.

As explained in Chap. 1, we approached the intercultural inquiries as a bottom-up process, whereby we supported the five teacher partners in developing their inquiries, while also taking a position of respect for each teacher's knowledge of their own class and context. As such, we probed and questioned the teachers, individually and as a group, as they began to frame their inquiries, but we refrained from prescribing specific intercultural outcomes and maintained a largely non-interventionist position with regard to other aspects of their planning and delivery.

Subsequent to the two-day hui, the teaching as inquiry model was used as an operational and reflective framework as the teachers proceeded to carry out the intercultural inquiries with their classes over the following two terms. These were documented by the research team, who observed their teacher partners' classes on at least three occasions, and undertook reflective 20–40 min debriefing conversations after each observation. At the end of the inquiry cycle in each of the five classes, we held

40–60 min summative interviews with each teacher, and 35–40 min focus group interviews with two groups of three to four students from each of the observed language classes (randomly selected from those who had consented to be interviewed)—in all, a total of 31 students over ten focus group sessions.

4.8.3 Phase III (February 2017–September 2017)

At the beginning of the 2017 school year, the five researchers and four Phase III teachers[6] met for another two days to share each teacher's Phase II inquiry and consider the Phase II findings. In order to take advantage of potential insights from delayed reflection, the teachers were asked to write two reflective pieces: in the first, to be completed prior to the meeting, the teachers reflected on the inquiries they had completed in Phase II; the second was a survival memo (Brookfield, 1995) where the teachers externalised their (tacit) reflections indirectly by passing on advice on intercultural teaching to a fictional new member of the project.

In preparation for Phase III, we explored the Newton et al. (2010) principles more deeply with the teachers, and went on to examine some of the pedagogical applications of intercultural principles as exemplified in Liddicoat (2008). Preliminary ideas for the Phase III inquiries were also explored, with the teachers deciding whether to continue with the same inquiry with their 2017 class (which in all cases apart from Lillian would be a new class) or develop a new inquiry. A similar cycle to that undertaken in Phase II was then followed, whereby we documented the inquiries through classroom observations, post-lesson reflective interviews and summative interviews with the teachers, and focus group interviews with two groups of students from each class—in this case, a total of 28 students over eight focus group sessions.

4.8.4 Phase IV (September 2017–December 2017)

In the final phase of the study, each teacher wrote a reflective account of their journey throughout the project, including the rationale for their pedagogical decisions at different points, challenges, "ah-ha" moments, and perceived outcomes of their inquiries. The team then worked together to synthesise the experiences that emerged from the teachers' research journeys in the form of a series of succinct "engaging examples of practice," following a model of case studies already available to support teachers to develop key competencies across the different learning areas of the NZC (TKI, 2015). We framed these as a professional learning tool and a resource to support other primary/intermediate school teachers with developing their own L2 programmes to enhance their learners' intercultural capability (East et al., 2018).

---

[6] As previously noted, Tamara was unable to take part in Phase III.

4.9 Data Analysis and Reporting

The use of a number of different data collection methods and sources added richness to our data and facilitated triangulation of emerging themes throughout the analysis stages. Close collaboration and consultation within the teacher-researcher team was an important aspect of the quality assurance processes throughout the project, and regular member checking contributed to the accuracy and interpretive validity of the findings (Miles et al., 2014). As explained earlier, extensive field notes were taken during each lesson observation, and all the individual interviews and focus group discussions were audio-recorded and transcribed. In keeping with the interpretivist paradigm, we then conducted an iterative thematic analysis, with initial inductive coding to identify emerging themes, and refinement of these through a collaborative process with discussions across the team at multiple points throughout the project.

The Phase I questionnaire, interview and observation data were analysed using three frameworks as interpretive lenses: the ten Ellis (2005) principles; the six Newton et al. (2010) principles; and the key competencies in the NZC. This provided us with detailed descriptions of the cases, including each teacher's conceptualisations of effective language pedagogy, and the influence of those conceptualisations on their L2 teaching practices at that point. The Newton et al. principles were also used as initial "touchstones" during the preliminary analysis by the five researchers of the data from the Phase II and Phase III classroom observations, teacher interviews and reflections.

We also noted in Chap. 2 that Byram (e.g., 1997, 2021) framed what he perceived was required for intercultural capability in terms of helping learners to develop several *savoirs*, or "knowledges." Byram (2009) introduced the notion of the interculturally competent L2 speaker as someone who possesses "some or all of the five savoirs of intercultural competence to some degree" (p. 327). We drew on Byram's *savoirs* model as a starting point to examine the student focus group responses and look for evidence of the extent to which the *students* reported intercultural gains.

The *savoirs* represent different dimensions of knowledge that are relevant to the general processes that contribute not only to interactions between two (or several) individuals but also to how social groups might behave both in the target language country and in the L2 learner's own country. The five components of the model are illustrated in Table 4.2. They should not be seen in isolation or assumed to develop in language users in a linear way. Rather, they should be seen as interacting components of the successful intercultural interlocutor. Thus, in reality, the *savoirs* form part of a whole where each component interacts with the others.

Byram (2021) regarded *savoir s'engager* as "a crucial element" in the development of intercultural capability (p. 59). In particular, *savoir s'engager* encourages language learners to "reflect critically on the values, beliefs, and behaviors of their own society … through comparative study of other societies" (Byram, 2009, p. 323). By way of expansion, East (2012) explained that this includes "comparison and contrast between cultures, and the space to explore the feelings evoked

Table 4.2 Byram's *savoirs*

Savoir	Definition	Essential positioning
savoir être (knowing how to *be*)	The ability to *accept* that one's own values, beliefs and behaviours are not necessarily the "right" or "only" ones, and to see how those values, beliefs and behaviours might look to an outsider	This is who I am (it is neither right nor wrong, it just is)
savoir comprendre (knowing how to *understand*)	The ability to *compare and interpret* documents or events from one's own culture alongside those from another culture	This is who I am in *comparison* with who you are
savoir apprendre (knowing how to *learn*)	The ability to *acquire* new knowledge of a culture and cultural practices	I need to know *more* about who you are
savoir faire (knowing how to *do*)	The ability to *apply* knowledge of a culture and cultural practices appropriately when interacting in real time with people from the target culture	I need to *apply* that knowledge as I interact with you
savoir s'engager (knowing how to *engage*)	The ability to *evaluate critically* the perspectives, practices and products in one's own and other cultures	I need to be willing to *evaluate critically* both who I am and who you are

by the encounter with the 'other'" (p. 141). This positioning is, however, as Byram et al. (2002) put it, "never a completed process." Rather, language users need to be "constantly aware of the need to adjust, to accept and to understand other people" (p. 7).

Regarding the focus group data, mapping intercultural development, and particularly Byram's *savoir s'engager* or "perspective shift," remains challenging—not least in the case of children. In the context of adult education, Mezirow's (2009) transformative learning theory has often been drawn on, but this was not appropriate for the young learners in our study. We considered, however, that the *savoirs* represented a theoretically grounded and relevant means of helping to identify and categorise any learning and intercultural shifts that may have taken place for the learners in our project.

As our analysis progressed, we developed five components of learning through which we examined the students' journeys:

1. knowledge of facts
2. noticing differences
3. openness to difference
4. comfortableness with difference, and
5. "third place" positioning.

4.9 Data Analysis and Reporting

We need to stress that while this framework provided an accessible lens through which to consider the students' intercultural gains, the five components (as with the *savoirs*) are not intended to represent fixed or linear levels of attainment. Rather, the components are intended to indicate the general direction of intercultural development, as opposed to rigid, lock-step, unidirectional or unidimensional progressions. Indeed, it became evident that these five components can and do co-exist in practice, and the students appeared to transition both backwards and forwards between different points during the intercultural explorations and as they discussed their experiences with each other.

Emerging themes from the teachers' and students' data were shared and discussed with the teachers during each of the two-day hui, and were examined more closely in concert with the teachers' own perceptions about their students' learning. As part of this process, the full team (teachers and researchers) also collectively examined a student focus group transcript, discussing possible indicators of the students' intercultural learning and development.

In Phase IV, the emergent themes and indicators of intercultural capability were revisited by the researchers, and, along with the teachers' final reflective statements, these informed the analysis for the engaging examples of practice as well as the accounts that follow in Chaps 5 and 6. In Chap. 7, we draw further on the constructs of collaborative action research (e.g. Burns, 1999, 2019), communities of practice (Lave & Wenger, 1991) and practitioner inquiry (Baumfield et al., 2012), among others, as we examine our journey as researchers and teacher educators, and analyse some "critical incidents" (Brandenburg, 2008; Tripp, 2012) that we identified as we looked back on the project.

4.9.1 Data Source Identifiers

It is important to note that, starting from our initial approach to the teachers and the schools, we secured teachers' consent to use their names in all public-facing documentation and in presentations. However, consistent with our undertakings to the students and their caregivers, all student data were anonymised. There are of course risks inherent in not anonymising all sources. This approach is nonetheless consistent with the requirement of the project's funder, New Zealand's Ministry of Education, that the project should be undertaken as a genuine and transparent teacher-researcher partnership through which reciprocal learning and growth are anticipated.

The remaining chapters include direct quotes from the data sources. The following conventions are used to identify the source of quotations:

- Teacher quotations: when it is not immediately apparent from the context, these are noted descriptively to indicate the source and/or timing where relevant (e.g. "Phase II hui").

- Student quotations (from focus groups): these are identified by pseudonyms for the students, followed by the language they were studying (which, therefore, identifies the teacher, but maintains the anonymity of the students). In the case of students studying Mandarin, they are distinguished by Mandarin 1 (taught by Lillian) and Mandarin 2 (taught by Kelly).

The next three chapters present the data we collected, with specific focus on the students (Chap. 5), the teachers (Chap. 6), and ourselves as researchers/teacher educators (Chap. 7).

References

Aitken, G., & Sinnema, C. (2008). *Effective pedagogy in Social Sciences/Tikanga ā Iwi: Best evidence synthesis iteration [BES]*. Ministry of Education. https://www.educationcounts.govt.nz/publications/series/2515/35263

Allwright, D., & Hanks, J. (2009). *The developing language learner: An introduction to exploratory practice*. Palgrave Macmillan.

Bagnoli, A., & Clark, A. (2010). Focus groups with young people: A participatory approach to research planning. *Journal of Youth Studies, 13*(1), 101–119.

Baumfield, V., Hall, E., & Wall K. (2012). *Action research in education: Learning through practitioner enquiry* (2nd ed.). Sage.

Bolstad, R., Hipkins, R., & Stevens, L. (2013). *Measuring New Zealand students' international capabilities: An exploratory study*. Ministry of Education.

Brandenburg, R. (2008). *Powerful pedagogy: Self-study of a teacher educator's practice*. Springer.

Brookfield, S. (1995). *Becoming a critically reflective teacher*. Jossey-Bass.

Burns, A. (1999). *Collaborative action research for English language teachers*. Cambridge University Press.

Burns, A. (2019). Action research: Developments, characteristics, and future directions. In J. Schwieter & A. Benati (Eds.), *The Cambridge handbook of language learning* (pp. 166–185). Cambridge University Press.

Butler, D. L., & Schnellert, L. (2012). Collaborative inquiry in teacher professional development. *Teaching and Teacher Education, 28*, 1206–1220.

Byram, M. (1997). *Teaching and assessing intercultural communicative competence*. Multilingual Matters.

Byram, M. (2009). Intercultural competence in foreign languages: The intercultural speaker and the pedagogy of foreign language education. In D. K. Deardorff (Ed.), *The Sage handbook of intercultural competence* (pp. 321–332). Sage.

Byram, M. (2021). *Teaching and assessing intercultural communicative competence: Revisited* (2nd ed.). Multilingual Matters.

Byram, M., Gribkova, B., & Starkey, H. (2002). *Developing the intercultural dimension in language teaching: A practical introduction for teachers*. Council of Europe.

Carr, W., & Kemmis, S. (1986). *Becoming critical: Education, knowledge and action research*. Falmer Press.

Cochran-Smith, M., & Lytle, S. (2009). *Inquiry as stance: Practitioner research for the next generation*. Teachers College Press.

Conway, C., & Richards, H. (2018). 'Lunchtimes in New Zealand are cruel': Reflection as a tool for developing language learners' intercultural competence. *The Language Learning Journal, 46*(4), 371–383.

References

Cook-Sather, A. (2008). 'What you get is looking in the mirror, only better': Inviting students to reflect (on) college teaching. *Reflective Practice, 9*(4), 473–483.

Creswell, J. W., & Plano Clark, V. L. (2011). *Designing and conducting mixed methods research* (2nd ed.). Sage.

Crotty, M. (1998). *The foundation of social research: Meaning and perspectives in the research process.* Sage.

East, M. (2012). *Task-based language teaching from the teachers' perspective: Insights from New Zealand.* John Benjamins.

East, M. (2014). Mediating pedagogical innovation via reflective practice: A comparison of pre-service and in-service teachers' experiences. *Reflective Practice, 15*(5), 686–699.

East, M., Tolosa, C., Biebricher, C., Howard, J., & Scott, A. (2018). *Enhancing language learners' intercultural capability: A study in New Zealand schools.* Languages Research NZ. https://learning-languages.tki.org.nz/Pedagogy-and-research

Ellis, R. (2005). *Instructed second language acquisition: A literature review.* Ministry of Education.

Ferguson, P. B. (2012). *Becoming a reflective practitioner.* The University of Waikato Teaching Development Unit.

Howard, J., Biebricher, C., Tolosa, C., Scott, A., & East, M. (2016). Principles and beliefs behind teachers' existing intercultural language teaching practices. *The New Zealand Language Teacher, 42*, 31–43.

Howard, J., Scott, A., & East, M. (2015). Sparkly and pink and bright: Investigating intercultural learning in a New Zealand primary language class. *The New Zealand Language Teacher, 41*, 34–47.

Kennedy, J. (2016). *Exploring opportunities for developing intercultural competence through intercultural communicative language teaching (ICLT): A case study in a Chinese as a foreign language classroom in a New Zealand high school* [Masters dissertation, Victoria University of Wellington, New Zealand].

Killion, J., & Todnem, G. (1991). A process of personal theory building. *Educational Leadership, 48*(6), 14–16.

Lave, J., & Wenger, E. (1991). *Situated learning: Legitimate peripheral participation.* Cambridge University Press.

Liddicoat, A. (2008). Pedagogical practice for integrating the intercultural in language teaching and learning. *Japanese Studies, 28*(3), 277–290.

Lincoln, Y. S., & Guba, E. G. (1985). *Naturalistic inquiry.* Sage.

Loughran, J. (2010). Reflection through collaborative action research and inquiry. In N. Lyons. (ed.). *Handbook of reflection and reflective inquiry: Mapping a way of knowing for professional reflective inquiry* (pp. 399–413). Springer.

Manfra, M. M. (2019). Action research and systematic change in teaching practice. *Review of Research in Education, 43*(1), 163–196.

Mezirow, J. (2009). Transformative learning theory. In J. Mezirow & E. W. Taylor (Eds.), *Transformative learning in practice: Insights from community, workplace, and higher education* (pp. 18–32). Jossey Bass.

Miles, M., Huberman, M., & Saldaña, J. (2014). *Qualitative data analysis: A methods sourcebook* (3rd ed). Sage.

Ministry of Education. (2007). *The New Zealand Curriculum.* Learning Media.

Muijs, D., Kyriakides, L., van der Werf, G., Creemers, B., Timperley, H., & Earl, L. (2014). State of the art—Teacher effectiveness and professional learning. *School Effectiveness and School Improvement, 25*(2), 231–256.

National Library of New Zealand. (n.d.). *Understanding inquiry learning.* https://natlib.govt.nz/schools/school-libraries/library-services-for-teaching-and-learning/supporting-inquiry-learning/understanding-inquiry-learning

Newton, J., Yates, E., Shearn, S., & Nowitzki, W. (2010). *Intercultural Communicative Language Teaching: Implications for effective teaching and learning—A literature review and an evidence-based framework for effective teaching.* Ministry of Education.

Oranje, J. (2016). *Intercultural Communicative Language Teaching: Enhancing awareness and practice through cultural portfolio projects* [Doctoral thesis, University of Otago, New Zealand].

Ramírez, E. (2018). *The intercultural dimension in language classrooms in Aotearoa New Zealand: A comparative study across languages and teachers' levels of proficiency* [Doctoral thesis, University of Auckland, New Zealand].

Schön, D. A. (1983). *The reflective practitioner: How professionals think in action.* Basic Books.

Schön, D. A. (1987). *Educating the reflective practitioner: Toward a new design for teaching and learning in the professions.* Jossey-Bass.

Scott, A. (2014). *Teachers of additional languages in New Zealand schools: A national survey and case studies.* [Doctoral thesis, Massey University, New Zealand].

Scott, A. J., & Butler, P. J. (2007). My teacher is learning like us: Teachers and students as language learners. *The New Zealand Language Teacher, 33,* 11–16.

Stake, R. (2006). *Multiple case study analysis.* Guilford Press.

TKI. (2015). K*ey competencies and effective pedagogy.* https://nzcurriculum.tki.org.nz/Key-competencies/Key-competencies-and-effective-pedagogy

TKI. (n.d.). *Collaborative teacher inquiry.* https://elearning.tki.org.nz/Professional-learning/Teacher-inquiry/Collaborative-inquiry

Tripp, D. (2012). *Critical incidents in teaching developing professional judgment.* Routledge.

Yin, R. (2014). *Case study research: Design and methods* (5th ed.). Sage.

Open Access This chapter is licensed under the terms of the Creative Commons Attribution 4.0 International License (http://creativecommons.org/licenses/by/4.0/), which permits use, sharing, adaptation, distribution and reproduction in any medium or format, as long as you give appropriate credit to the original author(s) and the source, provide a link to the Creative Commons license and indicate if changes were made.

The images or other third party material in this chapter are included in the chapter's Creative Commons license, unless indicated otherwise in a credit line to the material. If material is not included in the chapter's Creative Commons license and your intended use is not permitted by statutory regulation or exceeds the permitted use, you will need to obtain permission directly from the copyright holder.

Chapter 5
Journeys Towards Intercultural Capability: The Students' Voices

5.1 Introduction

In Chap. 4, we provided a full introduction to the two-year project that is the focus of this book, including the theoretical frameworks underpinning the study, and an introduction to the participants. In this chapter, we turn our attention to the inquiries[1] undertaken by the five teacher partners as they, for the first time, reframed their additional language (L2) programmes to incorporate an explicit intercultural stance with their 11–13 year-old beginner language learners.

The key focus of this chapter is on the students' journeys towards intercultural capability. To *contextualise* the voice that this chapter gives to the student participants, we start by presenting vignettes of what the *teachers* actually did with their students. We outline the inquiry foci that each teacher planned, along with the intercultural outcomes they hoped to achieve. We then present accounts of aspects of the inquiries, based primarily on classroom observations that documented some of the interculturally focused language lessons. The first part of the chapter does not therefore attend directly to the student voice. However, it presents data on the lessons and the teachers' actions, thereby outlining what the students experienced in the classroom and providing important background for the subsequent presentation of the students' perspectives.

In the second part of the chapter, we give voice to the student participants, drawing on data gathered from summative focus groups towards the end of Phases II and III of the project. Here we explore the impact of the new learning opportunities on the students' emergent intercultural growth, drawing primarily on the experiences and understandings the students themselves reported. The intercultural growth that the teachers perceived their students had made is also noted, along with some other,

---

[1] Please see Chap. 4 for a detailed overview of the "teaching as inquiry" model that was central to this project.

unanticipated, outcomes. We finish the chapter by reflecting on the learning reported by students, and parallel learning by the teachers, alongside issues and questions this has raised.

5.2 Contextual Background

As outlined in Chaps. 1 and 4, the participating teachers in our project taught Year 7 or 8 students (11+ to 12+ years of age) in the New Zealand primary/intermediate school context, and were reasonably typical of teachers in the primary/intermediate sectors. They had a range of language teaching experience (from two to ten years), although most had been class teachers for longer than that. All apart from Lillian (a first language [L1] speaker of Mandarin and essentially bilingual in Mandarin and English) had learnt the target language (TL) as L2 and reported their language proficiency to be at a beginner-intermediate level, that is, no higher than B1 on the Common European Framework (Council of Europe, 2001).

When the teachers were initially introduced to the literature on intercultural language teaching as part of a two-day familiarisation meeting (*hui*), two of the six principles proposed by Newton et al. (2010) became specific foci and had the most resonance for the teachers (see Chap. 7)—Principles 3 and 4:

- encourage and develop an exploratory and reflective approach to culture and culture-in-language;
- foster explicit comparisons and connections between languages and cultures (Newton et al., 2010, p. 63).

These two principles align strongly with the expected outcomes for beginner language students within the curriculum document (Ministry of Education, 2007), and are also reflected closely in published achievement objectives (Ministry of Education, 2009) and the goals outlined in the *Learning Languages* curriculum guide (Ministry of Education, 2016).

The Newton et al. (2010) Principles 3 and 4 became the primary (although not exclusive) foci as the teachers planned their lessons. In what follows, we present the teachers' lessons narratively (Chase, 2011) as snapshots of their inquiries as they unfolded. For ease of reference, Table 5.1 presents an overview of participants' language teaching experience, the languages they taught, the weekly time allocation and the focus of each teacher's intercultural inquiry topics in Phases II and III.

Although some of the chosen cultural topics are associated more with traditional "culture as artefact" approaches (Crozet et al., 1999), they can also be explored interculturally (Newton et al., 2010). As reflected in the accounts of the nine inquiries that follow, the intercultural stance is what each teacher intended.

Table 5.1 Participant background information

Participant	Lillian	Kelly	Kathryn	Mike	Tamara[a]
TL	Mandarin 1[b]	Mandarin 2	Japanese	French	Māori
TL proficiency	L1 speaker	Intermediate	Low-intermediate	Low-intermediate	Low-intermediate
Language teaching experience	4 years	2 years	6 years	10 years	2 years
Delivery structure per week	3 × 20 min per week	1 × 30–45 min per week	1 × 30 min over a six-day "week" cycle	2 × 30 min per week	Integrated across all learning areas
Phase II inquiry focus	School sports	Family and student life	Numbers and time	Food and drink	*Te ao kori* (the world of movement)
Phase III inquiry focus	School systems	Colour and clothing	Food culture in Japan	Schools and learning in different cultures	

[a]Tamara did not take part in Phase III of the project
[b]Student quotations in this chapter are identified as being from either Mandarin 1 or Mandarin 2 classes

5.3 Lillian

5.3.1 Phase II Inquiry: Discovering Different Perspectives of School Sports

For her first inquiry, Lillian aimed to problematise surface-level interpretations and develop her Year 7 learners' critical thinking. She particularly wanted her students to "become more empathetic and aware of contrasting perspectives" (Phase II hui) when exploring concepts. Images of children playing sports in China, which Lillian compiled from internet searches she conducted separately in Mandarin and English, formed the basis for her students' own inquiry learning cycles within Lillian's interculturally focused inquiry.

The students began the first observed lesson by sharing on a displayed Google document TL words and phrases that they were familiar with around the topic of sport. Working in pairs, they then orally shared five words and one sentence related to sports, focusing intently as they spoke in Mandarin to each other. They then watched two short video clips about a sports day at a junior high school in China, before reflecting on differences in two sets of images Lillian had downloaded from the internet. A search in English had produced a set of (arguably stereotypical) "unhappy" sports images, which predominantly portrayed a sense of compulsion, order and competitiveness. The video clips Lillian showed similarly depicted sport in China as a very regulated, almost militaristic, activity. In comparison, the images from a search in Chinese portrayed a more positive narrative. Lillian encouraged the class to critically explore, discuss and reflect on the similarities and differences.

When Lillian's students observed that the Chinese students seemed to have been forced into participating, she probed: "But, is that the whole picture? How do we know the reality is broader?"

Lillian took the discussion further in the next lesson, encouraging the students to consider the images from a range of perspectives. She prompted the class, "what do most people that are not from China usually see about school sport?" She then posed the particular inquiry question for this session, "what do most people from China want others to feel about school sports?" The students were very focused as they discussed and recorded different perspectives (in English). One student reported, "the Chinese want people to think they are really good at sport." Another suggested that people from China want others to think they are not forced to do it. Lillian scaffolded further reflection, guiding the students to think beyond homogeneous, "one country – one culture" conceptualisations: "Do all schools in China do sports this way? How do you know? What makes you think that?"

5.3.2 Phase III Inquiry: Using Senses and Feelings to Compare Schooling

Lillian noted that through the prompting and reflecting in the first inquiry, her students were beginning to challenge stereotypical views. She wanted to extend this further with her class as they moved into Year 8 the following year, aiming to foster exploratory mindsets through cultural comparisons and connections (Newton et al.'s [2010] Principles 3 and 4). The context for this was education in China.

The first observed lesson began with the students conducting research on their own devices about schooling for a student in China. Lillian prompted with questions such as "do they start school at 5? Are years organised in the same way?" As the students discussed some of their findings, Lillian drew attention to similarities and differences in practice, and invited a Korean student to make comparisons with the Korean school system. The students then watched a brief clip from a BBC documentary about a Chinese high school. Key messages included the school's allegiance to the Communist party, the strong academic focus, the teacher's role in students' success, and competition for university places. As the students discussed the video (in English), Lillian encouraged deeper reflection and explicit intercultural comparison: "How does this clip make you feel? How did it make you feel about if they failed their exam? What about the students who don't get the teachers' attention?" Alongside the cultural provocations, Lillian also guided the students as they added to a shared Google document to record their observations. When they watched a second video about school life, this time made by Chinese students, Lillian again probed to help the students decentre and consider their reactions further.

In the next observed lesson, Lillian showed the two videos again as triggers for further exploration and comparison. The students recorded their observations and reactions in four categories (what they see, what they hear, what they feel, and ideas generated). Most of the class engaged enthusiastically in the session that followed, comparing and contrasting the videos with their own experiences at school in New Zealand. In particular, they commented on the sense of pressure, attention on just one smart student in a class of sixty and that life seemed easier for them in New Zealand compared to students in China. One student went beyond reflecting from just a student perspective, speculating that the *teacher* in one of the videos may have felt proud to support the top students. Further discussion centred on what Lillian's class perceived as greater conformity in the Chinese schools, based on the students' uniforms, restrictions in voicing their opinions and disciplinary actions.

5.4 Kelly

5.4.1 Phase II Inquiry: Exploring Concepts of Family Through Language and Culture

For her first inquiry, Kelly wanted to give her class opportunities to compare and contrast their own values and beliefs with those held by people in China. She aimed to achieve this with her class of mostly Pasifika-heritage students by exploring aspects of family life.

Focusing initially on language, in the first lesson the students recalled words they already knew in Mandarin relating to family, and reinforced their familiarity by playing a game of *Memory*. Focusing on family size, Kelly then showed the students a photo of a family she had visited in China. In response to her question about why there was only one child in the photo, a student replied that it was because there were too many people (in China). Kelly expanded on this, explaining about China's one-child policy, the rationale for different rules for rural areas, and why some families preferred to have a boy. She also explained that the law had recently changed in China, but "there is a whole generation who grew up without siblings." The students explored how family life might be different for an only child in China, and compared this with their own (mostly larger) families. They also discussed similarities and differences between the types of activities the child in the photo did for fun, and activities they enjoyed themselves. The students then conducted a survey (in Mandarin) to elicit the number and gender of their classmates' siblings. This prompted a number of questions, including about who, specifically, counted as "part of a family."

The second observed lesson focused on the role of grandparents in China. The students played another game of *Memory*, which, this time, included Mandarin words for older and younger siblings, and formal and informal terms of address for parents. Kelly read an account in Mandarin about her own family, while the students wrote their understanding (in English) of what she was saying. This provided the opportunity for more explicit attention to culture-in-language, as Kelly also drew attention to the different names in Mandarin for maternal and paternal grandparents. It also provided a springboard for deeper intercultural reflection and comparison through discussion about the role of grandparents. The students then completed their own family tree and wrote about their families (in Mandarin), using Kelly's earlier account as a model.

5.4.2 Phase III Inquiry: Comparing Values and Beliefs Reflected in Colours and Clothing

At the time of her second intercultural inquiry, Kelly was at a different school, and had a Mandarin Language Assistant (MLA) working alongside her in her language classes. In contrast to the largely Pasifika school community in her previous school, the majority of the students were from New Zealand European or Asian backgrounds, including two fluent Mandarin speakers. As with Kelly's first inquiry, the aim was for her students to reflect, comparatively, on values and beliefs important to Chinese people—this time through explorations of colour and clothing.

As a warm-up exercise in the first observed lesson, Kelly named a series of colours in Mandarin and her students found instances of them around the room. Kelly then introduced an explicit intercultural focus, guiding the class as they discussed what they associated with *hóng sè* (red) in a Chinese context ("flag," "envelopes for new year," "lucky colour"), and compared their associations with the colour red in New Zealand ("stars on the flag," "war and blood," "strawberries [with pavlova])." After a game of *Go Fish* in Mandarin to reinforce the students' colour vocabulary, Kelly introduced the zodiac animal at that time (the rooster), and discussed its characteristics and associated colours. The students then played a barrier game, using prompts on the board to help them instruct their partner (in Mandarin) to colour a picture of a rooster.

The next observed lesson began with a PowerPoint presentation (in English) about *qí páo* (a traditional dress). The MLA drew attention to specific elements of the fabric and design, and clarified when a *qí páo* was usually worn. The students used posters of clothing labelled in *pīn yīn* to support them as they mimed putting on different garments when Kelly called them out in Mandarin. Reintroducing the intended intercultural focus, Kelly elaborated on the meaning of some colours within Chinese and Western cultures, and the students then "dressed" a picture of a puppet, following Kelly's instructions for it to be "labelled in Chinese."

In a subsequent lesson, Kelly introduced the connector *de* for use between an adjective and noun in Mandarin. Some of the students then used *de* as they worked in groups to describe clothing items worn by one of their classmates. After the MLA described some other traditional Chinese clothing, including *hàn fú* (which, like the Korean *hanbok*, is worn by men and women), the intercultural focus continued as the class discussed "skirts" for men in other cultures, with the students adding Scottish, Māori, Samoan and Tongan clothing as examples.

5.5 Kathryn

5.5.1 Phase II Inquiry: Noticing Similarities and Differences in the Use of Time

Teaching in an International Baccalaureate school, Kathryn saw a close alignment between her school's emphasis on reflective learning through student inquiries and Newton et al.'s (2010) Principle 3. Based on this and Principle 4, her first inquiry focused on comparing and contrasting the ways families in New Zealand and Japan use time. In a change from her previous teaching pattern, Kathryn planned to embed cultural aspects into all her lessons.

For the first observed lesson, Kathryn's goal was to develop the students' topic-related language repertoire, particularly in relation to numbers, as a foundation for their intercultural exploration of the use of time. As the students said their phone numbers, Kathryn guided them to notice how they were structured ("we cluster them a little"), before she explained that people in Japan say the word for "dash" when it is written between groups of numbers (e.g., 555 dash 55 dash 55). She introduced a further intercultural element when she later explained about the use of *moshi moshi* as a greeting for answering the phone. The students then practised writing phone numbers in Japanese.

In a later lesson, the students watched a video of Japanese people counting using their fingers. As the students then demonstrated how *they* counted on their fingers, Kathryn encouraged them to make comparisons, not only with the Japanese people they viewed in the video, but also with students in the class from different cultural backgrounds (Newton et al.'s [2010] Principle 5).

To gather up to date information for the inquiry, Kathryn arranged for students on an exchange to Japan (who were not part of the observed class) to document what their host families did in relation to time incidents and the concept of time. The class were to compare this with data they gathered about their own families' use of time. Kathryn began the next observed lesson with a discussion about the relative importance of time for different cultures and different people (such as farmers). The students contributed ideas about why time was important for them. They then watched a PowerPoint presentation that illustrated the concept of Japanese punctuality, and Kathryn gave some anecdotal examples that showed contrasting perspectives on the importance of being on time. To conclude the lesson, the students worked in pairs asking and answering questions in Japanese related to time.

5.5.2 Phase III Inquiry: Using Student Inquiries About Food for Intercultural Exploration

Noting that the intercultural elements in her first inquiry had heightened her students' interest and curiosity, Kathryn's goal for the next inquiry was for her students to go beyond cultural facts and surface-level comparisons, to consider "more the thinking behind" (Phase III hui) particular ways for doing things. Kathryn also wanted to guide her students to notice similarities as well as differences. Capitalising on her students' familiarity with inquiry learning and their strong digital literacy, Kathryn hoped that student-led inquiries around the theme of food in Japan would enrich her students' understanding of Japanese people, rather than just the language.

The unit began with predominantly language-focused lessons in which the students learned the names for food in Japanese, and some compatible sentence structures such as how to express "like," "dislike" and "love." They also watched video clips of Japanese food in a range of contexts, and learned about some of the cultural protocols around food. Kathryn then introduced the inquiry plan to the class, and suggested some themes that provided opportunities for the students to explore the dynamic nature of culture, such as changes in diet and attitudes to food over time. She also provided a list of websites and YouTube videos that might provide starting points as the students selected a focus for their inquiries.

As they researched their chosen topics over the following three lessons, most groups worked intently, organising the information they found into KWL charts (what we already *know*; what we *wonder*; what we have *learned*) in shared Google documents. Kathryn provided encouragement and probed, at times, to help students clarify the goals of their inquiries. She also emphasised to the students that cultural comparison was not an end in itself, and stressed the importance of deeper reflection on "why" in relation to the information they found.

In the next observed lesson, Kathryn used the arrival of other staff to her class as an authentic and context-appropriate opportunity to teach how to greet more than one person using the Japanese conjunction *to* (and). For the remainder of the lesson, the students drew on their KWL charts to create posters on topics such as Japanese school lunches, dining etiquette, tableware, the history and cultural significance of food presentation and the impact of diet on life expectancy. They subsequently shared these with the class.

5.6 Mike

5.6.1 Phase II Inquiry: Challenging Notions of "Normal" Through Food and Drink

Using food as a linguistic and intercultural framework, Mike's aims for his first inquiry were (1) to "challenge the idea of the 'normal' within [the students'] own cultures … to get an idea that there is no real normal," thereby helping his students to "create their own sense of identity" and develop "a greater idea of their own culture" (Phase II hui), and (2) for his beginner level students "to appreciate that culture is quite a complex idea … you can't just say 'people in France do this'" (Phase II interview). That is, he wanted his students to question what might be regarded as "normative," thereby challenging their own preconceived ideas. Importantly, however, Mike did not want these intercultural objectives to diminish the students' language learning opportunities.

In the first of the observed lessons, each student was to survey five classmates (in French) about what they ate for breakfast. Before they began, Mike elicited the appropriate etiquette and phrases for conducting a conversation with someone in French, and, incidentally, drew attention to a link between the dual functionality of *salut* in French and *aroha* in te reo Māori (both functioning as greetings of arrival *and* departure). Using a series of specified question/response structures and a list of five breakfast foods, the students conducted their interviews. They then worked in small groups to record their data in a histogram, with some groups adding an extra bar to represent the (majority of) students who had not eaten anything at all for breakfast. This provided an unexpected but timely segue for a discussion about assumptions and generalising, in which Mike confessed to the students that their survey results challenged his own preconceived ideas about what was "normal" for the class.

A "noticing" activity then followed, with the students watching a YouTube clip of a French family having breakfast. This served as a stimulus for intercultural reflection, during which Mike guided a discussion (in English) about similarities and differences between the video and the students' own breakfasts. The students observed: "they have breakfast together"; "they have all the food spread out on the table"; "[the French family] aren't in a rush"; and, "it's simpler [in New Zealand]." Mike speculated aloud about whether breakfast would be like this for all French families, and probed as the students offered further observations and recounted their experiences in other countries. The lesson concluded with Mike reminding the students that they had just seen "one video of one family in France"—they could not assume it was "typical."

The second observed lesson was similar in structure to the first, and similarly had dual language and intercultural goals. The students began by practising sentences in French in preparation for a survey activity intended to provide multiple opportunities for the students to use the target structures and vocabulary while they gathered data about how often they eat particular items of food. This time, though, many of the students employed a range of "avoidance strategies" and completed the activity with minimal TL use. In the cross-cultural comparison that followed, Mike encouraged the students to reflect on similarities as well as differences between the results of their survey and observations from videos of French meals they had viewed in intervening lessons. Despite Mike's further efforts to elicit some similarities, the students' focus remained almost exclusively on differences.

5.6.2 Phase III Inquiry: Reflecting on School Systems

Although Mike commented that the intercultural focus during his first inquiry added depth to his lessons, and his students "were *beginning* to dispel stereotypes about French culture" (Phase II interview, our emphasis), he wanted (as with Kathryn's second inquiry) to do more to guide his students to understand and appreciate commonalities *as well as* differences between languages and cultures. As a vehicle for this, Mike explored aspects of the French education system with his new Year 7 class, aligning the language objectives for the term, and drawing on "culturally rich resources" (Phase III interview) sourced through the internet to bring French schooling into his classroom. Mike aimed to use deeper reflective questioning throughout these lessons, instead of his earlier pattern of impromptu questions mainly at the end. He also hoped to achieve a "balance" between "the cultural element and the language element" (Phase III interview).

The students' schema for the second inquiry was activated using a video of a young French student reciting a poem about returning to school after the summer break. The class then compared their own feelings about returning after their recent holiday. In the next observed lesson, an authentic French school timetable was used as a medium for both language development and intercultural exploration. Most of the students quickly worked out the days of the week and the school subjects. They then compared the French school week with their own, focusing particularly on the length of the school day and having "free periods." Regarding days for attendance, Mike asked, "who'd be happy to go on Saturday, if you have Wednesday off?" This type of questioning led to a lively discussion about which system the students would prefer if they were able to choose, which they thought French students might prefer, and why. Towards the end of the lesson, when Mike asked a series of factual questions (in English) about the timetable, a larger than usual number of the students responded in French.

In the lessons that followed, the class read accounts about French children's daily routines, watched short videos of French students describing their day at school, and did more activities based around the French school timetable. There was a high level of engagement when Mike probed to elicit the students' thoughts and feelings about commonalities and differences throughout the lessons. Additionally, Mike drew attention to cognates and the origins of words at times, and explored instances of culture-in-language as they arose (Newton et al.'s [2010] Principle 3). In the fourth observed lesson, for example, a discussion about *petit déjeuner* ("small dinner") led to a comparison with the English *breakfast* ("breaking the fast"), which, in turn, led to a discussion about language and cultural change over time. In a later activity that included French addresses, Mike made links to a nearby town in New Zealand founded by French settlers, where the streets are still called *Rue*. Connections such as this appeared to pique the students' interest further, and some previously reticent students engaged enthusiastically in some of the discussions. The students used French to answer questions far more than Mike had experienced earlier, and incorporated French vocabulary they had not been explicitly taught.

5.7 Tamara

5.7.1 Phase II Inquiry: Making Connections Through Movement

Tamara's approach to teaching te reo Māori stems from her belief that no matter what the subject, "there is always a [Māori] component you can weave in" (Phase II interview). Applying this philosophy as much to *tikanga* (values and practices) as she does to language, it was not surprising that Tamara's intercultural goals for this inquiry were the integration of language and culture (Newton et al.'s [2010] Principle 1) and making connections between languages and cultures (Newton et al.'s Principle 4). She wanted her students to go beyond superficial comparisons, to make personal connections with Māori words, and, using Māori concepts, to make connections with each other within their diverse class and school setting. She recognised that this would also help develop her students' key competencies (see Chap. 3), particularly *relating to others*. Tamara selected *te ao kori* (the world of movement) as a conduit and theme for her inquiry.

In the first observed lesson, a traditional Māori games facilitator helped teach Tamara's Year 8 class how to play a game called *kī-o-rahi*. Tamara explained to the students that this is "all about *taniwha* (powerful creatures) and hunting … It's based on a Māori perception of how creatures move." An explanation about the *taniwha* myth provided the cultural context for how the game evolved. As they played the game, the students had opportunities to use the *kīwaha* (Māori colloquial expressions) they had been learning.

The facilitator made further cultural links in the next lesson, as she described how another game, *tapu ae*, relates to traditional Māori warfare. She interspersed Māori words with English as she explained that during *pā* (fortified village) wars, Māori warriors defended their women and babies (represented in the game by tennis balls on upturned cones within a circle at each end of the playing field). Assuming the roles of defenders, attackers and runners, the students then played the game, enthusiastically passing a ball along the playing area and trying to knock their opponents' "babies" out of their "nests." The game provided authentic opportunities for the students to use *kīwaha,* including side-line encouragements, such as *Hopukina!* (Catch it!), and *Ka mau te wehi!* (That's outstanding!). Some of the students carried flashcards to help reinforce these new phrases.

The intercultural focus on *te ao kori* continued in the next lesson as the class compared and reflected on movements across a range of cultures, including Irish dancing, *Siva Tau* (Samoan war dance), and striking a piñata (Mexico). Tamara introduced additional Māori vocabulary when the students needed it to describe some of the movements. The students also learned yoga poses with what Tamara termed "a Māori spin," making links between the sacredness of the head for Māori people and some other cultures. Tamara continued this cross-curricular intercultural approach in a later class about flight (in planes), and another about birds. Throughout the lessons, she drew on the diversity of the class as a pedagogical resource, encouraging students who had lived in other cultural contexts to contribute their experiences and understandings (Newton et al.'s [2010] Principle 5) as she guided the class to make connections—with each other, with their own heritages and with Māori language and culture.

5.8 The Students' Journeys: Emergent Intercultural Growth

Having provided overviews of the observed lessons, in what follows we turn our attention to the students' journeys during the inquiries, drawing primarily on the focus group discussions we had with the students at the end of each inquiry cycle (see also Howard et al., 2019). Using illustrative quotations, we explore the students' reported gains from the opportunities that the nine inquiries presented for intercultural growth as well as "what they *actually* learn from those practices" (Bolstad et al., 2013, p. 17). We follow the students' voices with a brief account of the intercultural growth their teachers perceived had been made.

5.8.1 Facts About the Target Cultures

When the students were asked what they had learned during the inquiries, some of the initial responses related to vocabulary, language functions and pronunciation. With regard to cultural learning, the responses frequently suggested an apparent focus on facts:

There's at least a billion people in China. (Asher, Mandarin 1)[2]

We learnt about the history of the Moa [extinct bird]. (Isla, Māori)

---

[2] Pseudonym.

5.8.2 Noticing Differences

It is possible that the initial factual focus noted above was due, at least in part, to how the opening focus group prompts used by the researchers were framed. Further probing elicited evidence that, within a range of intercultural thematic contexts, students were moved beyond factual knowledge to a position that demonstrated distinct noticing of differences, often triggered by videos they had watched:

> It's not like sports we know. (Simon, Mandarin 1)
>
> The homework and the pressure was bigger, and bigger classrooms and bigger expectations. (Hunter, Mandarin 1)

In many instances, it seemed that images and videos of the target cultures also prompted students to become conscious of their own cultural practices explicitly for the first time:

> Their baths – they would wash themselves off first, then they would hop in a bath to soak. (Cora, Japanese)

This heightened awareness of difference was often expressed comparatively:

> They don't move out of their house until they get married … [whereas] my oldest brother, he has moved out and he's not married. (Bruno, Japanese)
>
> We normally associate [red] with blood, whereas in China it's lucky. (Willow, Mandarin 2)

Not all students demonstrated acceptance of the differences they noticed. First-culture positioning was demonstrated when some of the students discussed what they perceived as peculiarities of practice—at least initially:

> They lock people out of school if they are late, but here we don't (Felix). But if it was not their fault and the bus was late or something they would still get locked out … it's kind of stupid. (Cameron, French)
>
> When you go to the market to buy the iconic breadstick … they would just wrap it in the middle … so it would just leave the rest of the world to touch it … I thought it was really gross and unhygienic. (Cleo, French)

There were further examples of reductive, homogeneous conceptualisations of cultures at the beginning of the inquiries. Gillian, for example, provided a perspective from before the opportunities to reflect on similarities and differences:

> I thought they were weird … three mums sitting at a coffee table eating frogs' legs and snails and doing evil laughs ... and [wearing] the berets. (Gillian, French)

In some cases, however, initial stereotypical understandings were later replaced with more open attitudes and a degree of self-awareness regarding personal positionalities. Declan (Mandarin 1), for example, initially viewed China "as a dark country … corrupted … bad … polluted," but demonstrated developing critical awareness as he later explained that movies had helped shape and reinforce some of his earlier perceptions. Other students, similarly, demonstrated developing abilities to recognise and question some of their initial stereotypes.

5.8.3 Openness to Difference

As the students reflected on similarities and differences, it was evident that some examples of noticing had led them to less rigid "our" and "other" culture standpoints. At times, they expressed this in terms of acceptance of different ways of "doing" and "being":

> Their school day starts earlier than ours and finishes later, and I think they've got quite a bit of homework they have to do each day ... If they want to do this, then it's not abnormal. It is unique to them. (Emmett, Japanese)

Likewise, two students from another class displayed acceptance of difference, and, further, demonstrated their growing reflective capacity as they discussed what they perceived to be a stricter school system:

> I would be pretty stressed [in a Chinese school], but it would help me learn more and be a better person. (Hunter, Mandarin 1)

> I kind of feel the same ... it would be even more stressful, but ... I would learn more and have more time to learn a lot more. (Rhett, Mandarin 1)

For some students, this also extended to empathy with people in situations they perceived would be challenging:

> I would probably feel pretty stressed because I probably deserve a good night's sleep. (Asher, Mandarin 1)

Other students illustrated the beginnings of deeper understandings when they made connections between target cultures and their own or others they knew about:

> Well, there are different tribes within the Māori, and [in China] they have different dresses and different languages. (Stella, Mandarin 2)

At times, increased openness to difference was evident in students' expressions of curiosity or "wonderings" as they considered the possibility of further cultural differences:

> Sometimes I wonder ... how they live ... [whether] their rules and stuff are different. (Isla, Māori)

> ... what church they go to, and how they've grown up. (Sage, Māori)

Reflection on practices in target cultures sometimes led students to make broad generalisations about perceived acceptability if these same practices were used in their own context:

> [In France] the girls usually go up to each other and kiss each other's cheek. In New Zealand, if people did that, they would find it creepy, and you would be alarmed. (Janice, French)

In this instance, the student later demonstrated the ability to view *herself* "as Other" (Kramsch, 2009, p. 18) as she reflected on greeting with a *hongi* (a traditional Māori greeting where noses are pressed together) in her own culture:

> Some of our Māori culture things that we do – people would think we are the weirdest people in the world, because we go up and [she demonstrated a *hongi*], but in other countries, they would be creeped out by that. (Janice, French)

5.8.4 Comfortableness with Difference

There is evidence that several students felt more comfortable with perceived differences as a result of the intercultural orientation in their L2 programmes. This was frequently expressed in terms of movement from an *"at first I thought..."* to a *"now I think..."* position:

> I used to think French people were amazing, magnificent, almost like dolls in a dolls' house, they needed to be put on display. But now I've learnt more about them, I think they are just normal people. They are just doing what their culture says. (Janice, French)
>
> At the start, I thought French people were weirdos, but now I think they are just normal people following their culture. (James, French)

Rather than minimising the differences they observed in an attitude of universalism, these two students had become less judgemental and more comfortable with cultural differences. This attitudinal change was also evident in an exchange where they reflected on possible future interactions with people from the target cultures:

> [Before] I probably would have imitated them and mocked them [but not] now I know their culture. (James, French)
>
> I don't think anyone who learnt about the culture would do anything like that. (Janice, French)

Having reflected on differences, other students were also beginning to understand, or at least think about, how they might engage themselves in interaction with people from the target cultures. Isla, in the Māori class, explained that she could greet Māori people in the community now *in Māori*, not because she did not know how to do this previously, but because she now felt more comfortable about doing it.

For some students, their increased comfortableness with difference was expressed in terms of acceptance and respect:

> You have to respect how [people from other cultures] are different to us ... you have to accept how they are and how they do things. (Khalessi, Mandarin 1)
>
> I understand them better and so I know why they do specific things unlike me or others ... so I kind of respect the other cultures. (Simon, Mandarin 1)

How this might look *in practice* was also discussed:

> I actually went to a Chinese restaurant and ordered it in Chinese ... letting them know that people care about their culture and want to learn more. (Tim, Mandarin 1)

Food appeared to be a salient distinguishing feature of other cultures in a number of discussions. It was also the vehicle through which another student expressed her growth in confidence to engage with cultural otherness. Having initially thought that eating French food "would be really weird," Janice announced enthusiastically at the end of the inquiry, "I really want to go there and try every food they've got." While, at first sight, this modified stance may appear superficial, it revealed a significant underlying shift, from a position of distance from the "other" to a place of willingness to enter comfortably into an intercultural experience that had previously been perceived as "alien."

5.8.5 "Third Place" Positioning

At least one student was explicitly aware that the intercultural exploration, for her, had been transformative. This was expressed simply:

> It has changed me, how I see things ... I normally would see it from that [monocultural] perspective, and now I look at another perspective. (Jade, Japanese)

The student focus groups also revealed that several students experienced learning gains in terms of coming to appreciate and value their own cultures and uniqueness alongside the cultures and uniqueness of others. It was apparent that some students were also beginning to understand what it meant to position themselves in a "third place." Although, at times, they struggled to articulate it, there is evidence above from the focus groups of movement towards spaces of "accommodation" (Liddicoat, 2008, p. 279) in which the students accepted cultural difference as non-threatening, and where their "first culture" positioning could be suspended without needing to discard their own sense of self.

We must nonetheless be cautious with extrapolations. We cannot confidently claim "third place" positioning for any of these students. The intercultural activities they engaged in did not include navigating different cultural perspectives with TL speakers, hence the students' capability to function *inter*dependently with cultural difference is not known. Similarly, articulations of change—such as Isla's intention to greet Māori people using Māori—were, at that point, still intentions rather than enacted. However, it is clear from reflective discussions with the teachers that they also recognised that intercultural learning gains were made by their students during the inquiries. The teachers' journeys in this project are explored in depth in Chap. 6. However, in what follows, we turn briefly to what the teachers reported in regard to their students' learning gains.

5.9 Teachers' Perceptions of Students' Intercultural Learning Gains

The intentional intercultural dimensions within the five teachers' language programmes provided valuable spaces to explore cultural similarities and differences, and help the students develop a greater openness to "otherness." This was particularly apparent in the Phase III post-lesson reflections. Kelly noted that her students had "been exploring stereotypes and discussing them openly." Mike similarly reported that the inquiries provided a context for "allowing students room to explore, challenging their pre-existing ideas." For Lillian, it was about her students "seeing the bigger picture."

An important outcome noted by all the teachers was that their students were beginning to make connections not only between the target culture and their own cultures, but also with students from diverse heritages within their own classes.

In terms of students' engagement with diversity and relating to others, Tamara noted that the inquiry had provided opportunities for genuine social interactions between the different cultures in her class, including the use of some Māori. The teachers also observed that, through the process of intercultural comparison and reflection, students were gaining insights into their own taken for granted values and practices. Mike explained it this way: "they were beginning to pick up some of their own culture as well … actually just looking and reflecting on your own culture … is an important part of it" (Phase II interview).

Examining similarities and differences across cultures also appeared to help move students towards an appreciation that culture cannot be reduced to a single set of beliefs and behaviours. In relation to actual *measurement* of growth within "the intercultural aspect," Mike pointed out that it was not as easy as with language acquisition. Nevertheless, he felt that his students "were beginning to dispel stereotypes about French culture. I think that was beginning to happen" (Phase III reflection). Lillian was also aware that, through prompting and reflection, her students were beginning to challenge stereotypical views, and "they can actually say to me 'well, you know, my friend so and so is from China, they don't celebrate this and also they don't do things in certain ways like that'" (Phase II interview). Tamara concluded that being able to take a different perspective was a key intercultural achievement for her class.

5.10 Unanticipated Outcomes

The student focus group discussions and teachers' reflections revealed that the students' learning journeys extended well beyond the explicit intercultural aims of the inquiries. That is, the students' journeys were not just towards intercultural growth, but also—encouragingly—appeared to lead to increased engagement, greater use of the target language, and heightened motivation for language use, language learning and intercultural interactions in the future. In what follows, we interweave some of the unanticipated comments from the students with the reflections of the teachers.

5.10.1 Increased Engagement

As the students reflected on the inquiries, there were frequent unprompted references to the zest they felt about the opportunities they had had to encounter and consider cultural differences during the interculturally focused activities:

> I enjoyed the fact that I've learned something not just from my culture – that I understand other people. (Brie, Mandarin 1)

> I really enjoy, like, the videos, and the new things we get to learn … they actually tell you more about [Japanese people]. (Carol, Japanese)

> I really enjoyed ... learning what other people do in their lives to see if they are like us. (Zian, Mandarin 2)
>
> I enjoyed learning about other cultures and how they look at things, and the differences and similarities. (Khalessi, Mandarin 1)

The students' enjoyment, enthusiasm and engagement was also a recurring theme in the teachers' post-lesson reflections (and something we pick up on in Chap. 6). Kathryn referred to her students' "passion" when she observed that they were "thoroughly enjoying what they are finding out and they are enjoying sharing it with other people too and discussing it" (Phase III). Lillian and Kelly also reported that their students were more engaged. Kelly attributed this to her students having opportunities to compare and make connections with their own cultures. Further to this, Mike felt that exploring similarities and differences between themselves and *similar-aged* students contributed to the heightened interest and engagement he observed in his classes.

5.10.2 Greater Use of the Target Language

The positive emotions the students expressed in relation to cultural aspects of their learning sometimes also extended to language learning:

> It's just fun learning another language and some of the things they do there to entertain themselves instead of what we do here. (Felix, French)
>
> I really enjoyed learning about the cultures and what they like doing over there and also the language itself. (Louis, Japanese)
>
> I feel good because we are not just learning English. [Mandarin] is very interesting. (Adam, Mandarin 2)

The teachers also perceived changes in their students' attitudes to language learning—not just in terms of engagement, but also their use of the TL. Lillian, for example, noted that her students were "really enthusiastic in the language learning while they're going through this process" (Phase III). Kelly noticed her students were more willing to ask for additional vocabulary items and (Mandarin) characters. Mike similarly perceived increases in his students' motivation for language learning, particularly in his second inquiry (Phase III). He attributed this to the "relevant, authentic and engaging context" the intercultural dimension provided, whereby "students enjoyed the challenge of 'decoding' the resources." He was excited to notice that, although he was spending less time on explicit language teaching during the inquiries, his students were using the TL more. He commented, "[i]t amazed me how much language they have actually learned. Quite obscure words that I never actually taught." In contrast to previous years, he noticed during the inquiries "the students' language use was fun and adaptive ... they were trying to communicate." Tamara also noted that her students appeared to gain in confidence to use the TL during the intercultural activities. This was also mentioned in the students' focus group discussions:

> We don't even really know we are doing it [speaking in Māori] because we are using it so much. (Isla, Māori)

5.10.3 Heightened Motivation for Future Language Use and Language Learning

Kathryn (teaching Japanese) felt that the increased motivation she perceived in her students derived from a sense of increased connection. She noted that although there was no guarantee that the students would continue with the language after intermediate school, "the culture … has really fulfilled the kids." She conjectured that the students' heightened interest may prompt them to study a language at high school, noting that "they feel related, I think, to Japan now" (end of Phase III).

The focus group discussions also suggested that increased cultural understandings the students had gained during the intercultural explorations manifested in greater confidence and positive attitudes towards engaging in the target languages in the future:

> If someone needs help, like in a mall, and they don't know their way around, you could help them. (Mae, French)

> I'll use it when I'm older, when I travel. (Cleo, French)

For some students, this extended beyond just the language they were learning during the inquiries, and indicated an openness to learn (and use) further languages if they had the opportunity:

> I would love to be able to speak to people from other cultures … we've got Chinese people [in our class]. (Isla, Māori)

5.11 Reflections on the Outcomes

As discussed in Chap. 1, the notion of interculturality has been the subject of extensive debate for decades now, with multiple and overlapping nomenclatures, interpretations and definitions contributing to what Dervin et al. (2020) referred to as "muddy roads" (p. 5) in this terrain. This lack of consensus as to what the intercultural dimension actually is raised important questions as we embarked on this project. What does it mean to enhance intercultural capability? What does it mean in relation to language learners? And how is it best evaluated? In response to these questions, we have presented what emerged from the student data as five components of learning (knowledge of facts, noticing differences, openness to difference, comfortableness with difference, and "third place" positioning). We chose these components as an effective lens for us to examine the students' journeys, and begin to explore the extent to which the students themselves reported intercultural gains. It is important to reiterate here that these five components are not conceptualised as either fixed levels of attainment, or unidirectional progressions (see Chap. 4). Rather, they act somewhat as roadside markers, where students' (contextual) positionality at a brief moment in time can be gauged, but from which movement, in *any* direction, is possible.

The students' voices reported above signal shifts—at least in some students—to increased recognition, acceptance and accommodation of cultural difference. Greater "appreciation of diversity" (Dervin, 2007, p. 8) was evident in relation to students' understandings of their own culture(s) as well as those of others. For some students, shifts were evident from initial fixed, stereotypical views to more moderated positions that allowed for spaces of "greyness" and less rigid language–culture associations. The focus group discussions also revealed glimpses of some students' growing recognition of the complexity of the notion of culture, and of relationships between languages and cultures. In addition to reporting greater openness to difference, some students demonstrated growing abilities to decentre and consider alternative perspectives. At least one student was also able to reflect on "the self as foreign"—a competency that Parks (2018, p. 120) suggested is an additional intercultural dimension, or *savoir*, to the five proposed by Byram (1997). Although variable across the students, these outcomes are encouraging.

The teachers similarly perceived that their students had made some worthwhile intercultural learning gains, although, again, these were variable, and were mostly reported by the teachers in somewhat tentative terms. Mike, for example, felt his students "were *beginning* to pick up some of their own culture" and "were *beginning* to dispel stereotypes," adding "I *think* that was beginning to happen" (Phase II interview, our emphases). Lillian similarly hedged when she reported "I *think* they have taken away with them that there are different perspectives at looking at things" (Phase III interview, our emphasis). This, then, raises questions about what type of growth, and how much, teachers can realistically expect when they integrate intercultural pedagogies into L2 programmes with learners of this age.

5.11.1 The Issue of Age

A key goal of intercultural language teaching is to facilitate a "shift in the positioning of learners, so that they are no longer rooted only in the experiences and identity derived from their existing cultures and languages" (Newton et al., 2010, p. 47). However, research from other fields indicates that the extent to which such a "shift" is possible for young learners may be constrained by factors beyond their own control, or that of their teachers.

Pre- and early adolescence—the age of the students in this study—are well documented as periods of considerable maturational developments. These manifest not just in visible characteristics, such as physical growth, but also in less visibly discernible attributes, such as cognitive changes (Berk, 2013). Certainly, it would be unrealistic to assume that the students in this study would have the same levels of reflexivity and criticality expected of older learners. More than this, however, the variability in cognitive, perceptual and neurobiological development in 11–13-year-olds suggests that wide variability in their growing intercultural maturity can also be expected. The students in this study were at differing stages of developing the reflective skills necessary for critical exploration of their own cultures. It is also likely they had experienced wide variability in the extent to which these skills had been fostered explicitly earlier in their education. Indeed, Lillian conjectured that her students had never been asked the types of questions she was posing during her inquiries.

In addition to the skills required for *self*-reflection, specific competencies are needed to make *inter*cultural comparisons and connections (Newton et al.'s [2010] Principle 4). Within an instructed context, this frequently requires students to consider life in cultural settings that are not physically present for them, and, further, are beyond what they have ever personally experienced. This was the case for most of the students in this study (with the possible exception of those learning te reo Māori), since cultural "otherness" was largely encountered in the inquiries indirectly (e.g., through video clips). Development of abstract and hypothetical reasoning skills that are necessary for intercultural comparative and reflective tasks generally begins at around 11–12 years of age (Byrnes, 2003). Hence, it is probable that the capacity for change in students' openness and comfortableness with cultural difference, or "shifts in position," is impacted by the (im)maturity of their developing propositional and abstract thought processes at that age (Berk, 2013).

Research from other disciplines points to further age-related factors that may impact intercultural growth. Social identity research, for example, indicates that an internally defined sense of self (which develops with both time and experience) is required in order to be able to accept difference without feeling threatened (King & Baxter Magolda, 2005). Studies have also found that stereotyping and in-group favouritism ("us" over "them") may be stronger in early adolescents than in older students (Tanti et al., 2011). Neurobiological research similarly suggests that negative out-group ("them" or "other") conceptualisations, such as those reported by some of the students in our study, may reflect age-related underlying capabilities that are still developing (see Howard et al., 2019, for a related discussion).

In summary, the extent to which maturational factors, such as those noted above, interact to impact on learners' developmental receptiveness for intercultural growth remains largely unknown. However, the growth reported by the 11–13 year-old students in our study is evidence of important steps towards intercultural capability that are possible for (at least some) learners of this age.

5.11.2 Affective Impacts

Of further interest, as we consider the outcomes of these intercultural inquiries, is the potential impact the inquiries had on other aspects of the students' language learning journeys. Certainly, the unanticipated outcomes (reported earlier) raise questions about the extent to which the intercultural dimension, in and of itself, influenced the students' overall engagement and sense of enjoyment, and further, the possibility of consequential impacts on their language learning and language use.

The role of socio-affective factors in L2 education has been the subject of extensive investigation since the early 1970s. Nevertheless, until recently, studies have focused predominantly on negative emotions, with anxiety, in particular, receiving significant attention (see Horwitz, 2010, for a timeline of research in this area). It is only in the last decade, as interest in positive affective variables across the wider educational sphere has increased, that positive emotions (such as enjoyment) have become more prominent in second language acquisition research (see, e.g., Dewaele & MacIntyre, 2014; MacIntyre et al., 2016).

Studies in educational psychology suggest that positive academic emotions play a key role in sustaining motivation (Pekrun & Linnenbrink-Garcia, 2014). This aligns with some of our findings. As noted earlier, students in the focus group discussions frequently referred to enjoyment, in relation to both the intercultural inquiries and language learning. There was evidence that the interculturally focused inquiries may have heightened some students' motivation, not just in relation to cultural understandings, but also in seeing themselves using the TL in the future.

Research also suggests that positive emotions foster behaviours such as "play, creativity, curiosity, and exploration" (Boudreau et al., 2018, p. 152). Again, this resonates with reports from the students and the teachers in our study. As we pointed out earlier, Mike (teaching French), for example, noted that his students' language use during his second inquiry was "fun and adaptive." The teachers and students also reported increased interest and curiosity. Boudreau et al. (2018) further suggested, specifically in relation to language learning, that positive emotions may "broaden the perspective of an individual learner, facilitating engagement with the language" (p. 152). This was also evident in our findings, with teachers reporting that their students had greater interest in acquiring new vocabulary and more *use* of the language during some of the inquiries.

Whether, and to what extent, positive emotions resulting from engagement in the intercultural inquiries influenced the students' language learning in this study remains conjecture. Enjoyment, in itself, can be associated with other factors, and its cause and effects in this study cannot be isolated from other variables. However, the possibility that integration of an intercultural dimension in language programmes may have a positive effect on students' language learning, and on their attitudes to language learning in the future, is exciting. Certainly, the unanticipated outcomes of this study signal this as a fertile area for further investigation.

5.12 Conclusion

The principal goal of our study was to support teachers as they aimed to integrate an intercultural dimension into their L2 programmes. The anticipated outcome was "shifts" in the student travellers as they journeyed towards greater understandings of themselves and cultural others. It is evident from the findings that, using Newton et al.'s (2010) principles as a guide, the teachers had certainly begun the process of "the bringing together of worlds" for their students. More than this, it seemed that the teachers were successful in "lighting a path" for their students' intercultural growth, and perhaps also for their language learning journeys, that they may otherwise not have embarked on. That said, evidence gathered from the teachers through reflective interviews after each observation and comments made during the two two-day hui (start of Phases II and III) revealed several tensions in practice.

In Chap. 6, we turn to the teachers, and uncover not only the positives they reported, but also the challenges they encountered, as they undertook their journeys with us.

References

Berk, L. (2013). *Child development* (9th ed.). Pearson.
Bolstad, R., Hipkins, R., & Stevens, L. (2013). *Measuring New Zealand students' international capabilities: An exploratory study*. Ministry of Education.
Boudreau, C., MacIntyre, P. D., & Dewaele, J.-M. (2018). Enjoyment and anxiety in second language communication: An idiomatic approach. *Studies in Second Language Learning and Teaching, 8*(1), 149–170.
Byram, M. (1997). *Teaching and assessing intercultural communicative competence*. Multilingual Matters.
Byrnes, J. (2003). Cognitive development in adolescence. In G. Adams & M. Berzonsky (Eds.), *The Blackwell handbook of adolescence* (pp. 227–246). Blackwell.
Chase, S. E. (2011). Narrative inquiry: Still a field in the making. In N. K. Denzin & Y. S. Lincoln (Eds.), *The Sage handbook of qualitative research* (pp. 421–434). Sage.
Council of Europe. (2001). *Common European framework of reference for languages*. Cambridge University Press.
Crozet, C., Liddicoat, A. J., & Lo Bianco, J. (1999). Intercultural competence: From language policy to language education. In J. Lo Bianco, A. J. Liddicoat, & C. Crozet (Eds.), *Striving for the third place: Intercultural competence through language education* (pp. 1–20). Language Australia.
Dervin, F. (2007). *An introduction to proteophilic competences*. http://citeseerx.ist.psu.edu/viewdoc/download?doi=10.1.1.602.9163&rep=rep1&type=pdf
Dervin, F., Moloney, L., & Simpson, A. (2020). *Intercultural competence in the work of teachers: Confronting ideologies and practices*. Routledge.
Dewaele, J.-M., & MacIntyre, P. D. (2014). The two faces of Janus? Anxiety and enjoyment in the foreign language classroom. *Studies in Second Language Learning and Teaching, 4*(2), 237–274.
Horwitz, E. (2010). Foreign and second language anxiety. *Language Teaching, 43*(2), 154–167.
Howard, J., Tolosa, C., Biebricher, C., & East, M. (2019). Shifting conceptualisations of foreign language teaching in New Zealand: Students' journeys towards developing intercultural capability. *Language and Intercultural Communication, 19*(6), 555–569.
King, P., & Baxter Magolda, M. (2005). A developmental model of intercultural maturity. *Journal of College Student Development, 46*(6), 571–592.
Kramsch, C. (2009). *The multilingual subject: What language learners say about their experience and why it matters*. Oxford University Press.
Liddicoat, A. (2008). Pedagogical practice for integrating the intercultural in language teaching and learning. *Japanese Studies, 28*(3), 277–290.

MacIntyre, P. D., Gregersen, T., & Mercer, S. (Eds.). (2016). *Positive psychology in SLA*. Multilingual Matters.
Ministry of Education. (2007). *The New Zealand curriculum*. Learning Media.
Ministry of Education. (2009). *Curriculum achievement objectives by learning area*. http://nzcurriculum.tki.org.nz/The-New-Zealand-Curriculum
Ministry of Education. (2016). *Learning languages curriculum guide: Version 4*. http://seniorsecondary.tki.org.nz/Learning-languages
Newton, J., Yates, E., Shearn, S., & Nowitzki, W. (2010). *Intercultural communicative language teaching: Implications for effective teaching and learning—A literature review and an evidence-based framework for effective teaching*. Ministry of Education.
Parks, E. (2018). *Communicative criticality* and *savoir se reconnaître*: Emerging new competencies of criticality and intercultural communicative competence. *Language and Intercultural Communication, 18*(1), 107–124.
Pekrun, R., & Linnenbrink-Garcia, L. (2014). *International handbook of emotion in education*. Routledge.
Tanti, C., Stukas, A., Halloran, M., & Foddy, M. (2011). Social identity change: Shifts in social identity during adolescence. *Journal of Adolescence, 34*(3), 555–567.

Open Access This chapter is licensed under the terms of the Creative Commons Attribution 4.0 International License (http://creativecommons.org/licenses/by/4.0/), which permits use, sharing, adaptation, distribution and reproduction in any medium or format, as long as you give appropriate credit to the original author(s) and the source, provide a link to the Creative Commons license and indicate if changes were made.

The images or other third party material in this chapter are included in the chapter's Creative Commons license, unless indicated otherwise in a credit line to the material. If material is not included in the chapter's Creative Commons license and your intended use is not permitted by statutory regulation or exceeds the permitted use, you will need to obtain permission directly from the copyright holder.

Chapter 6
Journeys Towards Intercultural Capability: The Teachers' Voices

6.1 Introduction

In Chap. 5, we presented overviews of the interculturally focused lessons the teacher participants had facilitated during the two inquiry cycles in our two-year project, alongside the intercultural learning that the students reported had taken place for them. We also included some reflections from the teachers regarding their students' perceived intercultural learning gains. Building on that initial presentation, this chapter continues an exploration of facets of the reflections of the five participating teachers on their inquiries over the duration of the project, including a more thorough discussion of their thoughts and reflections on their endeavours to promote the intercultural dimension in their teaching.

We have previously published some aspects of the teachers' stories emerging from Phase II of the project (Biebricher et al., 2019; East et al., 2017; Tolosa et al., 2018). In this chapter, we re-present key data emerging from Phase II and also include insights expressed by the teacher participants in Phase III. Findings are based on individual post-observation reflective teacher-researcher interviews that took place on at least three occasions during the two inquiry cycles, discussions among the teacher-researcher partners as a group during the two *hui* (two-day meetings) that took place at the start of each inquiry cycle, teachers' written reflections as their inquiries were ongoing, and summative written reflections once the inquiries had been completed (see Chap. 4 for more detail on all phases of the project, including data collection processes).

Chapter 5 presented a largely positive account of what the teachers did with their students in the course of the project and what the students reported that they had learned. This chapter starts with briefly contextualising the *challenges* faced in particular by primary/intermediate school additional language (L2) teachers in the New Zealand context. The chapter then looks at the teachers' reported developments in the course of the project, highlighting where those developments intersect for all or most of the participants. We identify those intersections as emerging themes and use them to present our findings. We portray the teachers' challenges as salient features of encountering a new construct and a different way of approaching their language teaching. Those challenges pave the way for reflection on what the participants appeared to learn as they continued on their journeys, leading to a presentation of the deeper insights and benefits the teachers identified by the end of Phase III of the project. We also draw readers' attention to the teachers' diverging experiences.

6.2 Contextual Background

In Chap. 3, we pointed out that New Zealand's teachers cannot rely on specific documents or support resources that outline how they might develop learners' intercultural capabilities, which (as we noted in Chap. 1) we define as "the ability to relate comfortably with people from diverse linguistic and cultural backgrounds, appreciating and valuing the learners' own cultures and uniqueness alongside the cultures and uniqueness of others" (Biebricher et al., 2019, p. 606). That is, two significant literature review reports (Ellis, 2005; Newton et al., 2010) provide bigger picture conceptualisations. However, as a consequence of the introduction of the revised *New Zealand Curriculum* (NZC) (Ministry of Education, 2007), language-specific support documents that proposed, in a step-by-step, hierarchical and sequential way, how teachers might teach the target language (TL) have officially been withdrawn. Teachers are now required to decide for themselves the content they would like to deliver within the overarching and quite generic expectations of the three strands of *Learning Languages* (*communication; language knowledge* and *cultural knowledge*). Furthermore, although achievement objectives for the *cultural knowledge* strand have been published (Ministry of Education, 2009), and these became a guide for us as we worked with the teacher partners in this project, they are provided as a general guideline. Thus, two key documents (Ministry of Education, 2007, 2009) offer teachers only limited guidance and no prescription in how desired intercultural outcomes should be achieved.

As a consequence of a lack of specific direction, teachers are reliant on their own knowledge and ideas as they attempt to incorporate an intercultural dimension into their language teaching.[1] This level of autonomy might seem like a benefit for teachers who are now free to be creative with their L2 classes. In many cases, however, it can be challenging, particularly for teachers who are less experienced. As we also noted in Chaps. 1 and 3, an additional challenge is the fact that many primary and intermediate teachers, like the ones in our study, are classroom teachers who may be encouraged by their schools to teach a language, but may not have received any specific teacher education, preparation or professional development to do so. Very often, they are on similar language learning journeys to their students and are learning and discovering the target language and culture alongside their students (Scott & Butler, 2007).

---

[1] This does not mean that no support resources are available. See Chap. 3 for a brief overview.

6.4 Preparing Teachers for Their Inquiry Cycles

Table 6.1 Participant inquiry foci

Participant	Lillian	Kelly	Kathryn	Mike	Tamara
TL	Mandarin	Mandarin	Japanese	French	Māori
Delivery structure per week	3 × 20 min per week	1 × 30–45 min per week	1 × 30 min over a six-day "week" cycle	2 × 30 min per week	Integrated across all learning areas
Phase II inquiry focus	School sports	Family and student life	Numbers and time	Food and drink	*Te ao kori* (the world of movement)
Phase III inquiry focus	School systems	Colour and clothing	Food culture in Japan	Schools and learning in different cultures	

6.3 The Participating Teachers

As explained in Chap. 4, the teachers in this project came from a variety of backgrounds, and taught different languages, in different school contexts, with varying structural affordances and constraints. They also differed by way of their pedagogical approaches, proficiency in the languages they taught, and the extent of their personal experiences within the TL cultures.

What all five of the teachers had in common from the outset of the project was their strong interest in ongoing learning to enhance their language programmes. However, none of the participants had formally undertaken any language-specific teacher education, although two teachers, Mike and Kelly, had participated in the year-long Teacher Professional Development Languages (TPDL) programme (see Chap. 3) several years prior to our project. These two teachers had therefore had a level of exposure to the ten principles of instructed second language acquisition (Ellis, 2005) and would have undertaken teaching as inquiry cycles focusing on aspects of the principles as part of that programme. Kathryn reported on only isolated, rare in-school professional learning and development (PLD) opportunities, while Lillian and Tamara reported that they had not participated in any language-related PLD.

Table 6.1. reminds readers of the inquiry topics selected by the participants (see also Table 5.1, Chap. 5).

6.4 Preparing Teachers for Their Inquiry Cycles

As we have made clear in previous chapters, our project aimed to support the participating teachers to incorporate an intercultural dimension into their L2 teaching by means of two interculturally focused teaching as inquiry cycles (Phases II and III of the project). Initial interviews with the teachers at the beginning of Phase I revealed that the teachers had limited or no knowledge and understanding of the six Newton et al. (2010) principles. Therefore, to prepare the teachers for their first inquiries, an initial two-day hui (Phase II) with the teachers framed the approach to developing L2 learners' intercultural capability through presenting and discussing these principles. We encouraged the teachers to focus on two specific principles for their inquiries:

- Principle 3: encourage and develop an exploratory and reflective approach to culture and culture-in-language.
- Principle 4: foster explicit comparisons and connections between languages and cultures (Newton et al., 2010, p. 64).

Achievement objectives aligned to these principles (Ministry of Education, 2009) are that students will:

- recognise that the target culture(s) is (are) organised in particular ways.
- make connections with known culture(s) (*Achievement Levels 1 and 2*).
- recognise and describe ways in which the target culture(s) is (are) organised.
- compare and contrast cultural practices (*Achievement Levels 3 and 4*).

The second inquiry cycle began with a further two-day hui (Phase III) where the teachers presented the outcomes of their initial inquiries to other participants, and continued their exploration of the intercultural dimension, this time focusing more on practical outworkings of the principles.

6.5 Initial Reflections

The final session at the end of the second day of the initial two-day hui provided the teachers with their first opportunity to reflect back on the input they had received and how this might inform their inquiries.[2] It was encouraging that, in line with the Newton et al. (2010) Principles 3 and 4 and the achievement objectives, the teachers were able to identify and articulate a desire to promote critical reflection on similarity and difference across cultures. Lillian spoke positively of "the goal of wanting the students to become more empathetic and more aware of different attitudes and perspectives … [and] actually compare and contrast the attitudes." Kelly wanted her students to "get an opportunity to learn and reflect upon the values and beliefs important to Chinese in comparison to their own." Mike's primary focus would become, "can students increase their intercultural awareness by noticing cultural differences and similarities presented in primary resources?" With a view to embedding intercultural learning into physical activity (game-playing), Tamara suggested that this "could be actually an opportunity to teach the games from a different culture and compare and contrast." The teaching as inquiry cycles became the vehicles through which the teachers' positive reception of the principles would be tested in practice.

---

[2] Unfortunately, Kathryn was unable to participate in this final session and therefore missed out on this collegial opportunity.

6.6 Challenges Encountered in Practice

While every teacher's personal and professional context and teaching situation was different, the teachers' reflections as they completed their inquiries highlighted some commonly experienced challenges, which we address below. These challenges ranged from: (1) a perceived lack of familiarity with an appropriate pedagogical approach and lack of confidence about how to help students explore intercultural aspects; (2) apprehension around addressing students' stereotyped beliefs about culture and finding appropriate responses; (3) balancing linguistic aspects and cultural aspects (i.e., how and to what extent language and culture could be integrated) and deciding which language to use to teach intercultural aspects (i.e., L1 or TL) and (4) time constraints when it came to researching, preparing and exploring intercultural aspects with learners.

6.7 Pedagogical Approaches

Although we encouraged a focus on the Newton et al. Principles 3 and 4 (as noted above), supported the teachers as they determined their topics and guided them as they began to plan their inquiries, we were committed to a non-interventionist approach whereby we would prescribe neither what the inquiries should be nor what pedagogical approach the teachers should follow with regard to the intercultural dimension. The project's focus was, rather, to observe how the participating teachers attempted to include intercultural aspects and to encourage critical reflection on their practice in debriefing conversations after lesson observations. The absence of an existing evidence-based teaching approach to develop L2 learners' intercultural capability led to a variety of challenges that the teachers reported over the duration of the project.

Lillian reported that she had decided to explore the intercultural dimension through a student inquiry learning approach, since this was an established pedagogical approach in her school with which her students were already familiar. Furthermore, she believed this would enable her to support her students' focus on constructing their own learning through discovery as they investigated and researched a specific intercultural theme, rather than by direct instruction. Lillian later acknowledged, however, that this decision turned out to be a challenge. Whereas the students were undertaking inquiry projects in other curriculum areas on a daily basis, Lillian was only able to facilitate the inquiry with her students once a week. As a consequence of a long time between lessons, she felt that students lost their focus in the inquiries.

Lillian pondered whether she needed to give her students more time to think about questions and create more opportunities and time for reflection. When reflecting on the extent to which she had achieved her goals, Lillian conceded at the end of Phase II that "we [were] kind of brushing on the surface," and the students' comments on cultural aspects lacked depth. She acknowledged that her students "were having difficulty in discussing what they [were] actually thinking," since this level of critical reflection was new to the students and potentially beyond what they were able to do at that time. Despite Lillian's best intentions to foster her students' intercultural understanding by her approach of encouraging students to reflect critically on culturally related behaviour and underlying values, Lillian concluded that, by the end of the whole project, she was not satisfied with the classroom discussions as they had not "gone in depth enough" (end of Phase III).

For the four teachers for whom the TL was also an L2, lack of knowledge about the target culture presented further barriers. Kelly, for example, noted that her own lack of cultural knowledge was a challenge when it came to focusing on culture. Feeling like a cultural "outsider", she was uneasy answering some of her students' questions. This was particularly the case when discussing "controversial subjects" like the Chinese one-child policy that she chose to address in her first inquiry. Not only did Kelly feel uncomfortable presenting the policy from an outsider's and foreigner's point of view, but she also felt that it was inappropriate to discuss underlying issues such as abortion with her students. The lack of prior guidance about how to deal with intercultural questions and her lack of in-depth knowledge of the target culture resulted in her "skirting around" (Phase II) some of the deeper discussion she had wanted for her students as they explored the values underlying family structures in China. Similarly, Kathryn, who, like Lillian, chose a learner-centred inquiry learning approach for her students, highlighted the additional challenge of students retrieving wrong information or misunderstanding and misrepresenting the information they had found. Because she felt "insecure about [her] lack of knowledge about the culture" (end of Phase III), she could not necessarily correct information students had compiled in their independent learning inquiries.

Although Tamara strongly identified as Māori and Pasifika and noted she had "all the passion and enthusiasm" for teaching te reo Māori, she also felt she "lacked knowledge" about cultural aspects and about how to help her students to explore the culture. In her opinion, reading "all the books and watching the movies" was not enough to portray and explore Māori concepts authentically, leaving her uncertain about how to approach intercultural aspects respectfully (Phase II).

Mike reported that, similarly to his colleagues, he lacked self-confidence teaching "culture" at the beginning of the project. He concluded that teachers lacking confidence would most probably not include intercultural aspects in their language lessons and would resort to only focusing on linguistic aspects. In an attempt to counterbalance his limited experience in French culture, Mike's chosen approach to developing his students' intercultural capability was to use authentic resources, often in the form of online video clips. His aim was to make his students aware of similarities and differences across cultures. Mike was eager to guide his students to understand the complexities and subtleties of culture, rather than enforcing a monolithic conceptualisation of "this is what the French do" (Phase II). At the same time, he endeavoured to guide his students to the realisation that cultures shared more aspects in common than had aspects that separated them. However, he found it quite challenging to achieve his goal of letting students discover the similarities themselves, and, in the end, he found he often had to revert to telling his students what the similarities and differences were.

In the course of the project, Mike had also become aware of other challenges. Recognising and realising differences in another culture was one thing, but an appreciation or even awareness among his students of their own different cultures was difficult to achieve and he acknowledged that he had "to think a bit more about that" (start of Phase III). A further challenge emerged when trying to assess his students' intercultural learnings. He pointed out that with language instruction you could, for example, "blitz vocabulary," whereas, because developing intercultural capability was "more long-term," he was unsure how to ascertain or measure what his students had learned. Since, in Mike's view, intercultural capability was linked to "observing and understanding," not only other cultures but also one's own, Mike felt that time limitations had not enabled him to facilitate sufficient cross-cultural reflection and came to the conclusion that this could not be achieved in a few school terms. Thus, as with Lillian, Mike perceived that the development of intercultural capability required a considerable investment of time.

The teachers' experiences and struggles highlight that, while the absence of an "approved" and successful model of how to explore the intercultural dimension is arguably a challenge for the specialist language teacher (see, e.g., Kennedy, 2016; Oranje, 2016), this is amplified for non-specialist teachers who are faced with their own limitations in terms of knowledge of both the TL and the TL culture, and also with incorporating an intercultural dimension into practice. This points to the systemic issues in the New Zealand delivery of L2 teaching which we outlined at the start of this chapter and which are supported in Lillian's reflection—the biggest challenge to achieving L2 teaching with an intercultural dimension was related to structural issues in the New Zealand primary and intermediate sector. According to Lillian, where non-specialist teachers were being asked to teach a language they did not speak, this contributed to a high turnover of staff and often resulted in L2 teaching starting "from the beginning again" (Phase III) as each new teacher attempted to teach the language. Short teaching sessions also presented an additional challenge. It was difficult for students to retain any learning from one lesson to the next. Lillian believed that in such a context it was unrealistic to include both language and culture. She concluded that only once there was "substantial systemic change" could intercultural aspects be incorporated successfully.

6.8 Addressing Stereotypes

Linked to uncertainty about including an intercultural dimension in a time-limited L2 context and perceiving themselves as cultural "outsiders," the participating teachers also expressed their concern about reinforcing stereotypical views of what it meant to represent a particular culture.

Mike early recognised that, in addition to being "nervous of me not having the culture knowledge myself," his students "don't have much cultural knowledge outside stereotypes" (Phase II hui). He was therefore apprehensive about perpetuating stereotypes and generalisations as he and his students explored aspects of French culture, although he was very aware that this was the opposite of what he wanted to achieve with his students. As we noted above, what helped Mike in practice was, for example, using video extracts in French as primary resources. These, he commented, helped him to solve his dilemma that "I don't know enough about French culture" (end of Phase II).

Similarly, Kelly was concerned about propagating stereotypes involuntarily when discussing cultural aspects. Kelly "worried about giving wrong information" (Phase II) and felt there was a danger of misrepresenting Chinese values and culture. She acknowledged at the end of the first hui, "I do need to take extra effort to research that I am teaching proper Chinese ideas." At the same time, she struggled to decide how much exposure her students should get to existing stereotypes, highlighting that she "just found it hard not knowing how far to go culturally, because there are so many stereotypes out there" (end of Phase II). This was a particular concern in her first inquiry as most of her students, according to Kelly, had no experience of interacting with someone from the target culture and therefore no opportunity to adjust their views through meeting somebody with an Asian background in their everyday encounters. That is, the majority of Kelly's students were of Pacific heritage and lived in neighbourhoods dominated by Pacific ethnicities. Furthermore, Kelly was aware that her students "don't always have positive comments to say about the Chinese people, because they don't know, and they hear silly things in movies and stuff like that." She noted the importance of "addressing that kind of thing in a respectful and proper way" (end of Phase II). While Kelly acknowledged the importance of realising, addressing and confronting her students', and potentially her own, stereotypical assumptions and was mindful that ignoring stereotypes would not change existing perceptions, she experienced this as an enormous challenge that she felt ill-equipped to deal with. She opted to try to avoid the stereotypes in her lessons because she felt she lacked suitable tools to address them.

In contrast to Kelly's avoidance strategy, Tamara chose to challenge some of her students' preconceived ideas, which surfaced when discussing intercultural aspects of playing sports. For example, Tamara reported that one of her students struggled to accept that in the French rugby team "there were a couple of men who were darker." In the discussion, Tamara challenged her student's view that "French people are white" and contested generalisations, querying the source of her student's assumption by asking "How do you know? Have you met every single person in France?" (end of Phase II). Tamara attributed the student's view to her upbringing in South Africa, noting that this might also potentially be a reflection of her parents' views. While Tamara acknowledged that this student's perceptions might not be altered through a few lessons, she saw it as a positive to raise the girl's and her other students' awareness and to be able to challenge students' stereotypical beliefs.

Lillian struggled with how she could challenge stereotypical views because she "want[ed] them to know you must not stereotype" (end of Phase II). She realised, however, that, by presenting them with stereotypical situations or perceptions (e.g., what a Chinese restaurant looks like), she might present stereotypes that her students may not even have been aware of before. When Lillian introduced various topics like food, sports or colour, she tried her best to illustrate that one could not generalise and that, in fact, everybody was different. However, Lillian found it challenging to elicit some of the discussion about stereotyping with her students. She commented that students were not used to reflecting on stereotypes, which (as we have already noted) made some of the ensuing conversations very superficial.

6.9 The Language–Culture Interface

A positive finding of this project was the evidence that participating in the project had made the teachers become aware of the importance of intercultural capabilities and the need to include an intercultural dimension in their L2 lessons, something that had only featured marginally or incidentally (if at all) prior to the project. It is also important to acknowledge what we stated in Chap. 5 that there were instances where TL use seemed to increase as the teachers grappled with the language–culture interface. Nevertheless, it was also clear that all participating teachers struggled with finding a balance between teaching language and addressing culture in their respective classrooms. It was also apparent that the teachers responded to this struggle in quite different ways.

Lillian felt that creating a balance between teaching language and focusing on culture, and "how to weave [culture] into language learning itself" (Phase II), remained one of the biggest challenges. Her approach to resolving the conflict between TL use and intercultural exploration led her to completely separate both components, having two language sessions per week focusing on Mandarin and one cultural session discussing Chinese culture in English (her students' learning inquiry).[3] This did not preclude *some* attention to language in the culturally oriented lessons (see Chap. 5). However, by the end of the project, Lillian commented, "I'm starting to see that it [the intercultural dimension] needs to be quite distinguished and focused and independent almost." She acknowledged the three-strand model of the NZC (*communication, language knowledge and cultural knowledge*), and recognised in *principle* that the model "intertwines everything together." However, in *practice*, "I think it is really hard to see the three together in one lesson" (end of Phase III)—hence an operational separation.

Kathryn acknowledged that she ideally wanted to maintain "a balance between the Japanese language and the Japanese culture" (Phase II). However, the struggle to find this balance led to conflicting thoughts as she aimed to determine what was more important. Kathryn acknowledged that culture was "valid and interesting," but she still wanted her students to develop their knowledge of the language, to, for example, "have that vocab and to learn to tell the time in that context" (end of Phase II). Nevertheless, over the duration of the project, Kathryn found herself shifting to a greater emphasis on the intercultural aspects, consequently giving up on attempting to achieve a balance.

---

[3] This was facilitated by the fact that the two language-oriented lessons were taken by a Mandarin Language Assistant, leaving Lillian free to undertake the remaining inquiry-focused lesson.

When prompted at the end of the second inquiry cycle to reflect on her previously experienced conflict regarding balancing linguistic and cultural aspects, Kathryn stated that, for her, the conflict had dissolved, and was something that, by the end, she was "far less stressed" about. She explained that, by focusing more on intercultural aspects, she was not able to include as much language, but she believed the focus on the intercultural was "making the students richer in their understanding of Japanese" (end of Phase III). She emphasised that the very limited time weekly for Japanese language teaching, and infrequent Japanese lessons, made it difficult for students to retain their knowledge of the TL. By contrast, Kathryn believed that the students' "retention of what they learn through the [cultural] inquiry will be strong." To her, focusing on intercultural learning "[builds] up the broader person" which she considered an important aspect in her teaching (end of Phase III). When Kathryn evaluated what she had gained in the project, she concluded that she had "achieved the cultural side" even though "the language side wasn't there." Although she taught the students some language, she believed that the extended focus on intercultural learning meant her students forgot most of their Japanese. However, in Kathryn's opinion the intercultural aspect had more long-term impact on her students.

Kelly reported that, as a consequence of the project, she had become very focused on not only teaching the language but also including cultural aspects of Chinese. Like the other teachers, Kelly found it challenging to balance language and culture in her Mandarin classes. Nevertheless, unlike Lillian who separated language and culture as two distinct dimensions and Kathryn who focused mainly on cultural aspects, Kelly attempted to integrate language and culture equally in her lessons. For Kelly, it was important to expose her students to as much Mandarin as possible and to allow her students to use as much TL as they could. However, she emphasised that her choice to focus on language meant that she had to grapple not only with the challenge of how much time or focus she could give to each aspect but also how much TL could realistically be used during intercultural discussions.

Inevitably, due to students' and Kelly's lack of adequate knowledge of Mandarin, the cultural discussions took place in English. As a result, including cultural discussion not only led to reduced time to focus on the language but also less exposure to Mandarin, which Kelly perceived as a disadvantage for her students. At the same time, Kelly conceded that being able to contribute to discussions in English was advantageous due to the range of students' questions and the nature of the discussions, and this certainly encouraged more students to engage in conversations and reflections. By the end, she noted, "I guess a natural part of my Chinese lessons has [now] become quite a lot of discussing and asking questions and reflecting." She continued, "it feels like that is how I start or finish every single Chinese lesson nowadays, which is quite nice." Although that meant "a lot more talking in English," at least this "gives that chance to reflect on a culture, which is good" (end of Phase III).

Tamara also struggled with including a high proportion of linguistic input. Her intercultural topic, an exploration and cross-comparison of how different cultures played games and celebrated in sport, had prompted her to try a hands-on approach to integrating language and culture. At the end of the first hui, she commented, "if we can play a game [with] all the instructions given in a language that's associated with whatever game it is," this could lead to reflection on "how do you feel about it, how do you find it?" Furthermore, if the focus were on "games around different cultures," the class would "want to look at the ethos behind it, what's in those countries? What kind of language is associated? What's appropriate? What's not appropriate?" She first provided linguistic resources for te reo Māori followed by her students playing different games and being encouraged to use the language as they played. However, Tamara noted that a specific focus on language was lost when she discussed other cultures and their corresponding games with her students, leading to a more generic lesson. Her own "survival-level" linguistic knowledge of Māori added to this challenge and resulted in very limited student exposure to the TL.

While it was positive for Mike to include culture into his language teaching and into his thinking about culture as "part of language teaching" (Phase II), it also created a challenge as to which language to choose when engaging with cultural content. Mike had originally proposed that he would organise the intercultural focus by having a "small segment dedicated entirely to cultures," such that "we stop the language learning … to talk [about] and discuss how the things were different" (Phase II hui). He was aware, however, of the danger that this might transform language lessons with cultural foci into "social studies lessons" (end of Phase II). Those lessons could arguably be taught outside a language setting and in a different curriculum area.

Mike stated that his goal for the future was to create lessons that could focus on both language and culture, without separating the aspects and without allowing one aspect to dominate. As Mike summed it up, whereas earlier in the project, "I would have been teaching them [language and culture] in isolation," by the end of the project he was "now relaxed a bit and just saying they need to be *exposed* to the culture … [but] the language can still be the focus" (Phase III, our emphasis). However, just how exactly he could achieve that balance remained unclear to him. Thus, it seemed that, for all teachers in the project, an added focus on the intercultural dimension came at the cost of less TL input, output and interaction.

6.10 Time Constraints

We have already signalled that lack of time was a perceived barrier for the participants. All five of the teachers agreed that time was a challenge in their attempts to include an intercultural dimension in their L2 classrooms, and this was certainly a factor in attempting to ensure more equal attention to language and intercultural aspects.

With regard to the teachers' participation in the project, Mike welcomed the time that this participation had allowed him for reflection, discussion and planning concerning intercultural aspects, and lamented the fact that these aspects might be missing beyond the research project. Similarly, Tamara was excited that the project had enabled her to observe other teachers' language lessons and to have professional conversations with teachers to discuss various language teaching approaches that she could reflect on and that she could adapt to her own approach. She was aware that her regular schedule beyond the project allowed no time to do any of this. Both Kathryn and Lillian stated as a learning outcome the importance of familiarising themselves with theoretical underpinnings and relevant literature to better understand how intercultural learning could be included in a language teaching approach.

Tamara, Kathryn and Kelly commented that, particularly as L2 speakers of the TL and as cultural "outsiders," they needed to spend extra time on planning how to include the intercultural dimension as well as familiarising themselves with the cultural aspects that might become the foci. At the end of Phase II, Tamara, for example, noted that, despite her Māori heritage, finding out about specific cultural aspects could be the "largest barrier to implementation," and Kathryn concluded that "researching the culture might be a step too far" for a busy teacher. Kelly commented that even after investing time researching cultural aspects, for example, via the internet, it was important to "verify your sources" with an L1 speaker or cultural expert "to ensure your knowledge of the culture is correct, up to date and relevant" (Phase III, survival memo).

Time was not only a factor for teachers' planning and reflecting on the intercultural aspects the teachers wished to explore. Time was also needed in class to ensure adequate or meaningful discussion of those aspects. In the context of her first inquiry, Lillian stated that a lack of time to discuss cultural aspects in depth led her to only focus on "vocabulary and grammar" at times, although she had planned to address topics in a different way. As she reflected on the outcomes of her second inquiry, with its comparative focus on schools in China and New Zealand, she commented, "I think a few of them [my students] have really … started to think about identity and really started thinking about 'oh, hold on, ok, so if you have 60 students in a class [in China], does the teacher actually know your name?'" Nevertheless, "the next step, *if I had more time*, would be 'so, how does that make you feel in terms of value, identity, the existence of yourself?'" (end of Phase III, our emphasis).

As stated earlier, Mike pointed out that intercultural discussions took time. Indeed, for Mike, the separation of language and culture, with language taking a back seat, was predicated on his belief that "I would have felt like there was not enough time to include it [the language]" (end of Phase III). Furthermore, he accepted that intercultural capability could only develop over time. For Mike, the key to intercultural capability was to "understand why we think that [and] why things are different" (end of Phase II), which, in his opinion, could only be achieved over a longer period of time and by continuous revisiting of intercultural aspects. He concluded that deepening this capability could not be achieved in a few lessons that focused on isolated cultural aspects. Kelly concurred that, in practice, time was a constraint, and commented (end of Phase III) that there really needed to be "another year of really doing it in depth" with her students.

6.11 Teachers' Reflections and Learnings from the Project

Having thus far in this chapter presented the challenges and limitations that the teachers encountered as they aimed to incorporate an intercultural dimension into their L2 teaching, in what follows we present the teachers' reflections on their learning gains by virtue of participation in the project over time. In particular, we focus on two aspects (1) the teachers' approach and (2) the need for critical reflection. Some aspects we present could be perceived as challenges and could therefore have been included in the previous section. However, the participating teachers identified the aspects we present below as what they had learned and what they could "take away" from the project, despite ongoing challenges in practice. We begin with teachers' learnings related to their approach to enhancing learners' intercultural capability, including the value of culture, the need for pedagogical content knowledge, the unpredictability of intercultural discussions, language use and a focus on similarities rather than differences between cultures. This is followed by teachers' expressed need for more enhanced critical reflection, not only for themselves but also for their students.

6.12 Realisations About the Teaching Approach

For Kathryn, one of the greatest areas of learning was the realisation that "students don't have to be perfect [in the TL] for there to be communication" and that "teaching about the Japanese people's lifestyles, beliefs, and culture [was] just as valid" as a focus on language (Phase II). Furthermore, Kathryn reported that, prior to the project, she had put herself under enormous pressure to develop her students' knowledge of the Japanese language, finding herself concerned about lack of progress. The project, and its emphasis on the intercultural, enabled her to feel her students did not have to "achieve an overwhelming amount of linguistic knowledge." She perceived that the NZC actually gave her permission to focus on cultural aspects. Reflecting back on her journey towards the end of the project, Kathryn explained:

> I didn't get it last year [in Phase II] … I didn't make that link enough … I think I was still trying to put cultural stuff in alongside the language in that short period of time. And now this year I [realised] I don't actually have to do language every lesson. The curriculum tells me to do culture, I can do culture, and so actually just focusing on that has really made a difference. [end of Phase III]

While this realisation was liberating for Kathryn, the flipside of focusing almost exclusively on culture was also a challenge, as mentioned in the previous section. Not using Japanese in her lessons also led her to ponder that she needed "to improve [her] Japanese again" (Phase III).

The project enabled Mike to become more aware of his teaching. For him, it was easy to "revert to teaching how you were taught" (Phase III hui), whereas the project had raised his self-awareness and encouraged him to include cultural aspects.

However, this newly introduced element of his teaching made Mike feel slightly "out of control" (Phase III hui) due to the unpredictability of intercultural discussion and his own lack of in-depth knowledge of the culture at times. Therefore, an important lesson for Mike was to accept unpredictable situations, in which he might feel out of his depth, and to make these a more integral part of his teaching. Mike stated that, prior to the project, he strongly believed in a focus on exclusive TL use where possible, but over the time of the project he came to accept the reality that discussions about culture would most likely need to be in English. Kelly came to a similar conclusion regarding follow-up discussions on intercultural aspects in English, but acknowledged that, in her view, introducing students to intercultural topics was possible in the TL. One of Kelly's realisations was that she believed her students would be capable of understanding those aspects in Mandarin, if she had prepared adequately. This would mean that her learners would be exposed to more TL input and that this could potentially tip the scales in favour of a balance between language and culture, something which she had perceived as a challenge.

Kelly noted that concentrating on intercultural aspects could inadvertently lead to a focus on differences between cultures. Once she had become aware of this tendency, she actively also tried to point her students to similarities between various cultures, including their own. While it was important for Mike to focus on both differences and similarities across cultures, he noticed, similarly to Kelly, that students found it more difficult to see common aspects. By the end of the project, he had come to realise that it was important to support his students to develop "an appreciation of their own culture ... just to be aware of it" (Phase III). In a similar vein, Kathryn noted shifts in her approach to addressing the intercultural over the duration of the project. She commented, "before I did this project, I would have wanted them [the students] to see the differences, now I want them to see the similarities" (Phase II). Rather than focusing on "the other," Kathryn stated that for her it had "become quite important ... the fact that we are the same," even though she acknowledged that at times "you may have to look harder" to find similarities. Nevertheless, Kathryn wanted her students to focus on what unites us rather than what divides. Like Kelly and Kathryn, Mike emphasised that there was no right or wrong when it came to culture and that, in his view, the teacher's role was to steer students away from generalisations and stereotypes and instead to enable them to relate to others.

As much as time was a challenging factor, it also played a part in the teachers' learnings. They acknowledged that it took time to implement changes in their own thinking and doing. At the same time, in her reflection at the end of the project, Kathryn reinforced that the perceived success of her intercultural inquiry was based on allowing students time for the project to develop and she "didn't rush it." Indeed, although Kathryn acknowledged that her second inquiry "was taking so much time," she commented nonetheless, "I gave them pretty much the time they needed, so it meant that they could really get into depth." She felt that, as a consequence, "they loved it; they really enjoyed it, and they feel knowledgeable, and they feel like they have a proper understanding, I think."

Overall, Kelly acknowledged the benefits of including intercultural aspects in her L2 teaching, but (as we previously pointed out) was mindful that it might take more time for her students' thinking and behaviour to change as a result of what they had learned over the years. A contrast for her was the type of students she was dealing with in her two teaching contexts. Her first school was "an environment where these kids don't know anyone Chinese. A lot of them might have said 'hello' to a Chinese person before that, but that would be about it" (end of Phase II). By contrast, in her second school, she found the intercultural exploration "much easier to bring up" because the students "don't seem to buy much into stereotypes … they've got such experience with the Chinese girls right here in the class and within the whole school," meaning "I don't think it is quite as foreign to them" (end of Phase III). This reflection points to the important dimension of students' own backgrounds and experiences, and the impact of these on the potential success of intercultural reflection.

6.13 Self-Reflection and Critical Thinking

All teachers highlighted the importance of increasing the ability to reflect critically on others' and one's own cultures. They emphasised that this reflection was equally as important for teachers as for students. For example, Kathryn pointed out that initiating an intercultural teaching inquiry required "honest reflection on your practice" (Phase III survival memo) but self-reflection was not limited to teaching practice; it also included one's beliefs about culture and as a person one had to be prepared to "let go of old beliefs." Kelly also commented that as a teacher she had to reflect on her perceptions and on her own culture and acknowledged "both my students and I struggled at times" (end of Phase II). Kelly's first set of predominantly Māori and Pasifika students expressed that they had come to know "more about Chinese families" than about their own. Kelly noted that her students most likely had not reflected much on their own culture before and mused that "people are often unaware of their own culture, particularly if they are part of the majority [within a cultural context]." She felt that an important part of "developing knowledge about another culture" was learning about and "identifying your own cultural practices, beliefs and values" (end of Phase II).

Another important dimension of critical reflection was the realisation that culture was not static, even within a particular cultural group. Mike's attempt to reflect critically and differentiate even further within a particular culture was echoed in the following comment: he encouraged his students to challenge a view of culture "as one thing" and to take "the idea of a 'typical' thing [within a culture] with a grain of salt" (Phase III). Towards the end of the project, Mike acknowledged, "I don't even think I could tell kids about Kiwi culture … my culture is quite different from what yours would be and I don't like the idea of me imposing my views on anyone else." For Mike, "the big thing was [that] we expose them to cultural elements, we try to question and get them questioning their own culture and they make their own judgement." There may be times when "we may not agree with their judgements." However, "we are just hopefully creating the environment where they are making more informed judgements" (Phase III hui).

Mike thus established that becoming aware of one's own culture went "hand in hand with questioning what a 'typical' person from a particular country looks like." The aim was to reflect on oneself and on others simultaneously. In this regard, Mike emphasised that it was important to "know which questions to ask" to elicit useful responses in an intercultural discussion and in guiding his students' reflections. Mike's learning for future planning was to "think more thoroughly about the questioning" and to "actually write the questions down ... rather than just discuss and make it up on the fly" (Phase III hui).

Like Mike, Lillian was passionate about increasing her students' critical thinking and wanted her students to recognise the complexities of culture and that "you don't identify a group of people as one culture" (Phase II), but, rather, people could belong to a multitude of cultures and 'culture' represented a range of perspectives. However, bringing students to this place of recognition was quite an ambitious goal, as it extended the concept of 'culture' beyond the static and uniform and challenged students' perception and understanding of it. For example, using the topic "sports in China," Lillian aimed to focus on raising her students' awareness of different perspectives on sports, not just interculturally but also intraculturally, that is, even within China and among Chinese people. In her approach to prompting critical thinking, Lillian started challenging labels and terminology, raising issues of who could be called "Chinese" in a globalised and internationalised world. Her goal was to challenge students' thinking patterns and ultimately "to make sure that we don't get kids to be narrow-minded" (Phase III hui).

Lillian stated the necessity to "challenge stereotypes," but, upon reflection, noted that prior to the project her school, herself included, "taught culture in a stereotype way" by focusing on aspects typical of a culture. As a person navigating multiple cultures herself, and who found herself "in between cultures" at times, Lillian saw exploring the intercultural dimension as an opportunity for young people in a similar situation. Reflecting on "why we do what we do" (Phase III hui) and realising the values underpinning those behaviours could, in Lillian's view, help with how young people positioned themselves within a range of cultures.

Tamara was enthusiastic about exploring underlying values and associated language and behaviour for different sports in different cultures. She also pointed out the need to reflect more generally beyond sports on "what do we do at home, what do our grandparents do?" (Phase II hui) so as to consider our behaviours and associated values in particular cultural contexts. That type of reflection was crucial both for her as the teacher and for her students. Students' reflections enabled some of them not only to bring in their "expertise" in a particular culture but also to "educate their classmates." However, Tamara's focus on sports also enabled some of her students to be confronted with their own stereotypes and prejudice, for example when the class looked at yoga. Tamara included words in te reo Māori in that context and students commented that it was "really weird" (end of Phase II) because in their perception yoga was linked to India. The assumption by some of Tamara's students that "only certain people do yoga and Pilates" sparked intercultural discussions between students from various cultural backgrounds and led to insights into the origins of and concepts underpinning both practices, while at the same time encouraging students to engage in a level of critical reflection into their own beliefs. She concluded by the end of Phase II that "looking at things differently" was a key thing she had achieved with her class during the inquiry.

6.14 Benefits of the Project

At the end of the project, the teachers were asked to reflect on the overall insights they had gained from the project. In what follows, we illustrate first where there was overlap among the teachers' final evaluations and reflections, which mostly focused on increased student motivation and increased critical reflection. We then point out additional insights from individual teachers.

6.14.1 Motivation and Student Engagement

In Chap. 5, we drew attention to the motivational dimension of the intercultural inquiries from the students' perspective. All participating teachers commented that focusing on intercultural aspects in their language teaching had led to increased student engagement and motivation. Kathryn was "quite amazed" about her students' "excitement" (Phase III) when it came to their intercultural learning inquiries, something she clearly had not anticipated to the extent that it was demonstrated. In Phase II, for example, they were "so excited about seeing the Japanese family schedule and comparing it to their own." Kelly echoed that one of the major positives of an intercultural focus for her was that her students were "engaged during language lessons and enjoyed learning the language as well as finding out about Chinese culture" (end of Phase III).

As we pointed out in Chap. 5, Lillian also noticed that her students were "definitely a lot more engaged than just teaching them, like, the actual characters and just the language of Chinese" (end of Phase II). She emphasised that there was a particular change in engagement for the boys in her classes. Before the project and its emphasis on intercultural learning, many students, but the boys in particular, were disengaged or even disruptive during language lessons. Focusing on intercultural aspects appeared to capture the boys' interest and encouraged them to participate more in discussions. Interestingly, the boys' engagement even stood out in comparison to the usually more actively involved girls in the language focused classes. Mike summed up the teachers' impression when he noted that "the main advantage" he could observe was "the increased student motivation."

Student motivation and engagement are arguably two of the principal goals for any teaching, especially as interest and motivation can support student learning. Achieving student engagement is, however, no easy feat. It cannot be taken for granted and, while desirable for both the teacher and the learner, is often not part of classroom reality. The fact that student interest in intercultural learning was not only affirmed, but highlighted as a main positive by all the participating teachers, despite their varying contexts, is noteworthy. Even with the lamented time constraints and largely varying approaches between teachers as they sought to include an intercultural dimension into their teaching, the outcome was the same: students enjoyed exploring intercultural dimensions even without a prescribed approach.

6.14.2 Increased Critical Reflection

The second overall positive of the intercultural project as perceived by the teachers was the increased critical reflection, both for themselves and for their learners. As indicated earlier in this chapter, the need for reflection and the opportunity to do so through the intercultural focus were two of the learnings for the participating teachers. Lillian noted that conversations about culture were "a success" because they encouraged her students to reflect critically on cultural ideas and beliefs, and "nobody [had] asked [the students] to think about that before" (Phase II). Although she realised that those critical thinking skills would take some time to develop, she was glad that she had at least begun to "raise awareness" and that discussions and reflections had started that process.

Kelly concurred that it was beneficial for her students to be presented with different cultures while reflecting on and making connections to their own. Mike also expressed the importance of developing critical thinking and reflection skills in his students. In his view, "the aim [was] not to teach children culture as this [is] unattainable and wrong—instead by including cultural elements in our learning and by intelligent questioning we can heighten students' awareness of culture, question their preconceived ideas and develop increased tolerance and respect" (Phase III survival memo). Mike's reflection highlights the fluidity of cultural aspects, or "unpredictability," as he called it in a previous reflection, but his comment also highlights an important desired outcome of intercultural language teaching: tolerance and mutual respect.

6.14.3 Additional Realisations

Apart from the two main foci mentioned above, some teachers emphasised additional benefits of the project.

One of Tamara's goals had been to try "to integrate Māori into everything we do" (Phase II). Participating in the project allowed her to "embrace the language" in her everyday teaching and to encourage her students to use te reo Māori every day. She had also valued the opportunity to "normalise" Māori into all aspects of teaching (beginning Phase II). This was a significant benefit to her and her students. Tamara's decision to integrate Māori into game-playing had enabled her students to "look at the values behind why Māori had these games, what was the purpose behind them

... and then ... relating it back to childhood games that the kids had played." She acknowledged that the "different games and looking at things differently" was the "big thing" she felt she had achieved with her class (end of Phase II). The moments for intercultural reflection were not just isolated to Māori, but included cross-cultural comparisons with other sports and pastimes.

For Kathryn, an important step forward was the acknowledgment and realisation that culture was a valid and important part of language teaching. In her view, the focus on culture allowed the students to get "the taste for it," potentially increasing "their desire to take a language anyway when they move into high school, because they are so interested" (end of Phase III). To her, therefore, a focus on culture was the gateway to an increased interest in language learning in her students.

Lillian also saw the inclusion of intercultural conversations and dimensions as a gateway, albeit a slightly different one. She looked at the project from the perspective of a "multicultural person," as she referred to herself in Phase II. An immigrant to New Zealand at the age of seven, Lillian explained that, for her, it was a positive change to include intercultural aspects into language teaching. When she came to New Zealand, "relating across cultures was just not talked about." She commented that reflection on different cultures would have made it easier for her to "find [her] identity" and to determine who she was as somebody "in between cultures." In Lillian's view, discussing others' cultures and becoming aware of one's own would make life easier for young multicultural students. Including intercultural aspects into teaching and reflecting on different cultures was thus a gateway and opportunity for her to contribute to the creation of a more respectful and knowledgeable multicultural society.

6.14.4 The Broader Context

It is noteworthy that the challenges experienced by the teachers participating in our project align in many ways with those of teachers in other studies (see Chaps. 2 and 3). The teachers' perceptions that they did not feel prepared enough and did not know how to enhance their learners' intercultural capabilities resonate, for example, with findings in Sercu's (2013) study. In this regard, teachers in Brunsmeier's (2017) study asked for a framework that would help them to include intercultural aspects and felt that they needed trigger questions that would support them as they worked with students. Liddicoat (2008) likewise pointed out the importance of upskilling teachers in posing questions that would enhance intercultural learning. Similarly, the teachers in our study felt that asking "the right questions" to elicit intercultural responses was a challenge.

The expressed challenge around balancing linguistic and cultural aspects in their language lessons is echoed in several other studies (see, e.g., Brunsmeier, 2017; Díaz, 2013; Sercu, 2005), and the lack of time to research, prepare and implement intercultural aspects is also acknowledged in previous studies (Castro et al., 2004; Díaz, 2013; Sercu, 2005).

Prior studies also highlight the crucial role of reflection, as expressed by teachers in our study. The teachers' perceived need to reflect on their own beliefs and values is also noted in studies by Liddicoat (2008) and Sercu (2005) and aligns with Moloney's (2008) perception that teachers are sometimes not aware of their own cultural understandings. The teachers in our study also emphasised that they aimed to foster critical reflection in their students and there was evidence to suggest that at least some of their students' abilities to see things from a different viewpoint developed over time (see Chap. 5). These findings concur with studies conducted in the United States where teachers reported that their students could reflect on different views (see, e.g., Despoteris & Ananda, 2017; Roher & Kagan, 2017).

6.15 Conclusion

In summary, it appeared that the main outcome of the teachers' learnings and perceived benefits of including an intercultural dimension in their language teaching was increased student motivation. This seemed to signal clearly students' readiness to learn about others and their interest in reflecting on other cultures as well as on their own. The teachers agreed that the exploration of culture was complex, but that it was important to expose their students to cultural aspects, and, as Mike had put it, to get them questioning their own cultures and making their own judgements. Although the teachers might not necessarily agree with the standpoints reached by the students, this was part of the teachers' acknowledgement that there was no "right or wrong" in culture, but, as Kathryn and Tamara agreed, it was their role as teachers to help their students to "see things from another viewpoint." Thus, although discussions might have unpredictable outcomes, lack depth, need time and require careful teacher preparation, including intercultural aspects and reflections can be seen as stepping-stones in the journeys towards relating comfortably to people from diverse linguistic and cultural backgrounds, and appreciating and valuing the learners' own cultures and uniqueness alongside the cultures and uniqueness of others, that is, intercultural capability (see also Biebricher et al., 2019).

In Chap. 7, we turn from the teachers to us as researchers and present critical dimensions of our own learning journeys in this project.

References

Biebricher, C., East, M., Howard, J., & Tolosa, C. (2019). Navigating intercultural language teaching in New Zealand classrooms. *Cambridge Journal of Education, 49*(5), 605–621.

Brunsmeier, S. (2017). Primary teachers' knowledge when initiating intercultural communicative competence. *TESOL Quarterly, 51*(1), 143–155.

References

Castro, P., Sercu, L., & Méndez-García, M. C. (2004). Integrating language-and-culture teaching: An investigation of Spanish teachers' perceptions of the objectives of foreign language education. *Intercultural Education, 15*, 91–104.

Despoteris, J., & Ananda, K. (2017). Intercultural competence: Reflecting on daily routines. In M. Wagner, D. Perugini, & M. Byram (Eds.), *Teaching intercultural competence across the age range: From theory to practice* (pp. 60–79). Multilingual Matters.

Díaz, A. (2013). Intercultural understanding and professional learning through critical engagement. *Babel, 48*(1), 12–19.

East, M., Howard, J., Tolosa, C., Biebricher, C., & Scott, A. (2017). Isolated or integrated? Should the development of students' intercultural understanding be separated from, or embedded into, communicative language use? *Babel, 52*(2/3), 20–25.

Ellis, R. (2005). *Instructed second language acquisition: A literature review*. Ministry of Education.

Kennedy, J. (2016). *Exploring opportunities for developing intercultural competence through intercultural communicative language teaching (ICLT): A case study in a Chinese as a foreign language classroom in a New Zealand high school* [Masters dissertation, Victoria University of Wellington, New Zealand].

Liddicoat, A. J. (2008). Pedagogical practice for integrating the intercultural in language teaching and learning. *Japanese Studies, 28*(3), 277–290.

Ministry of Education. (2007). *The New Zealand curriculum*. Learning Media.

Ministry of Education. (2009). *Curriculum achievement objectives by learning area*. http://nzcurriculum.tki.org.nz/The-New-Zealand-Curriculum

Moloney, R. (2008). You just want to be like that: Teacher modelling and intercultural competence in young language learners. *Babel, 42*(3), 10–19.

Newton, J., Yates, E., Shearn, S., & Nowitzki, W. (2010). *Intercultural Communicative Language Teaching: Implications for effective teaching and learning—A literature review and an evidence-based framework for effective teaching*. Ministry of Education.

Oranje, J. (2016). *Intercultural Communicative Language Teaching: Enhancing awareness and practice through cultural portfolio projects* [Doctoral thesis, University of Otago, New Zealand].

Roher, P., & Kagan, L. (2017). Using the five senses to explore cities. In M. Wagner, D. Perugini, & M. Byram (Eds.), *Teaching intercultural competence across the age range: From theory to practice* (pp. 60–79). Multilingual Matters.

Scott, A. J., & Butler, P. J. (2007). My teacher is learning like us: Teachers and students as language learners. *The New Zealand Language Teacher, 33*, 11–16.

Sercu, L. (2005). Foreign language teachers and the implementation of intercultural education: A comparative investigation of the professional self-concepts and teaching practices of Belgian teachers of English, French and German. *European Journal of Teacher Education, 28*(1), 87–105.

Sercu, L. (2013). Foreign language teachers and intercultural competence. What keeps teachers from doing what they believe in? In M. Jiménez Raya & L. Sercu (Eds.), *Challenges in teacher development: Learner autonomy and intercultural competence* (pp. 65–80). Peter Lang.

Tolosa, C., Biebricher, C., East, M., & Howard, J. (2018). Intercultural language teaching as a catalyst for teacher inquiry. *Teaching and Teacher Education, 70*, 227–235.

Open Access This chapter is licensed under the terms of the Creative Commons Attribution 4.0 International License (http://creativecommons.org/licenses/by/4.0/), which permits use, sharing, adaptation, distribution and reproduction in any medium or format, as long as you give appropriate credit to the original author(s) and the source, provide a link to the Creative Commons license and indicate if changes were made.

The images or other third party material in this chapter are included in the chapter's Creative Commons license, unless indicated otherwise in a credit line to the material. If material is not included in the chapter's Creative Commons license and your intended use is not permitted by statutory regulation or exceeds the permitted use, you will need to obtain permission directly from the copyright holder.

Chapter 7
Journeys Towards Intercultural Capability: The Researchers' Voices

7.1 Introduction

Findings from the two inquiry cycles undertaken by the teacher partners in this research project were presented in Chaps. 5 and 6. Chap. 5 outlined the inquiries as documented through classroom observations, alongside the students' reported intercultural learning gains. In Chap. 6, we focused on the teachers, and the reported challenges they encountered as they introduced an intercultural element into their language programmes, along with learning gains with regard to enhancing their students' intercultural capability.

In this chapter, we trace the evolution of the collaborative inquiries at the core of the project. We present our own journeys as researchers working with teachers who were both participants and research partners and document the realities and complexities of the intersecting processes of collaboration and independent inquiry that we aimed to foster in the project from its inception. We draw on diverse data sources, including project documents, audio-recordings and transcriptions of meetings, email archives and notes on discussions involving different members of the group, as well as the data from our work with the teacher partners. In our analysis in this chapter, we draw in particular on the literature and conceptualisations of collaborative action research (e.g., Burns, 1999, 2019), communities of practice (Lave & Wenger, 1991) and practitioner inquiry (Baumfield et al., 2012), to make sense of our journey.

Specifically, we document several "critical incidents" (Brandenburg, 2008; Tripp, 2012) that we identified as we reflected back on the project. Some of the incidents we describe may appear as normal occurrences in meetings, discussions or reflections, yet we identify them as *critical* in terms of how we saw their significance for the development of the project (Tripp, 2012) and for our own journey as researchers and teacher educators. Our purpose is to illuminate and interrogate the processes and enabling conditions of our collaboration and its outcomes, with a view to moving from the events themselves (the "what" and the "how") to understanding what these events meant for the project overall. In so doing, we contribute to a broader understanding of the complexities involved in the development of intercultural capabilities through the learning of an additional language (L2).

7.2 Contextual Background

As researchers, practitioners and teacher educators working in different capacities in diverse institutions, but with a common interest in teaching and learning languages, we were acutely aware of the challenges of the *Learning Languages* area of the *New Zealand Curriculum* or NZC (Ministry of Education, 2007). Our own previous research had identified the difficulties teachers of languages experience in the intermediate school sector as they develop their L2 programmes and aim to address NZC expectations (Biebricher, 2015; Howard, 2012; Scott, 2014; Tolosa et al., 2015). We wanted to gain a better understanding of the reasons behind the distance between what the NZC expects and what happens in classrooms. Specifically, we identified the *cultural knowledge* strand of *Learning Languages* as a particularly weak component of L2 programmes, despite rhetoric around the importance of helping learners to develop intercultural capability (see Chap. 3). A key dimension of the project from our perspective, as both researchers and teacher educators, was therefore to better understand the complexities of implementing the intercultural dimension in L2 programmes in primary/intermediate schools in New Zealand, with a view to enhancing language education both in and beyond our immediate context.

As we planned the project, we, as a team of five researchers, established a strong community of practice, with agreed shared goals and clarity in the functioning of the group. As we advanced the design of the project, the group grew to include the five teacher partners. The resulting group developed over time into a "collaborative inquiry" partnership (Burns, 1999, 2019; Butler & Schnellert, 2012; Scarino, 2014), with distinct roles and tasks (see Chap. 4). Specifically, the type of collaborative inquiry represented in our project involved "collaboration between researchers based in universities, undertaking funded projects and working with groups of teachers located in different schools" (Burns, 2005, p. 65), in order to investigate an issue of shared interest. Such collaborations aim to address the widely documented divide between theory and practice (Ball, 2000; Loughran, 2002; Zeichner, 1994).

Inviting teachers to become research partners signals a commitment to value their knowledge, experience and expertise; conversely, the teachers acknowledge the input from the researchers. The relationship develops reciprocally in that the researchers gain direct access to the experiences of teachers at the classroom level, while the teachers are supported in developing theoretical understandings of their practices or of curricular innovations. Working within a community of inquiry creates conditions for teachers to access rich resources and to engage in developing practice and learning as the researchers support and scaffold their engagement in the inquiry (Butler & Schnellert, 2012). Although the positioning of those involved in the researcher–teacher relationship may be different, they find a shared commitment to understanding the issue at hand. As suggested by Bevins and Price (2014), collaboration between academics and teachers can have the greatest impact when the purpose is clear and the members engage in processes of reflection and continuous dialogue.

As with all action research, the process of inquiry in the collaboration involves the systematic collection of evidence and the engagement in problem-defining, action-oriented, reflective and iterative cycles of inquiry with a shared goal (Timperley, 2011). Framed as such, the inquiry has the potential to "impact not only teachers' learning but also their practice in classrooms" (Butler et al., 2015, p. 2), thus offering an alternative to top-down dissemination and implementation of curricular innovations. However, a risk here is that the teachers do not retain full ownership over the inquiry since the issue to be investigated was first and foremost the researchers' agenda. To mitigate this possible threat, teachers engage in inquiry in their classrooms, while the researchers frame and relate these inquiries to the experience of others and to research literature and policy documents through a wider investigation, which would then inform the development and focus of a subsequent cycle of classroom inquiries. The ideal is that these inquiries become "virtuous cycles" (Wall & Hall, 2016) through which teachers develop a culture of reflection and research in their classrooms through their experience in the collaborative inquiry.

Furthermore, inquiries are opportunities "set up for teachers and researchers to construct knowledge collectively over time" (Burns, 2009, p. 294), although often with different aims. Whereas the researchers may engage in collaborative inquiry with the aim of solving a problem or introducing an innovation, the focus for teachers may be to "understand rather than change" their practices (Allwright & Hanks, 2009, p. 172). By integrating teaching, learning and research, the participants in the collaborative inquiry "construct pedagogical knowledge through dialectic interaction and critical exchange" (Burns, 2009, p. 294). Collaborative inquiry is thus regarded as an effective method both to support reflective practice and to generate valuable insights into practice. Our project was framed in the above light.

7.3 Beginning the Journey

A pilot project in 2015 had gathered initial evidence about how the intercultural dimension was being dealt with in schools (see Howard et al., 2015). The main project as reported in this book built on the pilot and took place in 2016 and 2017 (see Chap. 4).

Our decision to initiate a project where researchers and teachers would co-construct inquiry cycles positioned the teachers as co-researchers, thereby valuing their knowledge of practice and acknowledging their contributions to knowledge creation (Lave & Wenger, 1991). We wanted to ensure that all members felt they would benefit from participation in the project and that they could contribute equally to it as part of a democratic process of gaining and sharing knowledge and developing practices (Burns, 2015). We encouraged the teachers to exercise agency and autonomy as they undertook their own inquiries while also actively engaging with the wider investigation proposed by the researchers. Acting as knowledge brokers (McLaughlin et al., 2004), we scaffolded the teacher partners' development of their understanding of the intercultural dimension in L2 teaching, as well as of the inquiry process itself. As researchers, we thus developed roles common in these kinds of collaboration (McNiff, 2016): at times we were consultants who contributed research skills and theoretical knowledge; at other times we were facilitators who supported the teachers' inquiries; and sometimes we were critical friends.

7.4 Phase I

In a first step in working with the teachers, and before we had brought the teachers together as a group, individual researchers worked with individual teachers to establish rapport and develop the relationship of the pairs (Phase I). This initial step was crucial to the beginning of the project. As we noted in Chap. 4, when we first conceptualised the project, we approached schools where our institutions already had established relationships, and, in some cases we approached teachers we already knew through previous professional contact. However, a professional inevitability of the intermediate school sector is that teachers move to new positions. Once we started the project, we were working in schools we knew, but sometimes the teacher partners were new to the schools and new to us. Thus, Christine began working with a teacher whom she knew well and with whom she had an established relationship. By contrast, Martin, Constanza and Jocelyn were working with teachers they did not know.

We visited the teachers in their schools and collected baseline data about the school, the position of L2 teaching in the school, and the teachers' backgrounds, including their knowledge and understanding of language teaching pedagogies. As part of these data, we specifically asked the teachers about their knowledge of the ten Ellis principles (Ellis, 2005) and the six Newton et al. principles (Newton et al., 2010). We also observed at least two lessons and talked with each teacher about their teaching of languages. Besides the initial data collection, this first encounter also aimed to establish a shared purpose and initiate the development of mutual understanding and collegiality, all considered key components of collaborative efforts (Loughran, 2010). In those initial conversations, teachers expressed their commitment to the overall project and recognised the importance of establishing common goals. An important finding of the baseline data was the teachers' lack of knowledge of the Newton et al. principles and the concept of intercultural capability.

7.5 Phase II

The first full research team *hui* (meeting) with the teachers took place over two days in July 2016 and initiated Phase II of the project. We wanted to provide the teachers with a sense of the support available to them, ranging from "structural support" (Timperley, 2011) that allowed them to be released from their teaching to attend the hui, to support with understanding any new concepts through explanations that built on their experiences and prior knowledge (González et al., 2016). We anchored the start of the two days on the NZC itself, beginning with the development of key competencies (see Chap. 3) that we knew would provide common ground across teachers and schools. We also prepared short presentations on the theoretical aspects of the project, using the six Newton et al. (2010) principles, and including presentations by two researchers on the findings from their recent investigations into the implementation of the principles in New Zealand classrooms (Kennedy, 2016; Ramírez, 2018). Our aim was to provide a robust base for the teachers to understand the Newton et al. principles and to gain insights from others who had used these principles to interpret their own understandings of what they observed in classrooms.

We tried to provide a balance between the intellectual and procedural tools that we anticipated the teachers would need for the project, and thus build teachers' capacity to undertake research, and also eliciting from them what would be feasible for them given the realities of their work and their contexts. At the same time, we wanted to ensure that the aims we had set for the overall project were of mutual interest to all participants, albeit allowing room for individual inquiries. We therefore encouraged the teachers to narrow their focus on two of the Newton et al. (2010) principles, with particular guidance to consider Principles 3 and 4 (see Chaps. 5 and 6)—encouraging and developing an exploratory and reflective approach to culture, as well as fostering explicit comparisons and connections between languages and cultures. This balance between teacher autonomy to select the principles to focus on based on their contexts and teaching plan, and the researchers' nudging towards Principles 3 and 4, is illustrated in a comment made by Kelly at the start of the second day of the hui when we had asked the teachers to share how their thinking about the project had developed overnight and how they would describe what they were being asked to do:

> You mean, the idea of it [the project]? Picking a goal that will show good student outcomes and will really benefit them and their learning with regards to learning culture. Using these principles, particularly 3 and 4 which are quite important … What you guys said about your data and Juliet's [Kennedy - one of the guest researchers] study as well … show that these two, in particular, needed attention. Collecting results from … examples and data from students and myself, reflections and stuff like that … putting it together in some kind of a portfolio way to communicate what I've found.

Another illustration of the way the researchers supported ownership by the teachers was by reviewing and discussing the teaching as inquiry model commonly used in New Zealand schools (see Chap. 4) which the teachers would use to develop their situated inquiries. We wanted the teachers to see that although we acknowledged that we might have greater understanding of theoretical aspects, they already had the skills to develop their own inquiries, and they had intimate knowledge of their contexts. We were thus building a sense of mutuality which does not require all members of the team to be equally skilled in all areas of the project (Bevins & Price, 2014). Furthermore, we wanted the teachers to gain confidence in articulating their knowledge of practice and translating their contextual understandings to the whole group, what Passman (2002) called *going public.*

With regard to the choice of an inquiry model, we were mindful that "practice shifts are most likely to occur when teachers engage in practice-level inquiry, because it is at this level that teachers draw on resources and tools to define goals for students, strategically direct activity, monitor outcomes and make shifts accordingly" (Butler & Schnellert, 2012, p. 1208). Through the inquiries, we wanted the teachers to become "agentive actors and investigators within their own social contexts" (Burns, 2019, p. 166). All the teachers confirmed their familiarity with the teaching as inquiry model. Kathryn described it like this:

> We do a lot. There is a lot of teachers' reflection on our practice and a lot of 'what do I need to do?' which also needs 'how do I do that?' And so, we're very used to going out and find what we need and bringing in resources and how those are to be applied as well… [so I see a] very strong connection [with the proposed inquiries].

We were pleased that the teachers demonstrated enthusiasm to embark on the project. We closed the two-day hui by summing up our roles as researchers and motivating the teachers to start their individual inquiries—"maybe [we] challenged your thinking in the right ways and taking you to new directions, but this is what it's all about. It's about inquiring about something new and to see where it goes."

7.5.1 Critical Friend Conversations

As teachers embarked on their first inquiry cycle, they were supported closely by the researcher-partners who kept in regular email communication, visited the schools to observe lessons and held debriefing meetings with each teacher following a semi-structured interview format. These encounters were important in supporting the teachers' inquiries. We framed these debriefing meetings as "critical friend" conversations (Costa & Kallick, 1993) where the researchers' role was to support the teachers in framing and reframing their practices by moving from the concrete of their teaching and practices to the abstract (Loughran, 2010) of the Newton et al. (2010) principles, and vice versa. These conversations became catalysts for the teachers' reflections, helping them to move beyond the individual's thoughts and feelings and into the realm of research-informed practice.

The critical friend conversations developed differently for each researcher–teacher partnership. Since Martin, as Principal Investigator, was collating all the data from transcripts of our conversations for the milestone reports required by the project

7.5 Phase II

funder, he had a sense of these differences, as he pointed out in an email to the researcher team around halfway through the first inquiry cycle:

> ... several of us are working hard in the reflections to scaffold people into next steps—thanks for doing that! People may find it useful to listen, as an example, to the post-lesson reflections that Christine undertook with Kelly. Christine usefully probed Kelly to think further about how she could exploit some pretty key intercultural incidents, guiding her to think about how she could get the students to reflect on what they thought and how they felt.

In the transcript of Christine's debriefing with Kelly, they are discussing the topic of family that Kelly had selected for her beginner Mandarin class. Kelly had decided to include a discussion on the one-child policy in China, recognising that the mainly Pasifika students in her class would often come from larger families. The following excerpt from the debriefing illustrates the probing done by Christine as Kelly's critical friend:

Christine: You mentioned a lot of them [in China] grew up without siblings and I think that can be explored a little bit more: 'What would that feel like? What wouldn't you have?' And in comparison, 'what do you have here?' But also 'what are the challenges?' like, 'how many siblings in comparison?' I think you wanted to look at the values and the beliefs underneath. So possibly a little bit into that, if you looked at 'what does that feel like?'

Kelly: I didn't actually think of getting into that like that, but that is actually a really good idea, because if I do want to go on [to] the values. I think in my mind I keep focusing on the comparing and contrasting [Principle 4], you know what I mean. It's hard to try and think of all of them [the Newton et al. principles].

Christine: And one way can be to focus on this and go more in depth, and you would still compare and contrast. I think you would take it to a more emotional level or to think about 'what are the consequences of this?' Because otherwise it's on a factual level.

The ideal was that all of us would assume the probing and critical role that Christine was establishing with Kelly. However, since the circumstances of each partnership were different, occasionally the processes of developing a relationship, building trust and conceptualising the project had, comparatively, been somewhat more rushed and piecemeal. This meant that we felt that some of the teachers were operating with less conviction about the goals of the project and were engaging less critically. For some of us, this meant that we had to tread carefully and exercise professional courage (Alexander, 2010) to balance keeping the project moving forward with tactfully encouraging the teachers to engage more deeply, since their control of their own inquiries was crucial for the goals set for the project. We were, overall, encouraged to see that all the teachers did seem to be actively engaged with the project.

7.5.2 Promoting Reflective Practices

In order to support the teachers' reflective processes throughout the first inquiry cycle, we agreed to set up shared folders for each teacher in Google Drive so that they could archive documents relevant to the project alongside their reflections. For example, Kathryn included a file with a presentation she had given to her school's staff on her own involvement. She reported on her written reflection that she had told her colleagues, "the biggest takeaway for me so far is that it is just as important to be raising students' cultural awareness as it is to be teaching the language itself."

To further support teachers' reflections, Adèle, who was not working directly with any of the teachers in their school, offered to have critical friend reflective (written) conversations with each of the teachers. The teachers were encouraged to reflect at two levels as described by Farrell (2012) and to place these reflections in the folder. We first encouraged reflection at a descriptive level where teachers could regularly pause to consider and evaluate their actions. They were to follow that with a more focused reflection where they were to draw on the Newton et al. (2010) principles to evaluate their practices and search for evidence on the outcomes of their reflections. Accordingly, we suggested:

- jot down your reflections regularly in an ongoing reflections document if possible—even a couple of sentences a week.
- when you do get to reflect in a bit more depth, do have Newton et al.'s principles in mind—which ones come to the fore at this point? How can I enhance understandings? What questions should I ask next (of myself? My plan? The learners?).

Through these reflective exercises, we aimed to support the teachers in developing the ability to distance themselves from their practices in order to look into them with different eyes (Brookfield, 1995). These framings and reframings were not about justifying particular actions or decisions, but about seeing alternatives, because taking alternative perspectives offers insights into how and why a situation might be perceived in a particular way (Loughran, 2002).

The following thread illustrates how Adèle supported Kelly's reflection through praising progress and decisions made, posing questions about the planned inquiry, offering suggestions on how to collect evidence of students' intercultural learning, and encouraging deeper reflection:

> 9th August
>
> Looks like you're making great progress with the planning for your inquiry. I have a small question for you. Do you have a particular format (table/diagram/questions) that will frame (1) your own reflections? (2) the records of prior knowledge that the children will complete?

Kelly responded by apologising for a late reply and explaining that her plan was to ask each student to complete a Venn diagram on "family" in New Zealand and China to determine their prior knowledge of intersections and difference. Adèle's promptings continued as follows:

7.5 Phase II

26th August

Don't worry about when you come in here to "reply" to me—I'll be in and out every couple of weeks to keep the conversation going and will catch up on any responses at those times. The Venn diagram idea sounds like a good one.

When you talk to the students, it would be good to recall the questions you use, the prompts etc. to elicit their ideas and thinking. Some you will have thought ahead about, others might come on the spur of the moment … if you can remember, do keep a record of these for your notes. Helps to document your thinking and the process you went through … make sense? Have fun!

21st September

Hi again! Great to see your regular reflections and some data—I'm just about to listen to the audio file.

7th October

From your reflections and the audio snippet I can see that you are definitely focusing on the 4th principle in particular—you use explicit questioning …

One observation (not a criticism) from listening to the audio—towards the end you ask them to think of some adjectives or phrases to describe their families—some of the time you probe for further explanation—but I notice you only do that for the "negative" comments/phrases—these seem to dominate their responses, which I guess is why you later make a comment in your own notes about "unsettling descriptions of families."

Some extra ideas could have also come out if you probe the positive comments for more also—e.g., "what do you mean by caring?"

Despite the potential for feedback and direction available through the Google Drive initiative, and different attempts to motivate the teachers to write down and share their reflections with the research team, this channel for guiding reflections did not gain traction, and we decided to stop bringing this avenue for feedback to teachers' attention. Rather, we preferred to have the teachers invested in their own inquiries, since these were central to the work. Also, the debriefing interviews after observations still provided crucial opportunities for reflection.

As the inquiries progressed, evidence was emerging that teachers were able to facilitate a level of noticing of intercultural comparisons and contrasts with their students. However, it also became evident that "it is proving challenging to encourage teachers to take the next (harder) step of encouraging their students to *reflect* on how they think and feel about the comparisons and contrasts and, therefore, what the contrasts in particular *mean* for them as learners and developing 'intercultural interlocutors'" (Milestone Report, September 2016, our emphases). This was further confirmed in our summative interviews with the teachers and focus group interviews with the students at the end of Phase II. As there was a natural break at the end of the year, we decided to reflect on the issue ourselves and take appropriate actions as we prepared for Phase III of the project.

7.6 Phase III

In Phase III, the teachers were to embark on their second inquiry cycle, and with a new group of students, from the start of the new school year in 2017. The exception to this arrangement was Lillian who continued with the same group of students in the following school year. In the transition from one school year to the next, two teachers changed schools. This resulted in Tamara not being able to continue with the project and Kelly remaining in the project, but with a new school community. We carefully planned the second two-day hui where all researchers and teachers would come together so that we could provide spaces to deepen the teachers' reflection and learning.

From our analysis of data emerging from Phase II, we had identified several limitations in the inquiries regarding the collection of evidence of developing intercultural capability among learners. We saw this second hui as pivotal in our next steps with the teachers as co-researchers, and as a means both to value their own knowledge of practice and to recognise their contributions to the creation of knowledge (Lave & Wenger, 1991). We were mindful that our presentations of relevant concepts to the teachers had to be made "in ways to bring these concepts to bear on concrete practical activity, connecting them to their everyday knowledge and the goal-directed activities of teaching" (Johnson & Golombek, 2011, p. 2). After up to a year in the project, we wanted to give the teachers the opportunity to engage more actively as researchers, ensuring that they felt they would benefit from participation in the project and that they could contribute equally to it (Burns, 2015). Consequently, we started the meeting with the teachers sharing their insights from the Phase II inquiries and relating those to the analysis we had carried out. These were valuable opportunities for the teacher partners to hear from each other how their inquiries had gone. We also included a session that aimed to provide the teachers with first-hand experience of data analysis by getting them to examine a sample of the student data, and thereby gain some insight into the students' journeys to that point.

On the second day of the hui, each teacher was invited to describe their plans for the Phase III inquiries. We had suggested the following key questions as a guide to the teachers' planning and presentation:

- What will the second teaching as inquiry sequence look like in my school context?
- How might I evaluate my students' intercultural learning outcomes?
- How might my students record/document their intercultural reflections?
- How will you ensure that language and culture are inter-related?

It was at this juncture that a significant critical incident occurred. Our aim was to facilitate group discussion and input, aimed at clarifying aspects of proposed inquiry cycles as we supported the teachers in their planning. Lillian began to talk of a plan to help her students to understand how some practices can be seen differently by different cultures, thus helping to avoid stereotyping. As the group began probing into different aspects of her planning, it became evident that there was a disconnect between the focus and aims established for the project and Lillian's understanding

7.6 Phase III

of them. A long discussion (about an hour) ensued, where the group of researchers tried to address several mismatches that Lillian articulated with regard to the purpose of the project, the goals of language learning and the research process.

A number of issues emerged. It seemed at this point that Lillian perceived that we, as researchers:

- were trying to impose an agenda on the teachers;
- were going to formally assess student intercultural outcomes;
- had a narrow focus on intercultural gains (compare, contrast and reflect) and not on linguistic gains (despite our advocacy for an interface).

In response to the concern that we seemed to keep on pushing an agenda for a language–culture interface, Martin explained that our goal was "teasing out that language–culture relationship …" Before Martin could continue, Lillian asked for clarification to the teachers' group regarding what we expected to see in the students—enhanced intercultural capability or (by apparent contrast) knowledge of the language. It seemed Lillian perceived that we were only interested in the former and that we would assess that in a formal way. This time, Christine responded, "we are not assessing. I don't see myself assessing any of your students. I see myself as wanting to find out, but not assessing as in judging … I'm trying to find out what happens in a particular process." Jocelyn added, "it's an exploration that you are all going to do quite differently. From this perspective, the issues become, how is it working? And how you might decide to change it. There's no right and wrong."

Despite what we regarded as appropriate reassurances, Lillian questioned *why* it was important to get the students to the point of appreciating otherness. Jocelyn attempted an explanation: the purpose was "to work out how within a language programme we can be developing … beyond 'the cultural aspects' [signalling the practice of isolating cultural facts] to that sense of comfort in meeting with people from other different cultures and languages." Martin provided a more detailed description of how the project had arisen from the mismatch between what the NZC expected (i.e., the inclusion of an intercultural dimension) and what we knew was happening in practice (i.e., a focus on language to the [partial or total] exclusion of culture). He elaborated on the aims of the project and how we were working with the teachers to find out if there were workable ways to address the mismatch. He added a clarification of our intention as researchers—"as a researcher, I want to see what's the evidence that I have from your inquiries [as] to what works and what doesn't work and therefore how to inform the curriculum." Lillian acknowledged, albeit with apparent reticence, that an intercultural goal could potentially be achieved in the inquiry being planned, but argued that there could be no guarantee that this would actually help learners to be better communicators, apparently because the project was not interested in communication.

We encouraged Lillian to articulate her understanding of what we intended. It seemed that, from her perspective, the goal was to see whether culture could be integrated with language and whether that integration enhanced students' ability to communicate with TL speakers. Lillian thus wished to establish whether learners had increased in vocabulary knowledge of the target concept as well as whether or not there had been a shift away from stereotypical thinking. These conclusions gelled, to a large extent, with the direction of the project. Nonetheless, Lillian interpreted this stance as meaning that students would not be focusing on communication. She seemed adamant that what the teachers were looking for as outcomes were different from what the researchers were looking for, despite Christine's reassurance that "I don't think it's that different, honestly."

To draw the session to a close, Adèle added some important clarifications:

> We are not looking to prove anything. It's different ways to look at knowledge. We are not trying to prove that A equals B; or that if A happens, then B happens, and how to measure that. We are not looking to say what should be done for each of your inquiries. We are looking to see what is happening, how [it] is happening, how you are interpreting it … there is no right or wrong … And I know you want us to say 'this is exactly what we want from you or your students'. This is not that kind of study. We are not trying to find particular little things in a box. That's why it can be a little bit frustrating.

Adèle concluded by clarifying that the design of the research project was not confirmatory but, rather, exploratory, and that our position as researchers was to support the teachers' inquiries and decision-making.

This major critical incident was unexpected and disconcerting for us as researchers. Up to that point, we had thought that the teachers were clear about the aims of the project. After all, they had already been working with their research partner for almost a year and had already completed one interculturally focused inquiry cycle. That first year of the project had been designed to develop the community of inquiry and scaffold the teachers' engagement in the inquiry (Butler & Schnellert, 2012). We thought that we had established a reciprocal relationship where the research team was following the experiences of the teachers in their classrooms, while supporting them in developing theoretical understandings of their practices and the Newton et al. (2010) principles as a curricular innovation. As mentioned before, when we planned the second two-day hui (which took place at the beginning of Phase III), we knew that there were aspects of the project where we felt the teachers needed further scaffolding. We had anticipated that the teachers would need support in identifying means to evaluate their students' development of intercultural capability. However, we did not anticipate misunderstandings at the level of the goals of the project or uncertainties about the need to include an intercultural dimension in L2 teaching.

We concluded that the discussion that had taken place had probably made the teachers feel vulnerable and challenged when describing their practices. As Manfra (2019) asserted, "[a]ction research is predicated on changing practice through experience. This experience leads to disequilibrium, requiring teachers to question and affirm their professional knowledge" (p. 184). What we experienced as we were trying to co-construct knowledge with the teachers is described by Wall and Hall (2017) as the interaction of two principles: the principle of *disturbance* and the principle of *dialogue*. Our session based on critical dialogue had clearly created a disturbance in the teachers' views of their practices, leading one of the group to question the researchers and query some fundamentals of the project, in a sense asserting their own professional knowledge in light of disturbance to the equilibrium. In turn, as researchers, we learned that the dialogue that emerged was "more nuanced than simply talk" (Wall & Hall, 2017, p. 48), that is, despite our best efforts there were likely underlying tensions as the teachers might have perceived us as the "experts" in the context. Furthermore, we recognised that different teacher members of the collaborative inquiry were engaging differently in the inquiry processes. As Johnson and Golombek (2011) put it, "critical to the uneven and rather idiosyncratic nature of their [the teachers'] conceptual development was their own learning and teaching histories, the institutional and cultural contexts in which they were situated" (p. 5). We trusted, however, that, overall, the teacher partners felt supported through our interactions. Furthermore, a careful review of other interactions and debriefings with Lillian seemed to indicate that she did have more clarity about the project than this critical incident would indicate, and certainly the incident was not mentioned again as she embarked (positively) on the second inquiry cycle.

We decided to balance the hesitations and push-back of one teacher with the situation for the other three Phase III teachers. We also decided to guide the Phase III debriefing reflections with a revised set of questions that specifically addressed some of the issues that had arisen in the hui, and provided clear ownership by the teachers:

- If we compare this inquiry with last year's, what would you say are the changes you've made to planning the inquiry? What has caused those changes?
- Have you taken into account the inquiry cycle in your planning? [Use the inquiry cycle diagram—Ministry of Education, 2007, p. 35].
- Can you walk me through your planning to get to this lesson, or show me your planning?
- We discussed in the hui possible ways to evaluate students' language learning outcomes including intercultural outcomes. How do you plan to go about that? [reminder: pre- and post-Venn diagrams, or KWL tables—what we already know; what we wonder; what we have learned].
- What evidence will you collect from the students for this inquiry? [prompt: ways of documenting students' intercultural reflections].

We also made efforts to mitigate any sense of threat the teachers might be feeling as a consequence of a perceived power differential (Wang & Zhang, 2014) and brought it up with the group of teachers to convey how much we valued their own inquiries. To this end, a post-hui email to participants was sent by Martin:

> We wanted to re-iterate something that is very important for us in this project: the work you do with your own students should be work that you CHOOSE to do in the context of your own school. We are encouraging you to consider how language and culture fit together, and how, in the context of language learning, your students' intercultural skills may be developed. Within that overarching goal, we don't want to impose on you what you should do; rather, we want to encourage you to explore what is comfortable to you in light of your knowledge of your own students, using the NZC 'teaching as inquiry' cycle.

Towards the end of the semester, the milestone report of June 2017 recognised advances in the teachers' understandings of the Newton et al. (2010) principles and their own learning processes:

> The evidence available suggests that teachers have grown considerably by virtue of participation in the project. Observations of Lillian, for example, revealed a deeper understanding of the six Newton et al. (2010) principles, clearer appreciation of how to facilitate students' reflection on cultural similarities and differences, and greater awareness of the possibilities and challenges of including intercultural reflection into language learning (in particular, how to integrate language and culture—Newton et al.'s Principle 1).
>
> It was also very pleasing to see Kathryn make a presentation to her peers at a recent New Zealand Association of Language Teachers language seminar.[1] Her presentation revealed evidence of Kathryn's own professional learning and development by virtue of her participation in the project, but also of her students' learning. Kathryn spoke of her students' greater comfortableness not only with exploring cultural similarities and differences, but also with their own culture, and what they themselves brought to class. This, in our view (and hers), indicates a significant learning outcome on the part of her students.

We were pleased to see that, despite some uncertainties that had surfaced in the initial hui, the teachers were demonstrating in practice that their inquiries were having an impact on their learning, their students' learning and their classroom practices. As they conducted their new inquiries, we expected the teachers to become more conscious of how they were integrating the Newton et al. (2010) principles into their language teaching practices. By giving them control over the focus of their inquiries, we were "demonstrating a trust in their knowledge of their students' needs and the best way for them to be addressed" (Wall & Hall, 2017, p. 56).

As the Phase III inquiries began to draw to a close, the researchers and teacher partners realised that more time was needed to fully exploit the inquiry cycles. Therefore, a decision was made to extend the inquiry to the following school term (July to September), thus extending the original plan for Phase III. The end of that semester (early July) provided the space for the researchers to look back at the data collected so far in the second inquiry. We had the opportunity to meet as a research team at an international conference in Australia where we scheduled a full morning meeting. Central to the meeting were progress reports from each researcher on their work with the teacher partners, and key matters arising from Phase III of the project, as well as a discussion on Phase IV.

7.6.1 Challenges Emerging from the Inquiry Cycles

We were pleased with the developing evidence of comparison, contrast and reflection across cultures that appeared to be occurring. However, one core issue was emerging from our analysis of the teachers' inquiries: a separation that we all noticed between linguistic aspects and cultural aspects. That is, despite our attempts to encourage the integration of language and culture, it seemed that, in their planning and delivery of

---

[1] As we noted in Chap. 3, the "language seminars" or LangSems are one-day professional development opportunities organised on a biennial basis in different regions of the country by NZALT, the professional association of which many teachers of L2 in New Zealand are members.

lessons, the teachers—to varying degrees—separated the activities and discussions about cultural aspects from the teaching of the TL (see Chap. 6).

A crucial catalyst for our discussion on the language–culture divide was a keynote at the conference we were attending (Spada, 2018). With regard to the teaching of *language*, Spada revisited a question that had been at the forefront of her thinking for many years—whether attention to grammar should be integrated into, or isolated from, communicative activity and communicative language use. As we related what Spada was saying to New Zealand's three-strand model for *Learning Languages*, there were clear implications for the *language knowledge* strand: fully interwoven into the *communication* strand, standing as a separate component, or both. We started to contemplate whether that same analogy (integrated or isolated) could be applied to the *cultural knowledge* strand, and therefore to the data emerging from our project.

In particular, our analysis indicated that the students' intercultural reflections were carried out in English (the L1 of the majority of the students) as these seemed to be impossible in the TL for the beginner language learners. Of greater concern was that the teachers seemed to be conceptualising intercultural work as being achievable *only* by using English. We wondered whether we had inadvertently put teachers on a track where they had separated the language from the culture. We questioned our roles in the teachers' inquiries: had we failed as facilitators and knowledge brokers? Should we have directed the teachers differently? Despite the critical incident where one teacher had resisted a perceived attempt by us to impose a particular (separationist) agenda, we had decided to take a "non-interventionist" approach to our work with the teachers, refraining from judgement, for example, when we observed a language lesson that we perceived could have been improved. We had also decided to trust the teachers with their choices, since they knew their students and the possibilities of the project in their classrooms. However, in this critical incident, we wondered if that decision had been the wisest. Should the co-construction have been more directed? Furthermore, and again in light of one teacher's expressed reticence, we considered whether the teachers "misunderstood what was expected of them … interpreted things differently" (notes from July 2017 meeting).

Alternatively, were the teachers actually revealing in their emerging practices an important practical reality with regard to meaningful intercultural reflection of which we needed to take note? For example, compared to the first inquiry, Mike was using French less extensively in his teaching. Kathryn had almost abandoned any attention to linguistic aspects in her teaching and had, according to Constanza's observation notes, "moved 180 degrees to (inter)cultural teaching." Her planning had now focused exclusively on her students' group inquiries into Japanese food. Lillian had decided to teach Chinese language and culture in separate lessons. Mindful of a risk, Mike had already pointed out for himself, our meeting notes pointed to "the danger of this becoming a social sciences class." We acknowledged that, in the first two-day hui with the teachers (Phase II), we had foreshadowed (and aimed to guide the teachers away from) the possibility of the language–culture separation. We were disappointed at the emerging evidence that, despite our efforts to avoid this separation, a deeper separation of these two aspects was emerging in the teachers' classrooms. We were also puzzled about how to deal with this reality in what was left of the project and implications from the conclusions we would ultimately draw. As we noted in Chap. 6, the teachers expressed a concern that focusing on the intercultural appeared to detract from learning the language. In spite of several genuine efforts to embed the culture within the language (e.g., by facilitating intercultural exploration in clear alignment with a specific language focus), teachers struggled with a perceived incompatibility between L2 learning and intercultural reflection.

This critical incident and its resulting reflections on the classroom realities we were observing and their implications found expression in East et al. (2017), anticipated as a parallel publication to Spada (2018), where we speculated:

> Is intercultural understanding[2] better developed in an "integrated" model whereby intercultural noticing is interwoven with language in actual use? Or is it better developed in an "isolated" model whereby intercultural incidents are examined and reflected on outside of, or as an adjunct to, language in use? (p. 25)

As a result of our reflections, we drew several important conclusions which we take up in some detail in Chap. 8. At this juncture, it is important to note that our experiences and reflections were crucial as we embarked on the final stage of the project (Phase IV), where the focus would be on synthesising and publishing what had emerged from the teachers' journeys.

7.7 Phase IV

An important goal for Phase IV of the project was to capture each teacher's story through their eyes and their voice and complement the stories with alignment to the Newton et al. (2010) principles. We were hoping that these final reflective moments of looking back at the two years and the individual inquiries would provide further insights for all involved, including valuable insights into practice. We framed the stories as *Engaging Examples of Practice*, envisioned as short, teacher-friendly vignettes, to be made widely and freely available, so that other teachers of languages could read about the journeys of fellow teachers inquiring into the development of intercultural capability. As teacher educators, we knew that other L2 teachers would benefit from such a resource.

Thanks to additional funding, we were able to print a short-run of the stories in booklet form (East et al., 2018). The final publication integrated teaching, learning and research in ways that demonstrated how, through the project, we had co-constructed "pedagogical knowledge through dialectic interaction and critical exchange" (Burns, 2009, p. 294). The booklets were launched and distributed at the biennial international conference of the New Zealand Association of Language Teachers, held in Auckland in July 2018. We invited the teachers to participate in the

---

[2] In East et al. (2017) we used the term "intercultural understanding" rather than "intercultural capability" due to the primary target audiences (practitioners and researchers in Australia) who were more likely to be familiar with the former term (see Chap. 1).

launch as a way of giving closure to the project. After all, the booklet represented their journeys and their stories. Furthermore, the stories continue to be made available online as a key resource for L2 teachers in New Zealand (Ministry of Education, 2019).

7.8 Conclusion

The focus of this chapter has been on presenting our journey as researchers as we worked with the teacher partners who undertook two inquiry cycles in their schools, following the journey chronologically through each of the four phases of the project.

In all we did, we tried to balance the competing demands of the goals and expectations of a research project with respecting the rhythms and realities of each teacher's work. Similarly to the different paths the teachers took regarding their inquiries (as seen in Chaps. 5 and 6), their engagement with the larger inquiry was also diverse, no doubt reflecting their own prior knowledge, school context and experiences with L2 learning and teaching.

We were also mindful that, contrary to ideals of action research, the project had been developed by the research team and we ran the risk that teachers' ownership and agency could have been limited. In setting up different formats of meetings and opportunities to discuss issues, we aimed to open spaces for the teachers to contribute their ideas to the development of the project. We wanted them to be part of the process of inquiring into and reflecting on the inclusion of interculturality in their L2 programmes, and, through that, contributing to our understanding of bridging the distance between theory, curriculum and practice.

Throughout the project, the teachers were given opportunities to engage in productive and sustained reflection on different aspects of the project. We strongly believe that the inquiry process supported the teachers' developing understandings of their practices, in this case exploring the development of intercultural capability in their students. We found value in giving the teachers opportunities to understand the situated nature of learning and the relationship between practical and theoretical knowledge (Shulman, 1986). Through their inquiries, these teachers explored alternative solutions to pedagogical problems (Timperley et al., 2014).

When we conceived the collaboration, we were fully aware of the support that teachers require to embark on a project like ours. Despite the funded release time that we were able to provide for the teachers, and evidence of their engagement in the project and apparent genuine interest in the development of their learners' intercultural capability through their L2 teaching, we faced an important reality: the availability of time from the teachers was always limited, and did not allow for as full participation and commitment with the aims of the project as we would have liked.

A great deal occurred that was positive. Nevertheless, in this chapter, we have documented the realities and complexities of the processes of collaboration and inquiry that we experienced. Along the way, we identified key critical incidents that emerged as we undertook our own journey. The journey was by no means as straightforward as we had envisioned in the planning stages. Critical incidents represented significant points in the journey. In this chapter, we have aimed to tell the whole story and present a honest account of our project (McNiff, 2014). By sharing the process and its complexity, alongside unpredictable and surprising moments, and the ways that we addressed them, we join others who have described these endeavours as "messy" (Adamson & Walker, 2011; Butler & Schnellert, 2012; Timperley et al., 2014).

We started the project with the goal of giving the teachers a voice and valuing their knowledge and experience. Along the way, we found that listening to the teacher partners provided many insights not only on their work as teachers of languages but also on their efforts to grapple with a new construct and the difficulties they encountered. In turn, those reflections became central to our own understandings of the opportunities and challenges of implementing the intercultural dimension in L2 programmes. In the final chapter, we discuss the implications of all that we have presented in this and the preceding two chapters in light of the findings of research in other contexts.

References

Adamson, B., & Walker, E. (2011). Messy collaboration: Learning from a learning study. *Teaching and Teacher Education, 27*, 29–36.
Alexander, R. (2010). *Children, their world, their education.* Routledge.
Allwright, D., & Hanks, J. (2009). *The developing language learner: An introduction to exploratory practice.* Palgrave Macmillan.
Ball, D. (2000). Bridging practices: Intertwining content and pedagogy in teaching and learning to teach. *Journal of Teacher Education, 51*(3), 241–247.
Baumfield, V., Hall, E., & Wall K. (2012). *Action research in education: Learning through practitioner enquiry* (2nd ed.). Sage.
Bevins, S. C., & Price, G. (2014). Collaboration between academics and teachers: A complex relationship. *Educational Action Research, 22*(2), 270–284.
Biebricher, C. (2015). Effects of a professional development programme on New Zealand language teacher beliefs and teaching practice. In *The Asian conference on language learning 2015: Integrated practices: Creating experiences to enhance learning* (pp. 451–463). The International Academic Forum. http://iafor.org/archives/proceedings/ACLL/ACLL2015_proceedings.pdf
Brandenburg, R. (2008). *Powerful pedagogy: Self-study of a teacher educator's practice.* Springer.
Brookfield, S. (1995). *Becoming a critically reflective teacher.* Jossey-Bass.
Burns, A. (1999). *Collaborative action research for English language teachers.* Cambridge University Press.
Burns, A. (2005). Action research: An evolving paradigm? *Language Teaching, 38*(2), 57–74.
Burns, A. (2009). Action research in second language teacher education. In A. Burns & J. C. Richards (Eds.), *The Cambridge guide to second language teacher education* (pp. 289–297). Cambridge University Press.
Burns A. (2015). Renewing classroom practices through collaborative action research. In K. Dikilitas, R. Smith, & W. Trotman (Eds.), *Teacher-researchers in action*, (pp. 9–18). International Association of Teachers of English as a Foreign Language (IATEFL),

References

Burns, A. (2019). Action research: Developments, characteristics, and future directions. In J. Schwieter & A. Benati (Eds). *The Cambridge handbook of language learning* (pp. 166–185). Cambridge University Press.

Butler, D. L., & Schnellert, L. (2012). Collaborative inquiry in teacher professional development. *Teaching and Teacher Education, 28*, 1206–1220.

Butler, D. L., Schnellert, L., & MacNeil, K. (2015). Collaborative inquiry and distributed agency in educational change: A case study of a multi-level community of inquiry. *Journal of Educational Change, 16*, 1–26.

Costa, A., & Kallick, B. (1993). Through the lens of a critical friend. *Educational Leadership, 51*(2), 49–51.

East, M., Howard, J., Tolosa, C., Biebricher, C., & Scott, A. (2017). Isolated or integrated? Should the development of students' intercultural understanding be separated from, or embedded into, communicative language use? *Babel, 52*(2/3), 25–31.

East, M., Tolosa, C., Biebricher, C., Howard, J., & Scott, A. (2018). *Enhancing language learners' intercultural capability: A study in New Zealand's schools.* Languages Research NZ.

Ellis, R. (2005). *Instructed second language acquisition: A literature review.* Ministry of Education.

Farrell, T. (2012). *Reflective writing for language teachers.* Equinox.

González, G., Deal, J. T., & Skultety, L. (2016). Facilitating teacher learning when using different representations of practice. *Journal of Teacher Education, 67*(5), 447–466.

Howard, J. (2012). Teaching and learning languages in New Zealand primary schools: Principals' perspectives. *The New Zealand Language Teacher, 38*, 29–38.

Howard, J., Scott, A., & East, M. (2015). Sparkly and pink and bright: Investigating intercultural learning in a New Zealand primary language class. *The New Zealand Language Teacher, 41*, 34–47.

Johnson, K., & Golombek, P. (2011). *Research on second language teacher education: A sociocultural perspective on professional development.* Routledge.

Kennedy, J. (2016). *Exploring opportunities for developing intercultural competence through intercultural communicative language teaching (ICLT): A case study in a Chinese as a foreign language classroom in a New Zealand high school* [Masters dissertation, Victoria University of Wellington, New Zealand].

Lave, J., & Wenger, E. (1991). *Situated learning: Legitimate peripheral participation.* Cambridge University Press.

Loughran, J. (2002). Effective reflective practice: In search of meaning in learning about teaching. *Journal of Teacher Education, 53*(1), 33–43.

Loughran, J. (2010). Reflection through collaborative action research and inquiry. In N. Lyons (Ed.), *Handbook of reflection and reflective inquiry: Mapping a way of knowing for professional reflective inquiry.* (pp. 399–413). Springer.

Manfra, M. M. (2019). Action research and systematic change in teaching practice. *Review of Research in Education, 43*(1), 163–196.

McLaughlin, C., Black-Hawkins, K., & McIntyre, D. (2004). *Researching teachers, researching schools, researching networks: A review of the literature.* Cambridge University Press.

McNiff, J. (2014). *Writing and doing action research.* Sage.

McNiff, J. (2016). *You and your action research project* (4th ed.). Routledge.

Ministry of Education. (2007). *The New Zealand curriculum.* Learning Media.

Ministry of Education. (2019). *Enhancing language learners' intercultural capability: A study in New Zealand's schools.* https://learning-languages.tki.org.nz/News/Enhancing-Language-Learners-Intercultural-Capability-A-study-in-New-Zealand-s-schools

Newton, J., Yates, E., Shearn, S., & Nowitzki, W. (2010). *Intercultural communicative language teaching: Implications for effective teaching and learning—A literature review and an evidence-based framework for effective teaching.* Ministry of Education.

Passman, R. (2002, April). *Going public: Middle-level teachers build a learning community through reflective discussions.* Paper presented at the American Educational Research Association, New Orleans, LA.

Ramírez, E. (2018). Intercultural communicative language teaching (iCLT): A selection of practical points of departure. *The New Zealand Language Teacher, 44*, 18–30.

Scarino, A. (2014). Learning as reciprocal, interpretive meaning-making: A view from collaborative research into the professional learning of teachers of languages. *The Modern Language Journal, 98*(1), 386–401.

Scott, A. (2014). Wicked: The untold story of teachers of additional languages in New Zealand schools. *The New Zealand Language Teacher, 40*, 9–19.

Shulman, L. (1986). Those who understand: Knowledge growth in teaching. *Educational Researcher, 15*(2), 4–31.

Spada, N. (2018). Isolating or integrating attention to form in communicative instruction: A dilemma? *Babel, 53*(1), 7–12.

Timperley, H. (2011). *Realizing the power of professional learning*. Open University Press.

Timperley, H., Kaser, L., & Halbert, J. (2014, April). *A framework for transforming learning in schools: Innovation and the spiral of inquiry* (Centre for Strategic Education, Seminar Series Paper No. 234).

Tolosa, C., East, M., & Villers, H. (2015). Motivating 21st century learners: The impact of an online reciprocal peer-tutoring initiative for foreign language learning. In C. Koh (Ed.), *Motivating, leading and designing learning for the net generation* (pp. 137–149). Springer.

Tripp, D. (2012). *Critical incidents in teaching: Developing professional judgment*. Routledge.

Wall, K., & Hall, E. (2016). Teachers as metacognitive role models. *European Journal of Teacher Education, 39*(4), 403–418.

Wall, K., & Hall, E. (2017). The teacher in teacher-practitioner research: Three principles of inquiry. In P. Boyd & A. Szplit (Eds.), *International perspectives: Teachers and teacher educators learning through enquiry* (pp. 35–62). Wydawnictwo Attyka.

Wang, Q., & Zhang, H. (2014). Promoting teacher autonomy through university-school collaborative action research. *Language Teaching Research, 18*(2), 222–241.

Zeichner, K. M. (1994). Research on teacher thinking and different views of reflective practice in teaching and teacher education. In I. Carlgren, G. Handal, & S. Vaage (Eds.), *Teachers' minds and actions: Research on teachers' thinking and practice* (pp. 9–28). Falmer Press.

Open Access This chapter is licensed under the terms of the Creative Commons Attribution 4.0 International License (http://creativecommons.org/licenses/by/4.0/), which permits use, sharing, adaptation, distribution and reproduction in any medium or format, as long as you give appropriate credit to the original author(s) and the source, provide a link to the Creative Commons license and indicate if changes were made.

The images or other third party material in this chapter are included in the chapter's Creative Commons license, unless indicated otherwise in a credit line to the material. If material is not included in the chapter's Creative Commons license and your intended use is not permitted by statutory regulation or exceeds the permitted use, you will need to obtain permission directly from the copyright holder.

Chapter 8
Journeys Towards Intercultural Capability: Retrospective Reflections

8.1 Introduction

In the preceding three chapters, we have presented the findings of our two-year New Zealand Ministry of Education-funded study into the development of the intercultural capability of young beginner learners of an additional language (L2). We focused, respectively, on the students (Chap. 5), the teachers (Chap. 6) and ourselves as researchers/teacher educators (Chap. 7). In this concluding chapter, we draw each of the strands from Chaps. 5–7 together. In particular, we consider what we learned and the recommendations we would make, as both researchers and teacher educators, to move the debates about developing young L2 learners' intercultural capability further. Drawing on the three preceding chapters and aspects of the final report we submitted to our funder (East et al., 2018b), this chapter revisits the positive outcomes, along with the problems and challenges. We first present a summary of our key findings and then discuss the implications.

8.2 What We Found

Our first research question (RQ1) was this: How do stakeholders' understandings about enhancing language learners' intercultural capability change and develop over time?

In Chap. 1, we owned the reality that, for a host of reasons, the development of interculturality through L2 learning (in particular with younger learners) is a challenging enterprise. The challenge is exacerbated by the fact that the construct of "the intercultural" is murky (Dervin et al., 2020). By way of bringing some level of clarity, Dervin (2020) argued, "objectively, no one can claim to be right or wrong, better or worse in their visions of interculturality." He went on to suggest that, as a consequence, "one must be transparent about the way(s) one defines, problematises and uses the notion of interculturality" (p. 58). In our opening chapter, we presented transparently the definition of intercultural capability that we had set for ourselves, for the project and for RQ1—"the ability to relate comfortably with people from diverse linguistic and cultural backgrounds, appreciating and valuing the learners' own cultures and uniqueness alongside the cultures and uniqueness of others" (Biebricher et al., 2019, p. 606).

We also explained in Chap. 5 that, in line with our definition of intercultural capability, the Newton et al. (2010) Principles 3 and 4 became the primary (albeit not exclusive) foci for the five generalist teachers as they planned their lessons. This emphasis was in accord with two stated outcomes of the curriculum: that beginners with learning the target language (TL) might be expected, first, to recognise that the target culture is organised in particular ways, and, as they make progress, to be able to describe, compare and contrast cultural practices (Ministry of Education, 2009). These learning outcomes were designed to fulfil "the need to compare, contrast and establish relationships between concepts in their own and the foreign language" (Byram, 2021, p. 52). RQ1 specifically addressed the journeys of the different stakeholders as they engaged with practices that might lead towards the stated outcomes.

8.2.1 Students' Journeys: Developing Intercultural Capability

With regard to the students, there was evidence of nascent intercultural growth, and the emergence of *skills, abilities and knowledge* that might inform successful intercultural interactions, by virtue of comparison, contrast and reflection. Although, as we acknowledged in Chap. 5, this growth could not be described as linear or incremental (that is, it did not necessarily follow a particular upwards or deepening trajectory, but, rather, instances of learning and growth were discernible at different points), several key issues emerged.

Fundamentally, the students identified that their classroom experiences had introduced them to key facts or knowledge about the target culture that they may not have encountered previously. This led to a distinct noticing of differences, alongside greater awareness of their own cultural practices. These instances of noticing were often triggered by the videos they had been exposed to in lessons. In some instances, the students' first culture appeared to be regarded as normative, making the target culture "strange" in comparison. However, in other instances, initial stereotypical understandings became replaced with the ability to demonstrate greater openness to otherness, greater self-awareness regarding personal positionings, and greater questioning of initial stereotypes. There was also some evidence of comfortableness with a difference, expressed as a movement from *"at first I thought…"* to *"now I think…"* This led, for some students, to an increase in acceptance of and respect for difference.

8.2 What We Found

It was clear that the students in our study exhibited dimensions of Byram's (1997, 2021) *savoirs*, in particular with regard to comparative acceptance of self and others, and some emergent skills in critical evaluation. It was also clear that, although they were not necessarily able to express it as such, and although we acknowledged in Chap. 5 that we cannot confidently claim "third place" positioning for any of the students, some students were beginning to understand the meaning of such positioning. This could be described as a "comfortable and unbounded" space (Liddicoat & Crozet, 2000, p. 1), that is, a space of *accommodation* where users of an L2 are able to accept difference as something to be expected, rather than something to be threatened by, alongside a willingness to suspend a separatist "first culture" perspective. One student of French in Mike's class put it like this: "I think our culture, I think there is … almost a blend together … because sometimes we do the same things, sometimes we don't." This student went on to explain that this "blending" necessarily compelled people to confront difference and otherness without necessarily losing sight of their own positioning.

A student of Mandarin in Lillian's class suggested, "we should respect their culture and they should respect ours … like sharing everybody's cultures around, like knowing about different cultures." From this perspective, "we are all treated equally." Another in the same class ventured that, in light of an intercultural focus, "first of all, I understand them better and so I know why they do specific things unlike me or others." As a consequence, "I kind of respect the other cultures, and I kind of, well, replace my culture with the other culture so I can make my culture, like, better, I guess." This student went on to give an example that usefully illustrates a third place positioning, and what this student meant by "replace my culture with the other culture," even though the student could not articulate this in a more elaborate way:

> Everybody has a different culture … so it is sharing … [until] there is no such thing called 'country', like everybody will be just mixed up in a bunch, jumbled up in a salad. Instead of 'this is a tomato corner', 'this is a cucumber corner'—this is a 'salad corner.'

In interpreting this perspective in our final report (East et al., 2018b), we argued:

> a tomato and a cucumber do not cease to be by virtue of being in a salad, but they are no longer individual and standing alone; each contributes its own uniqueness to the whole, arguably making the whole a more complete expression by virtue of its contributing parts. (p. 12)

Over and above any student learning that appeared to have occurred as a consequence of explicit intercultural aims, the student focus group discussions revealed other aspects of the students' learning journeys. Most particularly, the students made frequent spontaneous references to increases in motivation and enjoyment as a consequence of opportunities to encounter and think about cultural differences.

The student discussions also suggested that increased cultural understandings manifested in greater confidence and more positive attitudes towards engaging with the TL in the future. As we noted in Chap. 5, these unanticipated outcomes highlight the possibility that the specific intercultural foci, *in and of themselves* and quite apart from language learning, influenced the learners' overall engagement and sense of enjoyment. They also point to the possibility that, as a result, these students might not only choose to continue with L2 study but might also find opportunities to put what they had learned into practice in future real contexts.

8.2.2 Teachers' Journeys: Developing Intercultural Teaching and Learning

A tangible benefit for the teachers, as noted in Chap. 6, was that the increased intercultural focus was a new dimension of language teaching and learning that they had not seriously considered up to that time. Lillian, for example, commented, "I do fully support that [this] is what language is all about. It's not just about teaching how to say it, the structure, but it is actually seeing the bigger picture." The intercultural focus had enabled the teachers to bring greater perceived relevance into their teaching, giving the learners opportunities to explore and challenge pre-existing ideas in self-reflective ways.

The teachers recognised that the inquiry learning cycles had prompted instances of deeper levels of critical reflection on the part of the students that helped to move them beyond generalised or stereotypical thinking—for example, an important driver for what Mike attempted to achieve in his classroom was, as he put it, "you can't just say 'people in France do this'." The inquiries, in the teachers' perception, also facilitated students' ability to make connections between the target culture, their own cultures, and the cultures of others in their class, in ways that illustrated that culture is dynamic and not static. Lillian explained, "they can actually say to me 'well, you know, my friend so and so is from China, they don't celebrate this and also they don't do things in certain ways like that'."

In parallel with what the student data had shown us, the teachers also noted an added motivational benefit to the intercultural foci that seemed to be absent when the focus was purely on language. For example, in Lillian's experience "[t]hey are definitely a lot more engaged than just teaching them, like, the actual characters and just the language of Chinese."

Despite the advantages, teachers perceived that they lacked sufficient knowledge of the target culture, and were concerned that they might as a consequence pass on inaccurate information or embed uninformed stereotypical thinking into their students. There was also perceived insufficient time to undertake intercultural exploration that they believed would really make a difference. Teachers were concerned that, going forward, they would simply not be able to sustain the level of intercultural inquiry they had been able to undertake by virtue of the project. In this regard, it was recognised that developing students' intercultural capability needed to be viewed as a longer-term goal, and something that required ongoing commitment over and above language teaching and learning—a hint, perhaps, that the intercultural was a bigger issue than one that could be addressed in the confines of a short language lesson.

That the intercultural exploration was viewed as "over and above" also indicated that, to varying degrees, the teachers were concerned that a focus on the intercultural detracted from learning the language, and that these teachers perceived L2 learning as largely about language. There was evidence of some genuine attempts to embed the culture within the language, for example by enabling the intercultural exploration to emerge from a specific language focus. Nevertheless, this was variable, and the teachers struggled with an apparent incompatibility between language learning and intercultural learning. This was perhaps most starkly expressed by Kathryn when she said towards the end of the project, "I think I achieved the cultural side, but the language side wasn't there just because the half hour wasn't long enough to be including the language and the culture." For Kathryn, the maintenance of balance was something that would exercise her once the project was completed. Lillian concurred that "a balance between the language structure learning as well as this [intercultural focus]" was "at the moment … a bit hard."

The segregation between language and culture was not always apparent. Tamara, in contrast to others, felt she had succeeded in her goal of "integrating Māori," through "not having a set lesson, but just embracing the bicultural nature of New Zealand through learning te reo" as part of the classroom programme. That is, "instead of saying 'we are going to be doing reading', right, *panui* [reading] time, and the kids, they just know it. Like, do you need to go to the *wharepaku* [toilet]? That kind of without it being 'I am doing Māori now'." Language use thus became "part of our *kaupapa* [programme] … part of what we do." However, seamless integration of *language* was arguably easier in a situation where Māori and English were often intertwined in daily lives. In the context of a nation in which te reo Māori is an official language with legal status, it is arguably easier to achieve greater integration than with a language (such as French or Japanese) that may be perceived as "other" or "separate," and that certainly does not feature in everyday life in the way that te reo Māori does.

8.2.3 Researchers' Journeys: Uncovering What Is Feasible

In Chap. 7, we took a step back from the students and the teachers, and considered our own journeys, primarily as researchers but also as teacher educators. For us as researchers, a number of events that we reported in Chap. 7 provided catalysts for our own reflection and growth as we grappled with what the teachers were experiencing. In particular, we focused on what we regarded as several "critical incidents" (Brandenburg, 2008; Tripp, 2012) that we identified through our reflections at different points in the research cycles.

We believed that the inquiry learning stance we were advocating fitted well with the constructivist learner-centred and experiential approach to learning underpinning the *New Zealand Curriculum* (NZC). The teachers confirmed their familiarity with the inquiry teaching and learning models, and so we believed that we were on relatively solid ground by advocating their use for learner-centred intercultural exploration. Our stance to supporting the teachers as they undertook their intercultural inquiries was framed from a mutual starting point.

Nonetheless, significant challenges emerged as the project progressed. We begin by summarising what we as researchers observed as challenges for the teachers in light of the findings of previous studies. First of all, it is noteworthy, and important to acknowledge, that the challenges experienced by the participating teachers align in many ways with those of teachers in other studies. These included feeling insufficiently prepared and uncertain what questions they should ask (Brunsmeier, 2017; Sercu, 2013), highlighting a need for upskilling in how to guide the conversations (Liddicoat, 2008). The challenge the teachers expressed around balancing linguistic and cultural aspects in their language lessons is also echoed in several other studies (see, e.g., Brunsmeier, 2017; Díaz, 2013; Sercu et al., 2005), and the lack of time to research, prepare and implement intercultural aspects has also been acknowledged (Castro et al., 2004; Díaz, 2013; Sercu et al., 2005).

Previous investigations also highlight the crucial role of reflection, as expressed by teachers in our project. The teachers' perceived need to reflect on their own beliefs and values is acknowledged by Liddicoat (2008) and Sercu et al. (2005) and is complemented by Moloney (2008)'s perception that teachers are sometimes not aware of their own cultural understandings. The teachers in our study also emphasised that they aimed to foster critical reflection in their students and at least some observed that their students' abilities to see things from a different viewpoint developed over time. These findings concur with studies conducted in the United States where teachers reported that their students could reflect on different views (see, e.g., Despoteris & Ananda, 2017; Roher & Kagan, 2017; Wagner et al., 2017).

Several significant challenges emerged by virtue of the context in which we were working. As previously stated, a key driver for us was to provide a balance between a top-down approach (whereby we as the researchers and the "experts" imposed both our theoretical understandings of "the intercultural" and how it might be developed in L2 classrooms) and a bottom-up approach (whereby we gave ownership to the teachers to discover for themselves what the intercultural meant to them alongside its development in each teaching context). However, and in line with the learner-centred and experiential emphases of the NZC alongside the important places for teaching as inquiry and inquiry learning in the curriculum, we deliberately placed greater emphasis on the teachers' own self-discovery, albeit a self-discovery that was guided by our prompting and input. As we acknowledged in Chap. 7, we wanted the teachers to become "agentive actors and investigators within their own social contexts" (Burns, 2019, p. 166).

Our navigation of a balance between top-down and bottom-up was not always easy. One critical incident (which we reported in Chap. 7) illustrated this for us in quite a powerful way. In the process of our second hui with the teachers in preparation for the second inquiry cycle, one of the teachers in the team expressed, in quite strong terms, a view that we, as researchers, had an agenda that we were imposing on the teachers and that we would formally assess in relation to student outcomes. This agenda, in this teacher's view, undermined the teacher's sense of autonomy and a consideration of what the teacher regarded as important for the classroom. We were concerned and surprised that this teacher, at least at this stage in the process and apparently in contrast to the other participants, perceived the imposition of a particular agenda rather than the negotiation of a shared agenda.

Our bottom-up stance was subsequently reinforced for the teachers in an email sent by Martin as Principal Investigator, in which he reiterated that the work that the teachers should carry out with their own students should be "work that you CHOOSE to do in the context of your own school." It was further clarified that we did not wish to impose a specific agenda but, rather, to encourage the teachers to explore what they were comfortable with in light of their immediate situations. Nonetheless, a largely bottom-up approach did raise significant issues which we will return to towards the end of this chapter.

Two other crucial tensions emerged as the project progressed, with which we wrestled quite extensively. The first of these was the tension between practising and using the TL versus utilising English as L1 as the vehicle for intercultural exploration. This led to the second issue—the extent to which the intercultural episodes needed to become separated from instances of TL use.

We were mindful that the teachers struggled as they attempted to juggle what they perceived as the primary goal of the project—intercultural comparison, contrast and reflection (which almost invariably required use of English)—and the primary goal of the L2 classroom—the learning of the language in question—which carried an assumption of maximal or exclusive TL use. In turn, the teachers struggled with the extent to which they could *integrate* the intercultural exploration into what they were doing in the classroom (i.e., interweave language with relevant episodes of cultural reflection and incorporate a culture-in-language position) and the extent to which they felt this intercultural exploration needed to be *isolated* from a language focus (i.e., dealt with in a separate and targeted way, albeit aligned in some way to the linguistic foci of the lesson or series of lessons). These two tensions became crucial issues for considerable reflection on our part (see our discussion of this in East et al., 2017). In what follows, we outline several theoretical considerations with regard to how L2 teaching and learning is perceived, both in the immediate context and beyond, that informed our reflections.

8.3 Language Teaching and Learning: Theoretical Considerations

8.3.1 Target Language or First Language Use?

The use of English for intercultural exploration, and what this might mean for a separation between language learning and intercultural exploration, begs more fundamental questions about how L2 pedagogy is perceived in the context. First of all, in the NZC the overriding goal of L2 programmes, and the core expectation of teachers' work, is clearly stated as *communication* in the TL. Also, as we have already made clear, the NZC encourages learner-centred and experiential pedagogical approaches in contrast to a top-down teacher-led model. For *Learning Languages*, a communicative and experiential L2 pedagogy is encouraged, for example, through the ten principles of the Ellis report (Ellis, 2005). As we outlined in Chap. 3, essentially it has been recommended that effective instruction in the L2 classroom would ensure a particular focus on fluency in the TL, predicated on extensive opportunities for learners to process language input, create language output and interact in the TL, alongside the development of implicit grammatical knowledge for purposes of effective communication.

Building on the ten Ellis principles as aligned to a learner-centred and experiential perspective, teachers have been encouraged to consider task-based language teaching (TBLT)—an approach we acknowledged in Chap. 1. In TBLT, however, "task" has taken on particular meanings and components which make it a specific phenomenon for L2 pedagogy.

To support teachers in achieving curricular aims from a task-based perspective, significant professional development has been provided for New Zealand teachers, particularly around the ten Ellis principles and TBLT. Thus, although in practice the enactment of TBLT in New Zealand classrooms is not mandated (and has also not necessarily been straightforward—see, e.g., Erlam & Tolosa, 2022), both TBLT and the principles that inform it have been extensively promoted (as we recognised in Chap. 3). As a consequence, approaches to L2 pedagogy in the New Zealand context place clear expectation on extensive TL use. That is, teachers are encouraged, according to Ellis (2005), to "[m]aximise use of the L2 inside the classroom," with the L2 becoming "the *medium* as well as the *object* of instruction" (our emphases), otherwise learners are "unlikely to achieve high levels of L2 proficiency" (p. 39). This brings into question the use of English as L1 as a component of curriculum delivery in the L2 classroom.

Although Ellis (2005) made the case that TL use should be *maximised* rather than *exclusive*, his principles appear to provide minimal scope for L1 use as a component of encouraging acquisition of the L2 in learner-centred ways. As a consequence, it should come as no surprise that teachers in the New Zealand context who have been exposed to the Ellis principles and professional development around TBLT would likely consider extensive TL use to be a significant component of learner-centred and experiential L2 pedagogy.

As we acknowledged in Chap. 1, however, TBLT does offer some potential for an integration between language and culture. Several authors have begun to explore the interface that can exist between TBLT and the development of intercultural capability (see, e.g., the study by Müller-Hartmann and Schocker [2018] that we noted in Chap. 2). With regard to the use of L1 in the context of TBLT, the value of the L1 as a mediating tool when completing L2 communicative tasks has been widely acknowledged (see, e.g., Seals et al., 2020). Learners may potentially use the L1 to support them in working at a higher level than might be possible if they only used the TL (Alegría de la Colina & García Mayo, 2009; Lightbown & Spada, 2020). As Swain and Lapkin (1995) put it, "[t]o insist that no use be made of the L1 in carrying out tasks that are both linguistically and cognitively complex is to deny the use of an important cognitive tool" (p. 269). Findings of studies have indicated that L1 use helps learners to manage the task and gives students opportunities to talk about the language they need to fulfil the task (Lasito & Storch, 2013).

Carless (2008) argued for "a balanced and flexible view of MT [mother tongue] use in the task-based classroom" (p. 336). An appropriate balance, according to Newton and Le Diem Bui (2020), "requires strategic and negotiated roles for L1 use and consideration of how it fits within the different phases of a task-based lesson" (p. 40). There is therefore precedent for *judicious, balanced and flexible* L1 use, even within a pedagogical approach such as TBLT that emphasises extensive use of the TL for purposes of input, output and interaction. This potentially creates room for intercultural explorations as "phases" of task-based lessons.

Nevertheless, the perception that teachers working within communicative or task-based paradigms should rely heavily on TL use (and avoid L1 use) is pervasive. We also acknowledged in Chap. 1 that exploration of the TBLT-intercultural interface is in its infancy. It is not likely to become part of the mainstream of the TBLT agenda for some time, if at all. As Scarino and Crichton (2007), for example, suggested, current approaches to language pedagogy do not sufficiently acknowledge the intercultural and do not help L2 learners to become intercultural. In the case of TBLT, TBLT and the intercultural are often seen as two distinct fields of scholarship (Adams & Newton, 2009). Exploring the intercultural within a communicative orientation to L2 pedagogy requires, as both Díaz (2013) and Crozet (2017) suggested, a *radical rethinking* of how language teaching may be conducted. This raises a further implication for our project.

8.3.2 Isolated or Integrated?

In the work we were undertaking with the teachers, we did not frame what we were encouraging the teachers to do as tasks as interpreted from a TBLT perspective. Additionally, the teachers in this study did not claim any substantial knowledge of or allegiance to TBLT or task use—even though two of them (Kelly and Mike) had undertaken the professional development programme reported by Erlam and Tolosa (2022). Kelly and Mike would therefore have been introduced to task-based ideas as part of exploring the ten Ellis principles, and did also aim to utilise tasks in their classrooms to some extent (e.g., Kelly's Mandarin as L2 classroom survey to elicit number and gender of classmates' siblings, and Mike's French as L2 classroom survey of breakfast items). Kelly and Mike were certainly able to use the survey tasks as segues into comparisons and contrasts across cultures; nonetheless, the intercultural reflections were separated from the TL practice as put into operation through the surveys, something that Mike worried could potentially be turning his class into a social studies lesson.

With regard to a separation in practice, a fundamental problem for the enactment of interculturally reflective activities in the New Zealand context is the exhortation, within the overarching goal of *communication*, to take into account *both* language knowledge *and* cultural knowledge. This is, however, to be done on the basis of two arguably largely mutually exclusive reports (Ellis, 2005; Newton et al., 2010)—even though Newton et al. argued that their report provided "an important sociocultural balance to the set of principles proposed by Ellis" (p. 72).

The isolated/integrated question was problematic in several respects. An initial problem was Newton et al.'s (2010) first principle—that an intercultural communicative approach integrates language and culture from the beginning. As we explained in Chap. 3, the intention of this first principle was to underline how language and culture are inextricably bound together, with the expectation that teachers will help learners to build conceptual bridges between language and culture right from the start of the language learning journey. This was seen as relatively easy to achieve, by highlighting, for example, the cultural content embedded in straightforward samples of language (and associated behaviours), such as greetings.

It is also important to acknowledge that the primary author of the Newton et al. (2010) report aligns himself strongly with the TBLT agenda and with task-based research. With regard to an interface between communicative approaches to language pedagogy and the intercultural dimension, Newton et al. (2010) suggested, "[t]he integration of culture and language is more easily achieved in classrooms informed by communicative language teaching and task-based language teaching ... since these approaches require active participation and experiential learning." They went on to argue, "the adoption of intercultural language teaching promotes a fuller realization of communication by focusing learners' attention on the effects of the implicit messages conveyed in their choice of linguistic forms and communication strategies" (p. 65). This argument further allows for an interface between TBLT and the intercultural dimension. A "fuller realization of communication" supports, for example, Kramsch's (2005) perspective that a communicative orientation must involve "more than just learning to get one's message across" (p. 551).

However, the Newton et al. (2010) report itself does not draw substantially on the task-based literature. Furthermore, it remains unclear how "more focused attention on the effects of messages" in the context of learner-centred experiential learning is to take place. It is also unclear how learners may be supported to take the next steps of comparison, contrast and reflection. More focused attention arguably requires some kind of intervention that might ask learners to step back from a particular interaction and articulate what they notice about it. As a consequence, even such a potentially *integrated* approach might require L1 as the vehicle through which the highlighting occurs, thereby potentially ultimately forcing a segregation between language and culture. The question then becomes whether the intervention and subsequent steps are better served in the TL or in the learners' L1, and therefore (to a greater or lesser extent) in *separation* from the language. The teachers in our study came to different conclusions as they encountered and reflected on the language–culture interface.

Certainly, a more integrated approach has arguably been taken up successfully in the Australian context. Morgan (2010), for example, presented a study that explored how an intercultural language focus might occur in a beginner Indonesian classroom. Even so, the intercultural exploration was facilitated in the L1 (something that Morgan accepted as valid).

It must also be acknowledged that Oranje's (2016) cultural portfolio projects (see Chap. 3) appeared to steer learners in the direction of undertaking reflection in English (rather than in the TL) in a relatively isolationist (discrete) way, thereby potentially minimising a strong language–culture interface and perpetuating a language–culture divide—even though a final presentation could be in the TL. Similarly to Oranje, Kennedy (2020) appeared to propose activities that would separate a language focus from an intercultural focus. Kennedy argued nonetheless that, if intercultural capabilities are to be developed among L2 learners, there needs to be "*intentional* [i.e., discrete] time for intercultural comparison and reflection in classrooms" (p. 427, our emphasis). She further maintained, "without *explicit inclusion* of intercultural pedagogies during class (involving discussing, comparing, connecting outside experiences with those in the classroom and reflecting), the skills, knowledge and traits which make up intercultural competence are not likely to evolve" (p. 437, our emphasis).

We will return to the integrated/isolated issue towards the end of this chapter. In what follows, we turn to our second research question (RQ2): What are the implications for language education going forward?

8.4 Implications for Language Education

We would like to suggest some broader implications gleaned from our project set in the New Zealand context and drawing on the teachers' experiences. We acknowledge that every teacher's setting and context are different. However, based on the participating teachers' experiences, we offer suggestions for teachers, whatever the context, who would like to include an intercultural dimension into their teaching of an L2 with a view to encouraging the development of intercultural capability. We see implications for planning, teaching and reflecting.

8.4.1 Planning

- Based on our findings, and in light of the findings of other studies, it is apparent that careful and thoughtful teacher planning is a prerequisite for moving learners towards greater intercultural capabilities.
- Teachers need time to invest in planning and researching the content they wish to use for intercultural reflection.
- Planning is also needed to verify selected cultural resources and to locate, where possible, L1 speakers who can evaluate these resources and point out any areas that may require particular attention (e.g., the perpetuation of biases or stereotypes).
- Teachers might benefit, at least initially, from planning content of lessons in detail, including writing down prompts, questions and ideas about how to guide a discussion focused on intercultural aspects.

- Teachers need to familiarise themselves with different pedagogical approaches that may be adopted for an exploration of the intercultural dimension and then plan their lessons based on a particular approach or as a mix-and-match from several approaches (e.g., approaches that may integrate the intercultural into, or alternatively isolate the intercultural from, language use).

8.4.2 Teaching

Implications for teaching based on our project relate to aspects of required professional learning and development (PLD), available resources and the selection of a viable teaching approach.

- Teachers would benefit from PLD that demonstrates how language and culture can be taught in conjunction and woven together. Existing PLD reports and resources could be used as starting points, but would need to be adapted to the local context (e.g., the "plurilingual and pluricultural competence" descriptors of the Common European Framework of Reference [Council of Europe, 2018] or the *Framework of Reference for Pluralistic Approaches to Languages and Cultures* [Council of Europe, 2010]).
- Teachers would benefit from PLD that supports them in asking the right kinds of questions, using prompts, and eliciting responses from students, as well as how to navigate and respond to stereotypical views. In our final report (East et al., 2018b), we suggested that possible questions might include:
  - What do I *learn* about the target culture through the input?
  - What *differences* do I notice? What *similarities*?
  - What do I *think* about the target culture through this input in relation to my own culture?
  - How will what I have learned and think *change the way I act* towards those from a different language and cultural background? (p. 13)
- Linguistic resources are needed that also present intercultural aspects, particularly if teachers wish to use the TL as they explore some of these aspects. The TL could be used, for example, to introduce an (inter)cultural feature, present topical material or initiate discussion by providing examples of the kind of language that may be used. Such resources do not seem to exist, at least for the New Zealand primary/intermediate school context (or indeed other contexts for young learners).
- Teachers need to be flexible and open to the possible directions that intercultural conversations could take. While thoughtful planning is helpful, teachers also need to accept the unpredictability of the conversations and of their students' opinions.
- Teachers need to accept and be comfortable with ambiguity. Culture is complex, and beliefs and values are not static, but dynamic.

- Acknowledging the diverse backgrounds of students in the classroom and allowing learners to uncover and discover their own cultural standpoints as they explore the intercultural with regard to the TL will create richer and more insightful discussions.

8.4.3 Reflecting

Teachers in our project considered reflection an important component for moving learners towards more enhanced intercultural capabilities.

- Teachers and learners should be encouraged to be open-minded and to reflect on their own cultures, values and beliefs. They also need to be aware of their own stance and allow room for differing opinions and perspectives.
- Teachers and learners could be encouraged to keep a reflection log or diary in an effort to raise awareness of their own values and beliefs as they encounter different aspects of the target culture. This could also sensitise them to different attitudes and behaviours in different situations and contexts.

8.5 Further Implications for Language Education

Our premise at the start of this book was that L2 programmes provided significant vehicles for an exploration of the intercultural. Considerable promise is held out at the *theoretical* level that a meaningful language–culture interface is achievable. However, classroom-based research studies, including our own, indicate that in *practice* there are significant challenges to be overcome, and the goal of developing intercultural capabilities as part of students' L2 learning journeys has had mixed success to date. The challenges have been attributed, in part, to teachers' unfamiliarity with the concept of intercultural capability, the absence or extreme variability of intercultural pedagogy within teacher education programmes, and ongoing uncertainty about expected intercultural goals and outcomes for different ages and stages (see, e.g., Brunsmeier, 2017; Díaz, 2013; Dervin et al., 2020; Hu & Byram, 2009; Oranje & Smith, 2018).

In our case, perhaps our efforts might have been more impactful if we had scaffolded the teachers more and had been more directive, and if we had provided the teachers with more examples of what could be done. Notwithstanding the constructivist principles on which we built this project, Kirschner et al.'s (2006) analysis of a range of studies led them to conclude that, in their words, "direct, strong instructional guidance" can be equally as effective as "constructivist-based minimal guidance" (p. 83), particularly when the learner is more advanced in expertise (as might be the case with currently practising teachers who are not absolute beginners or novices). As Conway and Richards (2018) made clear, there is a need for explicit PLD in order to help teachers to understand the distinction between culture and intercultural learning goals.

On the one hand, our findings suggest that, bearing in mind teachers' unfamiliarity with the concepts at hand alongside the innovative nature of the concepts, there is arguably greater room for direct instruction at the level of teacher education, or in scaffolding future research projects. On the other, lack of progress with the intercultural seems to be the case even when clear emphasis has been placed on teacher education and professional development initiatives. For example, despite the significant focus on the intercultural in Australia, teachers and learners are reported to have made limited progress (see, e.g., Díaz, 2013). The level of scaffolding might actually be an irrelevant variable (or at least a variable whose potential impact is over-stated).

In light of the challenges, López-Jiménez and Sánchez-Torres (2021) raise two tensions with regard to the intercultural in L2 learning that require some exploration. Noting that L2 language classrooms would *seem* to be particularly appropriate contexts for the development of intercultural competence, they argued nonetheless that L2 teaching and learning in many contexts continually focuses more on the development of communicative competence from a linguistic perspective than on the development of cultural and intercultural competencies. They also made the observation that intercultural competence is not usually located within a specific subject area of the curriculum. It is, rather, found within and across different subjects.

8.5.1 Implications for the L2 Classroom—Integrating Culture and Language

With regard to what is feasible within the L2 classroom, there is evidence from our findings that there can be a specific place for intercultural exploration. We caution, however, that L2 teaching and learning goals may need to be revised accordingly, with divergent goals across primary/intermediate and secondary sectors.

Our findings suggest that, despite the time limitations and the lack of teacher expertise at the primary/intermediate level, students *could* reflect, and intercultural awareness *could* be raised. We also noted instances of increased engagement and motivation, from both the students and the teachers. However, this seemed to be at the expense of teaching the language. That is, for the students, nothing appeared to be negative or counter-productive. For the teachers, the only perceived negative was the relative lack of target language input and growth. Even then, teachers were positive about the refreshed emphasis. One notion expressed in the teacher data was a sense of relief that the focus could be moved somewhat away from language (where some teachers felt that they lacked sufficient expertise), while recognising that meaningful, positive and motivating L2-related learning experiences could still be provided.

The clear and positive learning potential of intercultural exploration in L2 classrooms at the primary/intermediate levels leads us to speculate on whether, at these levels, the primary focus should move away from language and towards the cultural/intercultural. It would then make sense to support primary/intermediate teachers (who in the New Zealand context are not L2 specialists) with helping their students to develop their awareness of who they are in relation to others, including those in the class and those of the TL culture. This may provide a motivating and worthwhile foundation on which dedicated study of the TL might subsequently be built. More focused study of the language may then perhaps be left to secondary school specialists, who require time to ensure that linguistic/communicative goals are met.

Indeed, at the time of planning and discussion around the introduction of *Learning Languages* in the NZC, Barnard (2004) had suggested that, depending on the TL selected, the goal of communicative competence was effectively unrealistic in the primary/intermediate years. This, he maintained, was due not only to the limited hours available for instruction but also to the lack of suitably qualified and experienced teachers. Barnard went on to argue that it might be more worthwhile to aim for "a limited measure of linguistic and intercultural competence" (p. 215). The first (linguistic) could provide learners with "a basic conceptual framework for future study," and the second (intercultural) could be achieved "through the interactive use of attractive and socioculturally relevant media" (pp. 215–216). He asserted that, in such an approach, "[t]he exclusive use, or even a dominant use, of the target language is not necessary for a limited attainment of linguistic and intercultural competence" (p. 216).

Barnard's (2004) propositions do not preclude an exploration of language, but provide space for intercultural reflection without the anxiety, for both teachers and learners, of having to reach a certain level of linguistic proficiency. Furthermore, these suggestions align with what the teachers in our study, whom we encouraged to find out what was most comfortable and feasible for them in their contexts, actually ended up doing—with a good degree of success.

8.5.2 Implications Beyond the L2 Classroom—Isolating Culture from Language

Another conclusion that we reach is that the intercultural is so much bigger than language learning. This would make L2 programmes, in and of themselves, insufficient. Additionally to the L2 classroom (or even as an alternative), we suggest that the development of interculturality needs to be a whole-school endeavour, offered across the curriculum, and supported by school-wide PLD.

Furthermore, we reach the conclusion that moving the intercultural beyond the L2 classroom would enable L2 teachers (particularly at the secondary level) to provide more focus on the *language* to be learned. After all, learning the *language* does remain a central priority of the communicative classroom and of aligned assessments. This does not mean that cross-cultural issues and a language–culture interface cannot or should not be addressed (theoretical models of communicative competence regard sociolinguistic competence as a key component). However, the intercultural speaks to the broader ideals of education that may be better addressed in a cross-curricular way (as proposed, for example, in the principles, values and key competencies articulated in New Zealand's curriculum document that we referred to in Chap. 1). The primary/intermediate context, with its merging of subject boundaries and a flexible timetable, provides a viable vehicle for incorporating an intercultural dimension *across* the curriculum. Nevertheless, a stronger cross-curricular approach to developing learners' intercultural capability raises questions around feasibility in a secondary sector that appears to remain wedded to discrete subject boundaries.

8.5.3 Reconciling the Language–Culture Interface in the New Zealand Context

Notwithstanding arguments for the broadening out of intercultural exploration across the curriculum, and recognition of the persistence of linguistic foci in L2 classrooms, in East et al. (2018b) we strongly recommended that, with regard to L2 classrooms in New Zealand, work needed to be done to reconcile the perceived incompatibility between two influential but quite distinct reports (Ellis, 2005; Newton et al., 2010). This work, we suggested, might include the preparation and presentation of a revised set of overarching principles. At the very least, these principles would need to take into consideration to what extent the currently existing principles *can* be reconciled. Any reconfiguration would need to offer teachers clear guidance about navigating the intercultural dimension of L2 learning.

We concede that, given the different theoretical frameworks and arguments that underpin the recommendations of the two reports, reconciliation may simply not be possible. With regard to second language acquisition or SLA (as represented in Ellis, 2005), it seems possible to fall back on relatively developed and stable theoretical frameworks and an aligned history of practice. This does not mean that theory and practice have not been questioned over many years—as Mitchell et al. (2019) put it, there can be "no 'one best method', however much research evidence supports it, which applies at all times and in all situations, with every type of learner" (p. 406)—but it does mean that there are established theoretical and empirically tested bases on which the Ellis principles are built. Also, as we noted in Chap. 1, mainstream researchers into SLA have tended, by and large, not to consider interculturality as a component of either theories of SLA or empirical studies into SLA. With regard to the intercultural (as represented in Newton et al., 2010), the situation is murkier (see, e.g., Dervin et al., 2020). ICLT as an attempt at reconciliation is an interesting proposition, but seems limited in face of the realities and constraints of L2 classrooms.

If reconciliation between the two sets of principles is not possible, this needs to be owned, and careful consideration needs to be given to how the intercultural in the context of L2 learning is to be framed. We have suggested potential ways forward for L2 teachers, but acknowledge that perhaps a cross-curricular approach would be a more effective means of achieving greater intercultural outcomes. Particularly in light of the ongoing tendency for L2 teachers (whether specialist or non-specialist) to view *language* teaching as a priority, and an increasing emphasis on the removal of separate subject barriers and greater cross-curricular experimentation, a cross-curricular approach would not necessarily undermine the intercultural endeavour, and may even enhance its viability by recognising that interculturality necessarily crosses discrete boundaries.

Our own reflections, as both the researchers and the teacher educators working alongside the teachers in this study, led us to the following conclusion:

> … dichotomous thinking (isolated or integrated) is likely to diminish rather than enhance the students' learning experiences. There is arguably no one best path to helping students to acquire intercultural understanding. The choice must surely depend on several factors, including the intercultural goal(s) the teacher has in mind. It is not a question of 'either/or'. It is a question of 'both/and.' (East et al., 2017, p. 30)

That is, we see the importance of both *integration* (exploration of the language–culture interface in L2 classrooms) and *isolation* (opportunities to step back from the language—whether in or beyond the L2 classroom—to explore, compare, contrast and reflect on similarity and difference in behaviours, practices and actions). In this regard, we argued that it was important for teachers not to "erect an artificial divide" (East et al., 2017, p. 30), by making the assumption that L1 use inevitably means that the intercultural focus is not integrated or, indeed, must be separated. For example, Kelly's and Mike's class surveys to elicit (in the TL) the siblings students have or what students ate for breakfast could be followed up with explorations (in the L1) of what students think about differences they have encountered, not only between themselves in class but also through a consideration of what they may have noticed from TL sources. In East et al. (2017), we went on to note that the challenge for teachers is to determine the conditions in which an isolated or integrated focus on developing intercultural capability is more appropriate. These, we acknowledged, will likely vary from situation to situation, and from class to class.

8.6 Limitations and Directions for Further Research

In our final report to the funder (East et al., 2018b), we identified several limitations to this study. These limitations remain apposite.

First, this was a locally situated small-scale study where teachers (regardless of their level of knowledge and understanding) are guided to operate within specific parameters articulated in such documents as the NZC (Ministry of Education, 2007), and the Ellis (2005) and Newton et al. (2010) reports. This local contextualisation provides both benefits and constraints, but limits both the generalisability of our findings and the extent to which the intercultural inquiries selected by the teachers can be implemented in other contexts without modifications. Even so, the project was built on the belief that intercultural inquiries will likely be most effective when they are personalised to teachers' own contexts. Furthermore, we believe that what the teachers did can be useful springboards for other teachers, hence the "engaging examples of practice" that we produced (East et al., 2018a).

Second, the teachers in our project held a range of understandings and beliefs about, and developed a variety of practices concerning, the place of culture and the intercultural dimension in their teaching of languages, including a stance that emphasised facts about the target culture. Also, these primary/intermediate school teachers, unlike their secondary school counterparts, had not undertaken any specific initial teacher education focused on L2 pedagogy (although some had engaged in a level of PLD). They were in these regards not untypical of teachers in this context (see Chap. 1). This contextual reality meant, however, that observed shifts in these teachers' learning and practices, and the incremental steps taken by the teachers, were less extensive and more modest than we had anticipated or hoped for. This may have been intensified by our deliberate non-interventionist stance whereby we did not direct and instruct the teachers in how to approach the intercultural and in what the foci of their inquiries should be. Rather, and in line with a constructivist approach to teaching and learning, we guided the teachers, and questioned them as they worked through the process themselves.

Third, self-report data are, in themselves, potentially limiting. We sought to enhance the validity and reliability of our findings by triangulating data using several sources of evidence. Additionally, the young age of the students limited these students' ability to articulate clearly the level of intercultural gains that they had reached, in particular with regard to the "third place." The indications of students' third place positioning were often embedded within more superficial comments. They could easily have been missed and required careful extrapolation. These comments did, however, represent learning gains by virtue of the sowing of "small intercultural seeds."

Further studies would benefit from investigating scaffolding and direction as variables that might influence teachers' understanding and practices. These may include taking into account the implications for planning, teaching and reflecting that we presented earlier in this chapter. Additional studies would also benefit from collecting a broader range of evidence on students' learning and intercultural gains. For example, ongoing reflective journals might enable evidence of exploration and gain to be gathered as part of the *process* of intercultural reflection, rather than relying on a summative snapshot. Additionally, researchers (and teachers) may wish to draw on instruments that have been designed to measure the intercultural dimension. Revised CEFR descriptors might provide a useful starting point.[1]

---

[1] It must be acknowledged that, just as intercultural competence remains a somewhat murky construct, its assessment remains an issue of debate, beyond the scope of the project we have reported here.

8.7 Conclusion

It is important in closing to restate the assertion we made both in Chap. 1 and towards the beginning of this chapter—that the development of the intercultural dimension through language learning (particularly with younger students) is mired by challenges. Its implementation represents what Dervin et al. (2020) described as one that follows "diverse and uneven pathways," with its implementers forced to confront "personal and pedagogical risk, growth, … struggle and frustration" (p. 9).

The project we have presented in this book represented a new journey for both the teachers and their students. It also represented a new journey for us as researchers and teacher educators, despite our strong familiarity with the requirements of the NZC. Furthermore, the journeys have not been unidimensional for any of the stakeholders. Sometimes there was wandering off the path; at other times there were roadblocks to be overcome; at others, the pathway would have benefitted from being better lit.

The journeys for all of us were predicated on attempting to make sense of the NZC and its three-strand model for L2 learning—the core *communication* strand and the supporting *language knowledge* and *cultural knowledge* strands. We have ended up still in a place of uncertainty about how best to integrate the intercultural into L2 classrooms, and have reached what we now see as clear (and perhaps irreconcilable) tensions in the NZC's three-strand model. It seems that the New Zealand system is asking teachers to do things that they actually cannot do, or at least not do well within their contextual constraints.

We acknowledge that the goals of ICC as articulated by Byram (e.g., 2021) are positive, and certainly seem to have suited the European context at a particular time very well. While our study has aimed to address a perceived gap in knowledge with regard to younger learners (as noted, e.g., by Byram, 1997), the reality is that it is very challenging to realise more fully the goals of interculturality with such learners, as has been demonstrated in other contexts.

Nevertheless, the evidence from our study is that the teachers (and the learners) did make positive progress, even as the teachers, in particular, encountered struggles, questions and frustrations as they took risks to implement something new. We as researchers and teacher educators also made progress as we engaged reflectively with what we observed and drew conclusions about what seemed to be realistic and achievable in the context. Although we cannot claim fundamental shifts in learning or practice, there were glimpses of steps forward in line with our operational definition of the construct of intercultural capability, and, given the significant constraints, we believe that what all the stakeholders in our project achieved was noteworthy. The stakeholders in our project certainly did get their boots dirty as they made their journeys towards enhanced intercultural capability in L2 classrooms. Nonetheless, we encourage all stakeholders, whatever the context, to continue the journeys. Their experiences will provide further illumination along the way.

References

Adams, R., & Newton, J. (2009). TBLT in Asia: Constraints and opportunities. *Asian Journal of English Language Teaching, 19*, 1–17.

Alegría de la Colina, A., & García Mayo, M. (2009). Oral interaction in task-based EFL learning: The use of the L1 as a cognitive tool. *International Review of Applied Linguistics in Language Teaching, 47*(3/4), 325–345.

Barnard, R. (2004). The diverse aims of second language teaching: Implications for New Zealand primary schools. *New Zealand Journal of Educational Studies, 39*(2), 207–221.

Biebricher, C., East, M., Howard, J., & Tolosa, C. (2019). Navigating intercultural language teaching in New Zealand classrooms. *Cambridge Journal of Education, 49*(5), 605–621.

Brandenburg, R. (2008). *Powerful pedagogy: Self-study of a teacher educator's practice*. Springer.

Brunsmeier, S. (2017). Primary teachers' knowledge when initiating intercultural communicative competence. *TESOL Quarterly, 51*(1), 143–155.

Burns, A. (2019). Action research: Developments, characteristics, and future directions. In J. Schwieter & A. Benati (Eds.), *The Cambridge handbook of language learning* (pp. 166–185). Cambridge University Press.

Byram, M. (1997). *Teaching and assessing intercultural communicative competence*. Multilingual Matters.

Byram, M. (2021). *Teaching and assessing intercultural communicative competence: Revisited* (2nd ed.). Multilingual Matters.

Carless, D. (2008). Student use of the mother tongue in the task-based classroom. *ELT Journal, 62*(4), 331–338.

Castro, P., Sercu, L., & Méndez-García, M. C. (2004). Integrating language-and-culture teaching: An investigation of Spanish teachers' perceptions of the objectives of foreign language education. *Intercultural Education, 15*, 91–104.

Conway, C., & Richards, H. (2018). 'Lunchtimes in New Zealand are cruel': Reflection as a tool for developing language learners' intercultural competence. *The Language Learning Journal, 46*(4), 371–383.

Council of Europe. (2010). *Framework of reference for pluralistic approaches to languages and cultures*. Council of Europe Publishing.

Council of Europe. (2018). *Common European framework of reference for languages: Learning, teaching, assessment. Companion volume with new descriptors*. Council of Europe Publishing.

Crozet, C. (2017). The intercultural foreign language teacher: Challenges and choices. In M. Dasli & A. Díaz (Eds.), *The critical turn in language and intercultural communication pedagogy* (pp. 143–161). Routledge.

Dervin, F. (2020). Creating and combining models of Intercultural Competence for teacher education/training—On the need to rethink IC frequently. In F. Dervin, R. Moloney, & A. Simpson (Eds.), *Intercultural competence in the work of teachers: Confronting ideologies and practices* (pp. 57–72). Routledge.

Dervin, F., Moloney, R., & Simpson, A. (Eds.). (2020). *Intercultural competence in the work of teachers: Confronting ideologies and practices*. Routledge.

Despoteris, J., & Ananda, K. (2017). Intercultural competence: Reflecting on daily routines. In M. Wagner, D. Perugini, & M. Byram (Eds.), *Teaching intercultural competence across the age range: From theory to practice* (pp. 60–79). Multilingual Matters.

Díaz, A. (2013). Intercultural understanding and professional learning through critical engagement. *Babel, 48*(1), 12–19.

East, M., Howard, J., Tolosa, C., Biebricher, C., & Scott, A. (2017). Isolated or integrated? Should the development of students' intercultural understanding be separated from, or embedded into, communicative language use? *Babel, 52*(2/3), 25–31.

East, M., Tolosa, C., Biebricher, C., Howard, J., & Scott, A. (2018a). *Enhancing language learners' intercultural capability: A study in New Zealand's schools*. Languages Research NZ.

References

East, M., Tolosa, C., Biebricher, C., Howard, J., & Scott, A. (2018b). *Enhancing the intercultural capability of students of additional languages in New Zealand's intermediate schools*. Teaching and Learning Research Initiative, Final Project Report.

Ellis, R. (2005). *Instructed second language acquisition: A literature review*. Ministry of Education.

Erlam, R., & Tolosa, C. (2022). *Pedagogical realities of implementing task-based language teaching in the classroom*. John Benjamins.

Hu, A., & Byram, M. (2009). *Intercultural competence and foreign language learning: Models, empiricism, assessment*. Gunter Narr Verlag.

Kennedy, J. (2020). Intercultural pedagogies in Chinese as a foreign language (CFL). *Intercultural Education, 31*(4), 427–446.

Kirschner, P. A., Sweller, J., & Clark, R. E. (2006). Why minimal guidance during instruction does not work: An analysis of the failure of constructivist, discovery, problem-based, experiential, and inquiry-based teaching. *Educational Psychologist, 41*(2), 75–86.

Kramsch, C. (2005). Post 9/11: Foreign languages between knowledge and power. *Applied Linguistics, 26*(4), 545–567.

Lasito, & Storch, N. (2013). Comparing pair and small group interactions on oral tasks. *RELC Journal, 44*(3), 361–375.

Liddicoat, A. (2008). Pedagogical practice for integrating the intercultural in language teaching and learning. *Japanese Studies, 28*(3), 277–290.

Liddicoat, A., & Crozet, C. (Eds.). (2000). *Teaching languages, teaching cultures*. Language Australia.

Lightbown, P., & Spada, N. (2020). Teaching and learning L2 in the classroom: It's about time. *Language Teaching, 53*(4), 422–432.

López-Jiménez, M. D., & Sánchez-Torres, J. (Eds.). (2021). *Intercultural competence past, present and future: Respecting the past, problems in the present and forging the future*. Springer.

Ministry of Education. (2007). *The New Zealand curriculum*. Learning Media.

Ministry of Education. (2009). *Curriculum achievement objectives by learning area*. http://nzcurriculum.tki.org.nz/The-New-Zealand-Curriculum

Mitchell, R., Myles, F., & Marsden, E. (2019). *Second language learning theories* (4th ed.). Routledge.

Moloney, R. (2008). You just want to be like that: Teacher modelling and intercultural competence in young language learners. *Babel, 42*(3), 10–19.

Morgan, A.-M. (2010). Me, myself, I: Developing concepts of self and identity in early years language classrooms. *Babel, 44*, 26–34.

Müller-Hartmann, A., & Schocker, M. (2018). The challenge of thinking task-based teaching from the learners' perspectives: Developing teaching competences through an action research approach to teacher education. In M. Ahmadian & M. Garcia Mayo (Eds.), *Recent perspectives on task-based language learning and teaching* (pp. 233–257). De Gruyter.

Newton, J., & Le Diem Bui, T. (2020). Low-proficiency learners and task-based language teaching. In C. Lambert & R. Oliver (Eds.), *Using tasks in second language teaching* (pp. 33–48). Multilingual Matters.

Newton, J., Yates, E., Shearn, S., & Nowitzki, W. (2010). *Intercultural communicative language teaching: Implications for effective teaching and learning—A literature review and an evidence-based framework for effective teaching*. Ministry of Education.

Oranje, J. (2016). *Intercultural communicative language teaching: Enhancing awareness and practice through cultural portfolio projects*. Doctoral thesis, University of Otago, New Zealand.

Oranje, J., & Smith, L. (2018). Language teacher cognitions and intercultural language teaching: The New Zealand perspective. *Language Teaching Research, 22*(3), 310–329.

Roher, P., & Kagan, L. (2017). Using the five senses to explore cities. In M. Wagner, D. Perugini, & M. Byram (Eds.), *Teaching intercultural competence across the age range: From theory to practice* (pp. 60–79). Multilingual Matters.

Scarino, A., & Crichton, J. (2007). *Why the intercultural matters to languages teaching and learning: An orientation to the ILTLP programme*. University of South Australia.

Seals, C. A., Newton, J., Ash, M., & Nguyen, T. B. T. (2020). Translanguaging and TBLT: Crossovers and challenges. In Z. Tian, L. Aghai, P. Sayer, & J. Schissel (Eds.), *Envisioning TESOL through a translanguaging lens—Global perspectives* (pp. 275–292). Springer.

Sercu, L. (2013). Foreign language teachers and intercultural competence. What keeps teachers from doing what they believe in? In M. Jiménez Raya & L. Sercu (Eds.), *Challenges in teacher development: Learner autonomy and intercultural competence* (pp. 65–80). Peter Lang.

Sercu, L., Bandura, E., Castro, P., Davcheva, L., Laskaridou, C., Lundgren, U., & Ryan, P. (2005). *Foreign language teachers and intercultural competence: An investigation in 7 countries of foreign language teachers' views and teaching practices*. Multilingual Matters.

Swain, M., & Lapkin, S. (1995). Problems in output and the cognitive processes they generate: A step towards second language learning. *Applied Linguistics, 16*(3), 371–391.

Tripp, D. (2012). *Critical incidents in teaching developing professional judgment*. Routledge.

Wagner, M., Perugini, D. C., & Byram, M. (Eds.) (2017). *Teaching intercultural competence across the age range: From theory to practice*. Multilingual Matters.

Open Access This chapter is licensed under the terms of the Creative Commons Attribution 4.0 International License (http://creativecommons.org/licenses/by/4.0/), which permits use, sharing, adaptation, distribution and reproduction in any medium or format, as long as you give appropriate credit to the original author(s) and the source, provide a link to the Creative Commons license and indicate if changes were made.

The images or other third party material in this chapter are included in the chapter's Creative Commons license, unless indicated otherwise in a credit line to the material. If material is not included in the chapter's Creative Commons license and your intended use is not permitted by statutory regulation or exceeds the permitted use, you will need to obtain permission directly from the copyright holder.

Ingram Content Group UK Ltd.
Milton Keynes UK
UKHW020140050723
424579UK00003B/95